blue monday

Chynna Clugston Flores

Inbetween Days

3

blue m

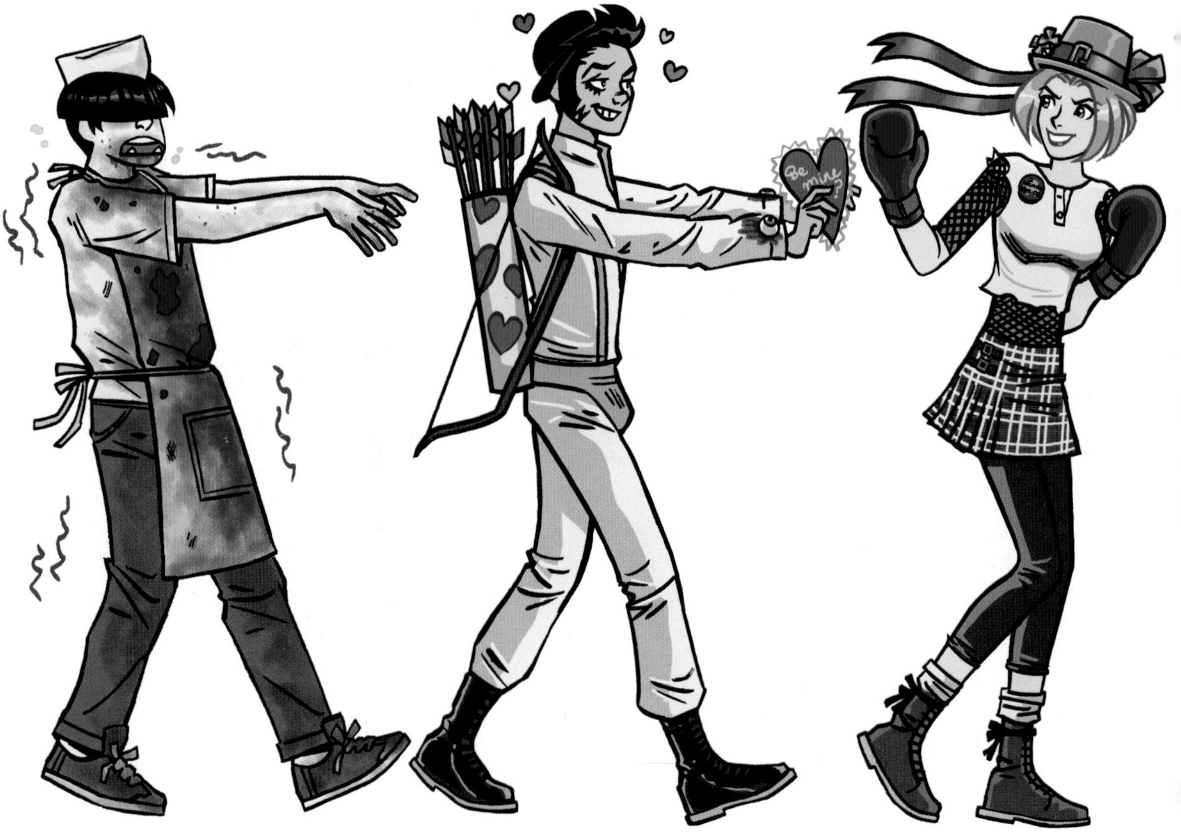
Be mine?

Chynna Clugston Flores
Writer & Illustrator

Jordie Bellaire
Colorist

Bryan Lee O'Malley
Letterer

Drew Gill
Book Design

Jamie S. Rich
First Edition
Schmeditor

Ian Shaughnessy
Remastered Edition
Schmeditor

Chynna Clugston Flores
Cover & Chapter Break Art and Colors, Crummy Hand-Lettering

Guy Major
Original Cover Colorist

Dan Brereton
Halloween Pin-Up

Steven Birch
Logo Design

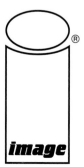

IMAGE COMICS, INC.
Robert Kirkman—Chief Operating Officer
Erik Larsen—Chief Financial Officer
Todd McFarlane—President
Marc Silvestri—Chief Executive Officer
Jim Valentino—Vice-President

Eric Stephenson—Publisher
Corey Murphy—Director of Sales
Jeff Boison—Director of Publishing Planning & Book Trade Sales
Chris Ross—Director of Digital Sales
Jeff Stang—Director of Specialty Sales
Kat Salazar—Director of PR & Marketing
Branwyn Bigglestone—Controller
Sue Korpela—Accounts Manager
Drew Gill—Art Director
Brett Warnock—Production Manager
Meredith Wallace—Print Manager
Tricia Ramos—Traffic Manager
Briah Skelly—Publicist
Aly Hoffman—Events & Conventions Coordinator
Sasha Head—Sales & Marketing Production Designer
David Brothers—Branding Manager
Melissa Gifford—Content Manager
Drew Fitzgerald—Publicity Assistant
Vincent Kukua—Production Artist
Erika Schnatz—Production Artist
Ryan Brewer—Production Artist
Shanna Matuszak—Production Artist
Carey Hall—Production Artist
Esther Kim—Direct Market Sales Representative
Emilio Bautista—Digital Sales Representative
Leanna Caunter—Accounting Assistant
Chloe Ramos-Peterson—Library Market Sales Representative
Marla Eizik—Administrative Assistant
IMAGECOMICS.COM

BLUE MONDAY created by Chynna Clugston Flores.

BLUE MONDAY, VOL. 3: INBETWEEN DAYS. First printing. July 2017. Published by Image Comics, Inc. Office of publication: 2701 NW Vaughn St., Suite 780, Portland, OR 97210. Copyright © 2017 Chynna Clugston Flores. All rights reserved. Contains material originally published in single magazine form as BLUE MONDAY: DEAD MAN'S PARTY, BLUE BELLES, LOVECATS, NOBODY'S FOOL, EVERYTHING'S GONE GREEN, & EVERYBODY PLAYS THE FOOL. "Blue Monday," its logos, and the likenesses of all characters herein are trademarks of Chynna Clugston Flores, unless otherwise noted. "Jingle Belle" is TM & copyright © Paul Dini. "Image" and the Image Comics logos are registered trademarks of Image Comics, Inc. No part of this publication may be reproduced or transmitted, in any form or by any means (except for short excerpts for journalistic or review purposes), without the express written permission of Chynna Clugston Flores or Image Comics, Inc. All names, characters, events, and locales in this publication are entirely fictional. Any resemblance to actual persons (living or dead), events, or places, without satiric intent, is coincidental. Printed in the USA. For information regarding the CPSIA on this printed material call: 203-595-3636 and provide reference #RICH–720403. For international rights, contact: foreignlicensing@imagecomics.com. ISBN: 978-1-63215-874-1.

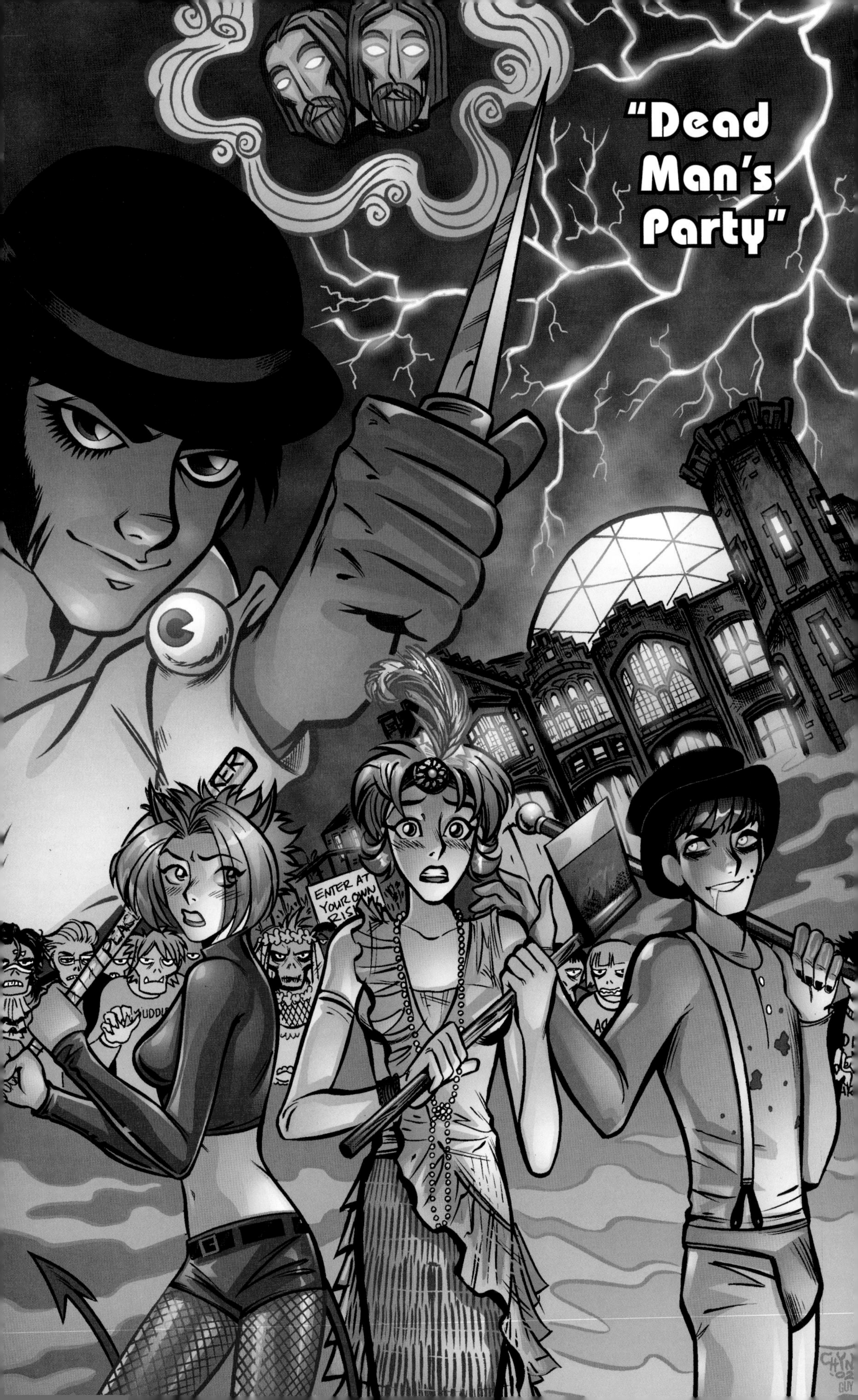
"Dead Man's Party"
ENTER AT YOUR OWN RISK

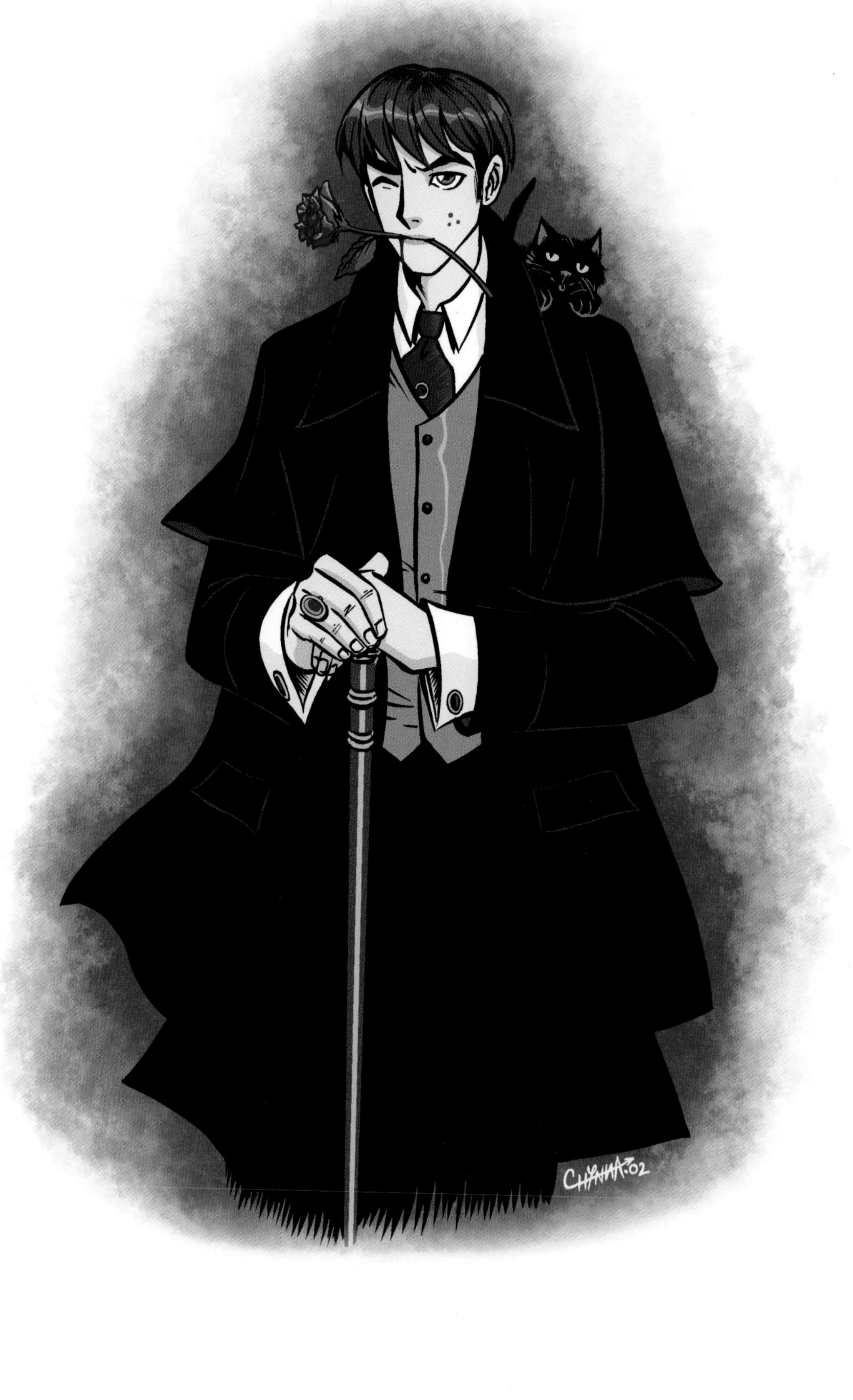

OINGO BOINGO "NO ONE LIVES FOREVER"

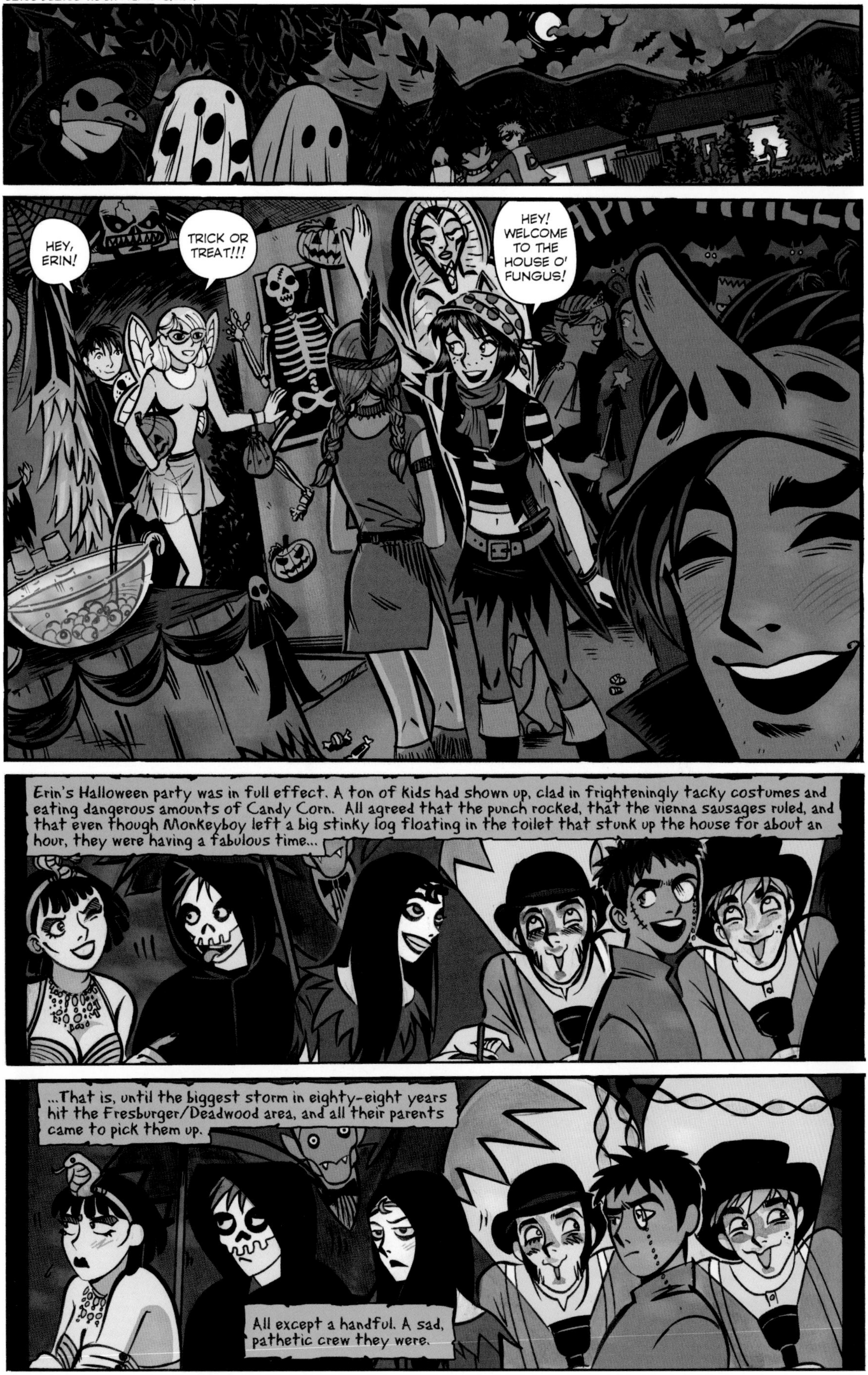
HEY, ERIN!
TRICK OR TREAT!!!
HEY! WELCOME TO THE HOUSE O' FUNGUS!
Erin's Halloween party was in full effect. A ton of kids had shown up, clad in frighteningly tacky costumes and eating dangerous amounts of Candy Corn. All agreed that the punch rocked, that the vienna sausages ruled, and that even though Monkeyboy left a big stinky log floating in the toilet that stunk up the house for about an hour, they were having a fabulous time...
...That is, until the biggest storm in eighty-eight years hit the Fresburger/Deadwood area, and all their parents came to pick them up.
All except a handful. A sad, pathetic crew they were.

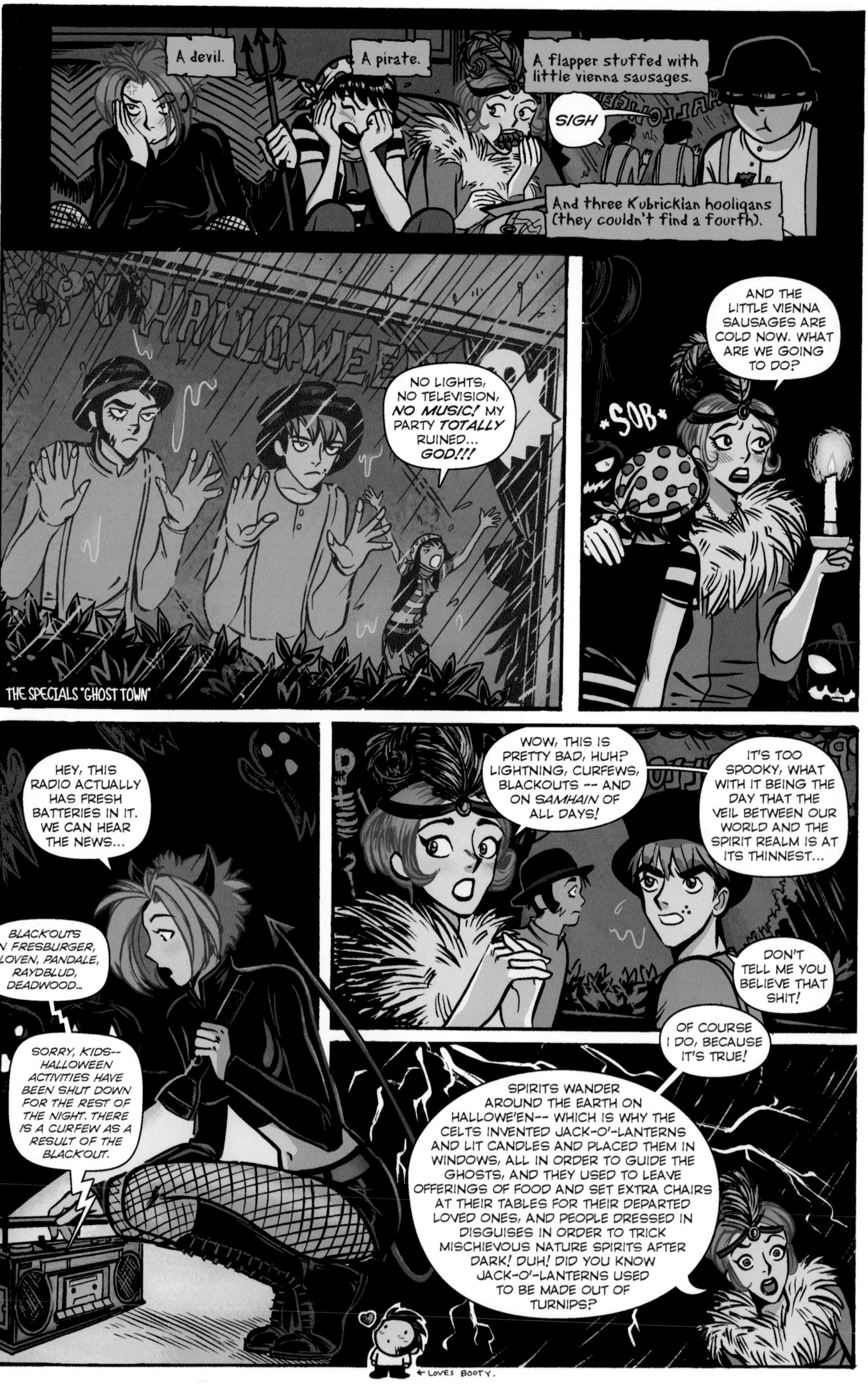
A devil.
A pirate.
A flapper stuffed with little vienna sausages.
SIGH
And three Kubrickian hooligans (they couldn't find a fourth).
NO LIGHTS, NO TELEVISION, NO MUSIC! MY PARTY TOTALLY RUINED... GOD!!!
THE SPECIALS "GHOST TOWN"
AND THE LITTLE VIENNA SAUSAGES ARE COLD NOW. WHAT ARE WE GOING TO DO?
SOB
HEY, THIS RADIO ACTUALLY HAS FRESH BATTERIES IN IT. WE CAN HEAR THE NEWS...
BLACKOUTS IN FRESBURGER, CLOVEN, PANDALE, RAYDBLUD, DEADWOOD...
SORRY, KIDS-- HALLOWEEN ACTIVITIES HAVE BEEN SHUT DOWN FOR THE REST OF THE NIGHT. THERE IS A CURFEW AS A RESULT OF THE BLACKOUT.
WOW, THIS IS PRETTY BAD, HUH? LIGHTNING, CURFEWS, BLACKOUTS -- AND ON SAMHAIN OF ALL DAYS!
IT'S TOO SPOOKY, WHAT WITH IT BEING THE DAY THAT THE VEIL BETWEEN OUR WORLD AND THE SPIRIT REALM IS AT ITS THINNEST...
DON'T TELL ME YOU BELIEVE THAT SHIT!
OF COURSE I DO, BECAUSE IT'S TRUE!
SPIRITS WANDER AROUND THE EARTH ON HALLOWE'EN-- WHICH IS WHY THE CELTS INVENTED JACK-O'-LANTERNS AND LIT CANDLES AND PLACED THEM IN WINDOWS, ALL IN ORDER TO GUIDE THE GHOSTS, AND THEY USED TO LEAVE OFFERINGS OF FOOD AND SET EXTRA CHAIRS AT THEIR TABLES FOR THEIR DEPARTED LOVED ONES, AND PEOPLE DRESSED IN DISGUISES IN ORDER TO TRICK MISCHIEVOUS NATURE SPIRITS AFTER DARK! DUH! DID YOU KNOW JACK-O'-LANTERNS USED TO BE MADE OUT OF TURNIPS?
←LOVES BOOTY.

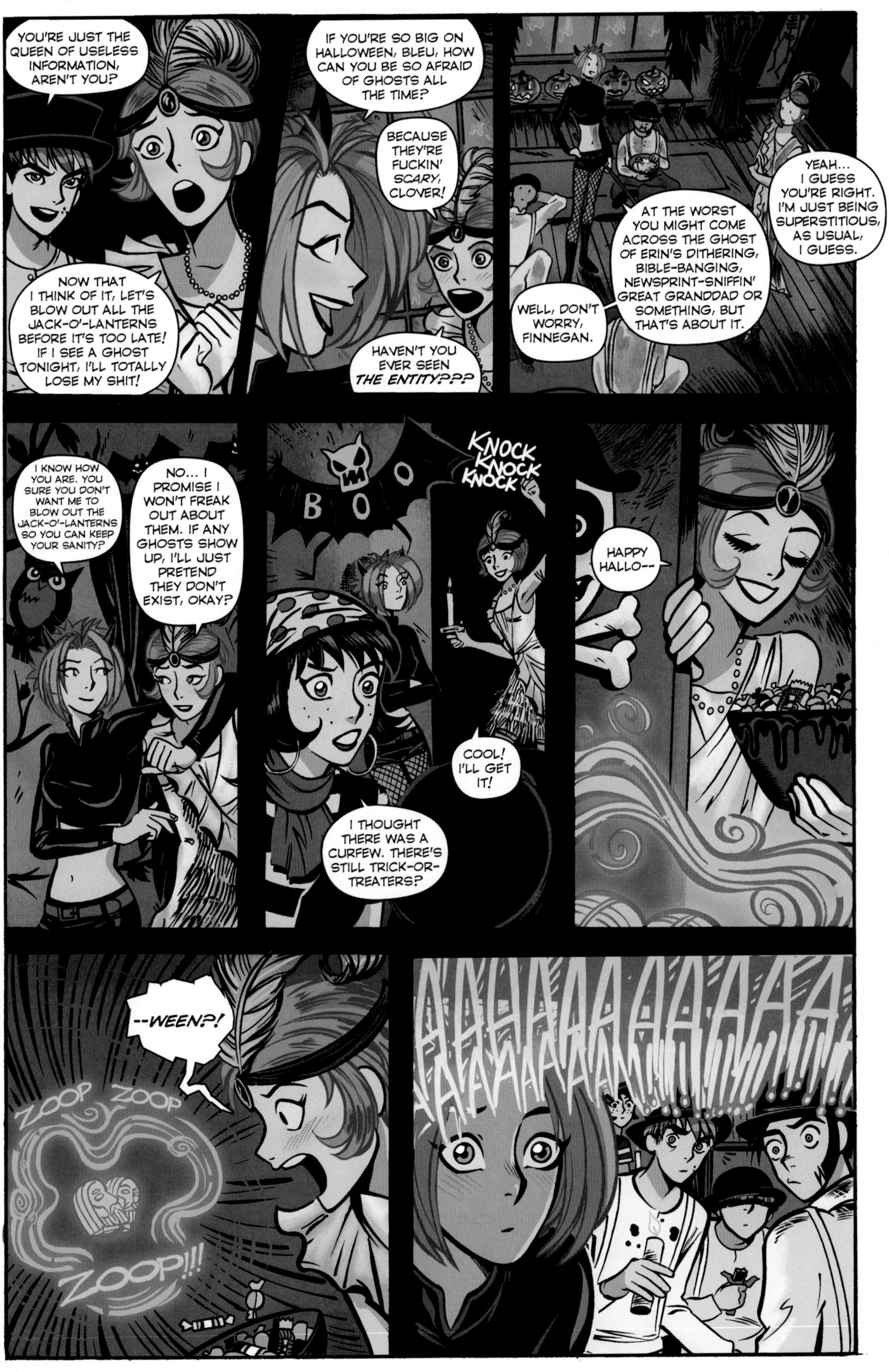
YOU'RE JUST THE QUEEN OF USELESS INFORMATION, AREN'T YOU?
NOW THAT I THINK OF IT, LET'S BLOW OUT ALL THE JACK-O'-LANTERNS BEFORE IT'S TOO LATE! IF I SEE A GHOST TONIGHT, I'LL TOTALLY LOSE MY SHIT!
IF YOU'RE SO BIG ON HALLOWEEN, BLEU, HOW CAN YOU BE SO AFRAID OF GHOSTS ALL THE TIME?
BECAUSE THEY'RE FUCKIN' SCARY, CLOVER!
HAVEN'T YOU EVER SEEN THE ENTITY???
WELL, DON'T WORRY, FINNEGAN.
AT THE WORST YOU MIGHT COME ACROSS THE GHOST OF ERIN'S DITHERING, BIBLE-BANGING, NEWSPRINT-SNIFFIN' GREAT GRANDDAD OR SOMETHING, BUT THAT'S ABOUT IT.
YEAH... I GUESS YOU'RE RIGHT. I'M JUST BEING SUPERSTITIOUS, AS USUAL, I GUESS.
I KNOW HOW YOU ARE. YOU SURE YOU DON'T WANT ME TO BLOW OUT THE JACK-O'-LANTERNS SO YOU CAN KEEP YOUR SANITY?
NO... I PROMISE I WON'T FREAK OUT ABOUT THEM. IF ANY GHOSTS SHOW UP, I'LL JUST PRETEND THEY DON'T EXIST, OKAY?
BOO
KNOCK KNOCK KNOCK
COOL! I'LL GET IT!
I THOUGHT THERE WAS A CURFEW. THERE'S STILL TRICK-OR-TREATERS?
HAPPY HALLO--
--WEEN?!
ZOOP ZOOP
ZOOP!!!
AAAAAAAAAAAAAAAAAAAAAAA

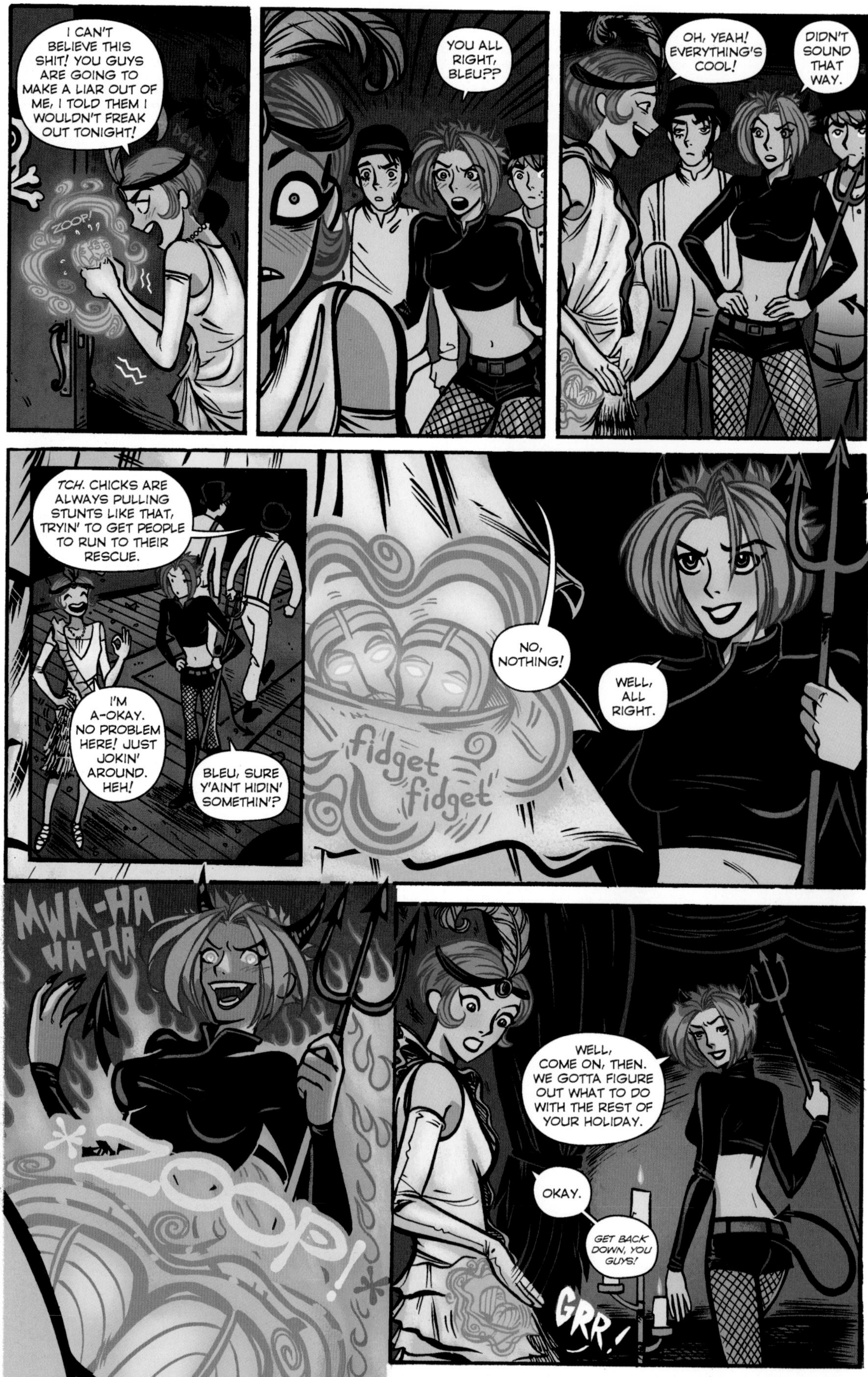
I CAN'T BELIEVE THIS SHIT! YOU GUYS ARE GOING TO MAKE A LIAR OUT OF ME, I TOLD THEM I WOULDN'T FREAK OUT TONIGHT!
ZOOP!
YOU ALL RIGHT, BLEU??
OH, YEAH! EVERYTHING'S COOL!
DIDN'T SOUND THAT WAY.
TCH. CHICKS ARE ALWAYS PULLING STUNTS LIKE THAT, TRYIN' TO GET PEOPLE TO RUN TO THEIR RESCUE.
I'M A-OKAY. NO PROBLEM HERE! JUST JOKIN' AROUND. HEH!
BLEU, SURE Y'AINT HIDIN' SOMETHIN'?
fidget fidget
NO, NOTHING!
WELL, ALL RIGHT.
MWA-HA HA-HA
ZOOP!
WELL, COME ON, THEN. WE GOTTA FIGURE OUT WHAT TO DO WITH THE REST OF YOUR HOLIDAY.
OKAY.
GET BACK DOWN, YOU GUYS!
GRR!

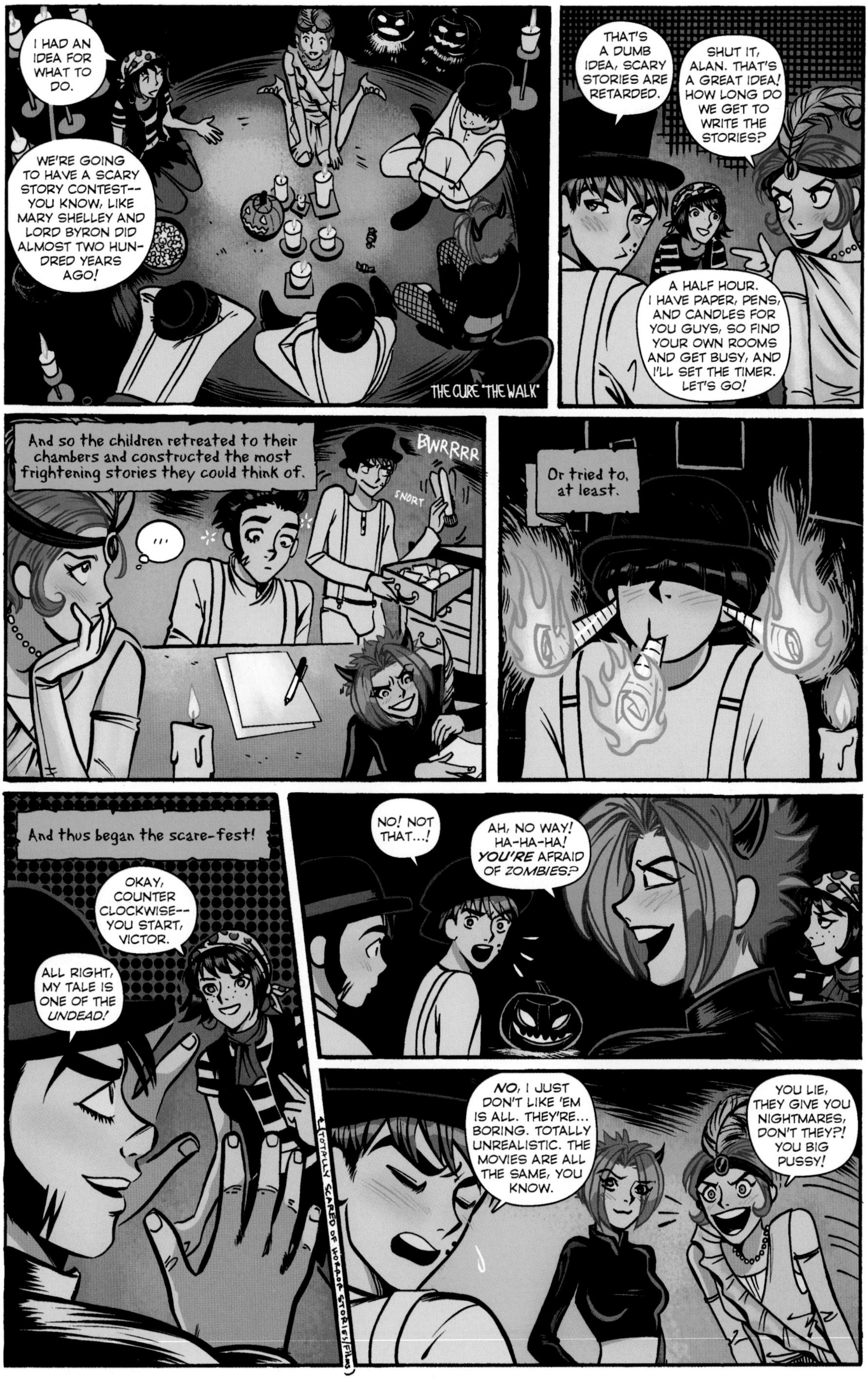

I HAD AN IDEA FOR WHAT TO DO.
WE'RE GOING TO HAVE A SCARY STORY CONTEST-- YOU KNOW, LIKE MARY SHELLEY AND LORD BYRON DID ALMOST TWO HUNDRED YEARS AGO!
THE CURE "THE WALK"
THAT'S A DUMB IDEA, SCARY STORIES ARE RETARDED.
SHUT IT, ALAN. THAT'S A GREAT IDEA! HOW LONG DO WE GET TO WRITE THE STORIES?
A HALF HOUR. I HAVE PAPER, PENS, AND CANDLES FOR YOU GUYS, SO FIND YOUR OWN ROOMS AND GET BUSY, AND I'LL SET THE TIMER. LET'S GO!
And so the children retreated to their chambers and constructed the most frightening stories they could think of.
BWRRRR
SNORT
...
Or tried to, at least.
And thus began the scare-fest!
OKAY, COUNTER CLOCKWISE-- YOU START, VICTOR.
ALL RIGHT, MY TALE IS ONE OF THE UNDEAD!
TOTALLY SCARED OF HORROR STORIES/FILMS
NO! NOT THAT...!
AH, NO WAY! HA-HA-HA! YOU'RE AFRAID OF ZOMBIES?
NO, I JUST DON'T LIKE 'EM IS ALL. THEY'RE... BORING. TOTALLY UNREALISTIC. THE MOVIES ARE ALL THE SAME, YOU KNOW.
YOU LIE, THEY GIVE YOU NIGHTMARES, DON'T THEY?! YOU BIG PUSSY!

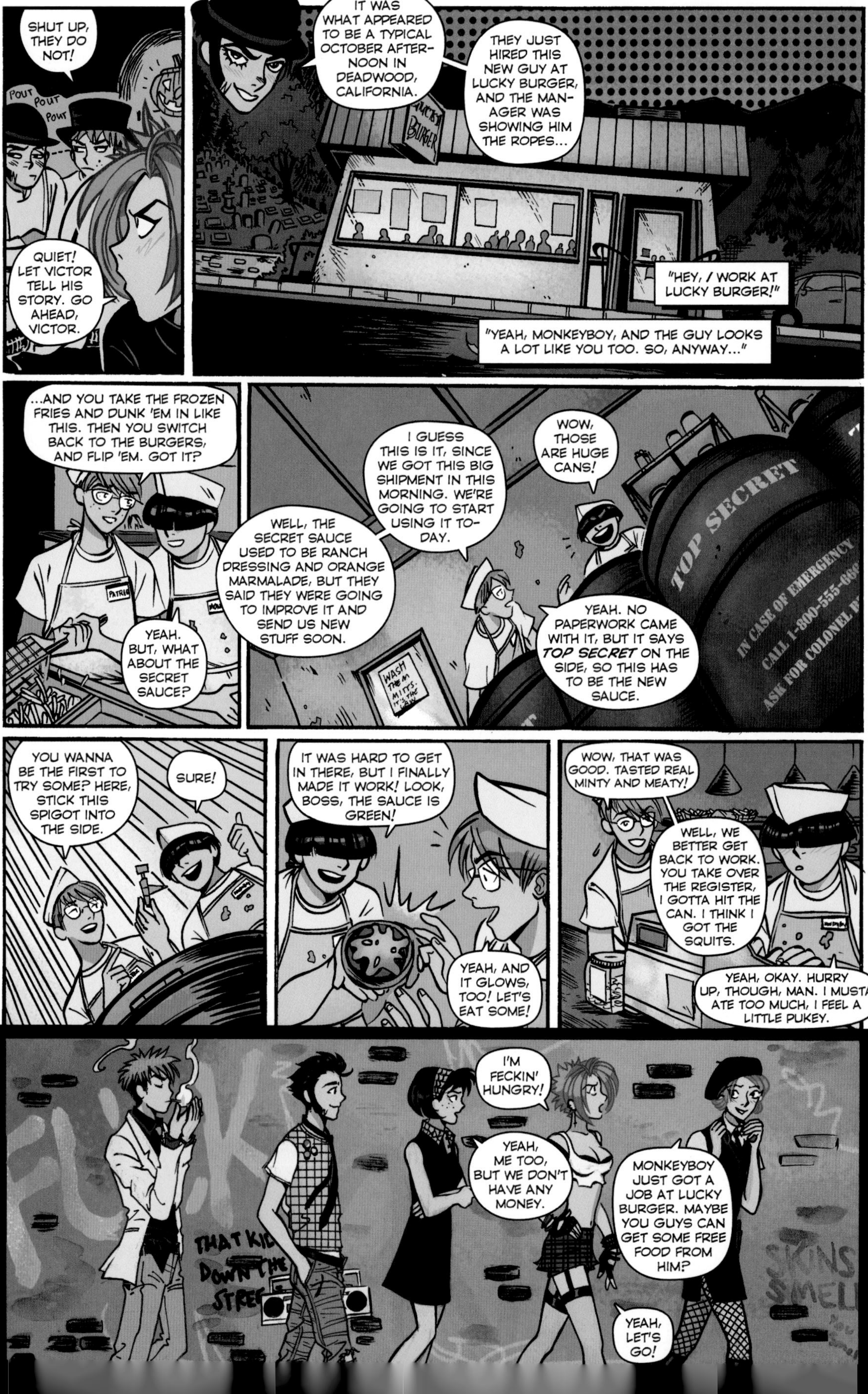
SHUT UP, THEY DO NOT!
POUT POUT POUT
QUIET! LET VICTOR TELL HIS STORY. GO AHEAD, VICTOR.
IT WAS WHAT APPEARED TO BE A TYPICAL OCTOBER AFTER-NOON IN DEADWOOD, CALIFORNIA.
THEY JUST HIRED THIS NEW GUY AT LUCKY BURGER, AND THE MAN-AGER WAS SHOWING HIM THE ROPES...
"HEY, I WORK AT LUCKY BURGER!"
"YEAH, MONKEYBOY, AND THE GUY LOOKS A LOT LIKE YOU TOO. SO, ANYWAY..."
...AND YOU TAKE THE FROZEN FRIES AND DUNK 'EM IN LIKE THIS. THEN YOU SWITCH BACK TO THE BURGERS, AND FLIP 'EM. GOT IT?
YEAH. BUT, WHAT ABOUT THE SECRET SAUCE?
WELL, THE SECRET SAUCE USED TO BE RANCH DRESSING AND ORANGE MARMALADE, BUT THEY SAID THEY WERE GOING TO IMPROVE IT AND SEND US NEW STUFF SOON.
I GUESS THIS IS IT, SINCE WE GOT THIS BIG SHIPMENT IN THIS MORNING. WE'RE GOING TO START USING IT TO-DAY.
WOW, THOSE ARE HUGE CANS!
YEAH. NO PAPERWORK CAME WITH IT, BUT IT SAYS TOP SECRET ON THE SIDE, SO THIS HAS TO BE THE NEW SAUCE.
TOP SECRET
YOU WANNA BE THE FIRST TO TRY SOME? HERE, STICK THIS SPIGOT INTO THE SIDE.
SURE!
IT WAS HARD TO GET IN THERE, BUT I FINALLY MADE IT WORK! LOOK, BOSS, THE SAUCE IS GREEN!
YEAH, AND IT GLOWS, TOO! LET'S EAT SOME!
WOW, THAT WAS GOOD. TASTED REAL MINTY AND MEATY!
WELL, WE BETTER GET BACK TO WORK. YOU TAKE OVER THE REGISTER, I GOTTA HIT THE CAN. I THINK I GOT THE SQUITS.
YEAH, OKAY. HURRY UP, THOUGH, MAN. I MUSTA ATE TOO MUCH, I FEEL A LITTLE PUKEY.
I'M FECKIN' HUNGRY!
YEAH, ME TOO, BUT WE DON'T HAVE ANY MONEY.
MONKEYBOY JUST GOT A JOB AT LUCKY BURGER. MAYBE YOU GUYS CAN GET SOME FREE FOOD FROM HIM?
YEAH, LET'S GO!

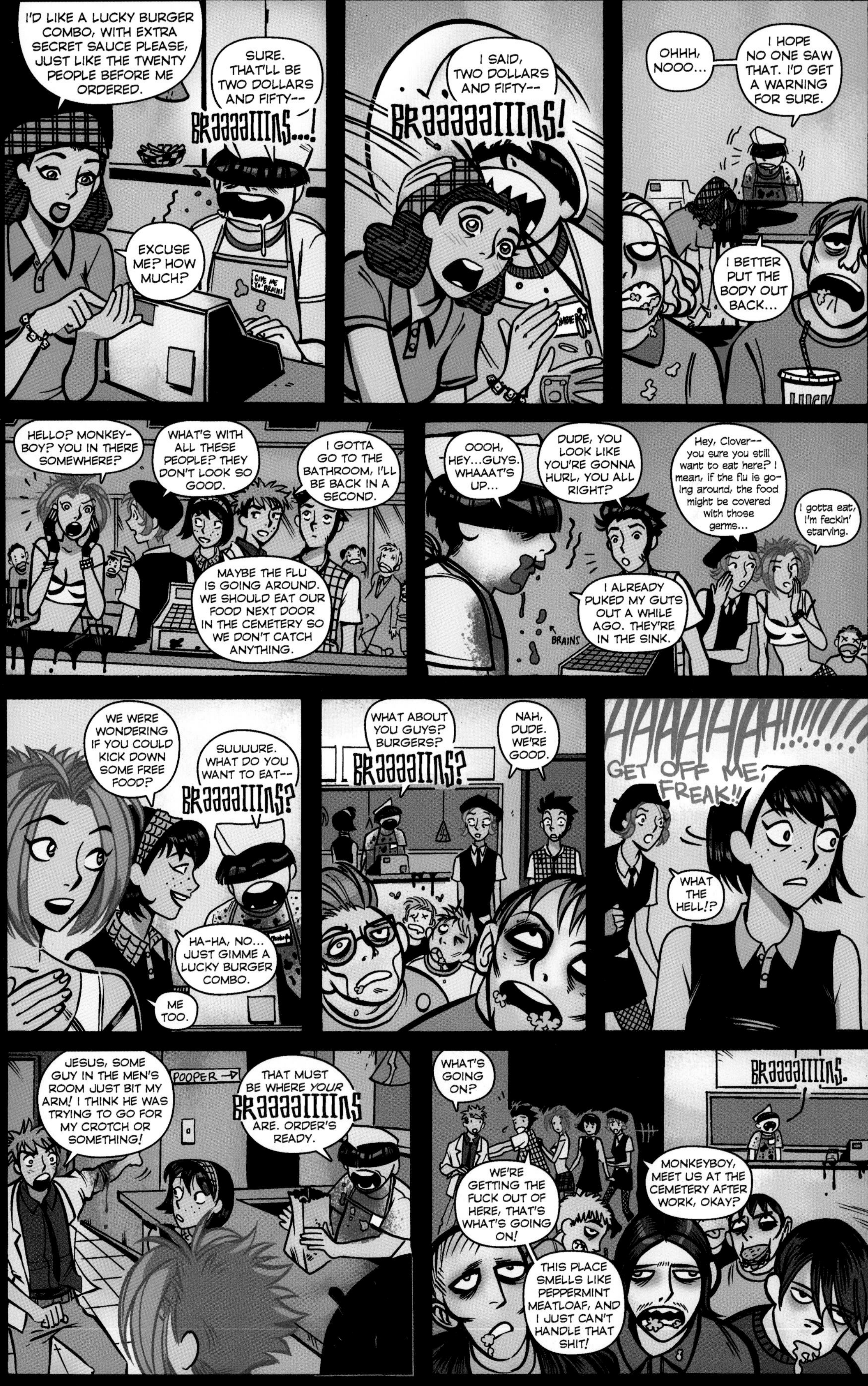
I'D LIKE A LUCKY BURGER COMBO, WITH EXTRA SECRET SAUCE PLEASE, JUST LIKE THE TWENTY PEOPLE BEFORE ME ORDERED.
SURE. THAT'LL BE TWO DOLLARS AND FIFTY--
BRAAAAIIINS...!
GIVE ME YO' BRAINS
EXCUSE ME? HOW MUCH?
I SAID, TWO DOLLARS AND FIFTY--
BRAAAAAIIINS!
OHHH, NOOO...
I HOPE NO ONE SAW THAT. I'D GET A WARNING FOR SURE.
I BETTER PUT THE BODY OUT BACK...
HELLO? MONKEY-BOY? YOU IN THERE SOMEWHERE?
WHAT'S WITH ALL THESE PEOPLE? THEY DON'T LOOK SO GOOD.
I GOTTA GO TO THE BATHROOM, I'LL BE BACK IN A SECOND.
MAYBE THE FLU IS GOING AROUND. WE SHOULD EAT OUR FOOD NEXT DOOR IN THE CEMETERY SO WE DON'T CATCH ANYTHING.
OOOH, HEY...GUYS. WHAAAT'S UP...
DUDE, YOU LOOK LIKE YOU'RE GONNA HURL, YOU ALL RIGHT?
I ALREADY PUKED MY GUTS OUT A WHILE AGO. THEY'RE IN THE SINK.
BRAINS
Hey, Clover-- you sure you still want to eat here? I mean, if the flu is going around, the food might be covered with those germs...
I gotta eat, I'm feckin' starving.
WE WERE WONDERING IF YOU COULD KICK DOWN SOME FREE FOOD?
SUUUURE. WHAT DO YOU WANT TO EAT--
BRAAAAIIINS?
HA-HA, NO... JUST GIMME A LUCKY BURGER COMBO.
ME TOO.
WHAT ABOUT YOU GUYS? BURGERS?
BRAAAAIINS?
NAH, DUDE. WE'RE GOOD.
AAAAAAH!!!!!!!!
GET OFF ME, FREAK!!
WHAT THE HELL!?
JESUS, SOME GUY IN THE MEN'S ROOM JUST BIT MY ARM! I THINK HE WAS TRYING TO GO FOR MY CROTCH OR SOMETHING!
POOPER
THAT MUST BE WHERE YOUR BRAAAAIIIINS ARE. ORDER'S READY.
WHAT'S GOING ON?
WE'RE GETTING THE FUCK OUT OF HERE, THAT'S WHAT'S GOING ON!
THIS PLACE SMELLS LIKE PEPPERMINT MEATLOAF, AND I JUST CAN'T HANDLE THAT SHIT!
BRAAAAIIIINS.
MONKEYBOY, MEET US AT THE CEMETERY AFTER WORK, OKAY?

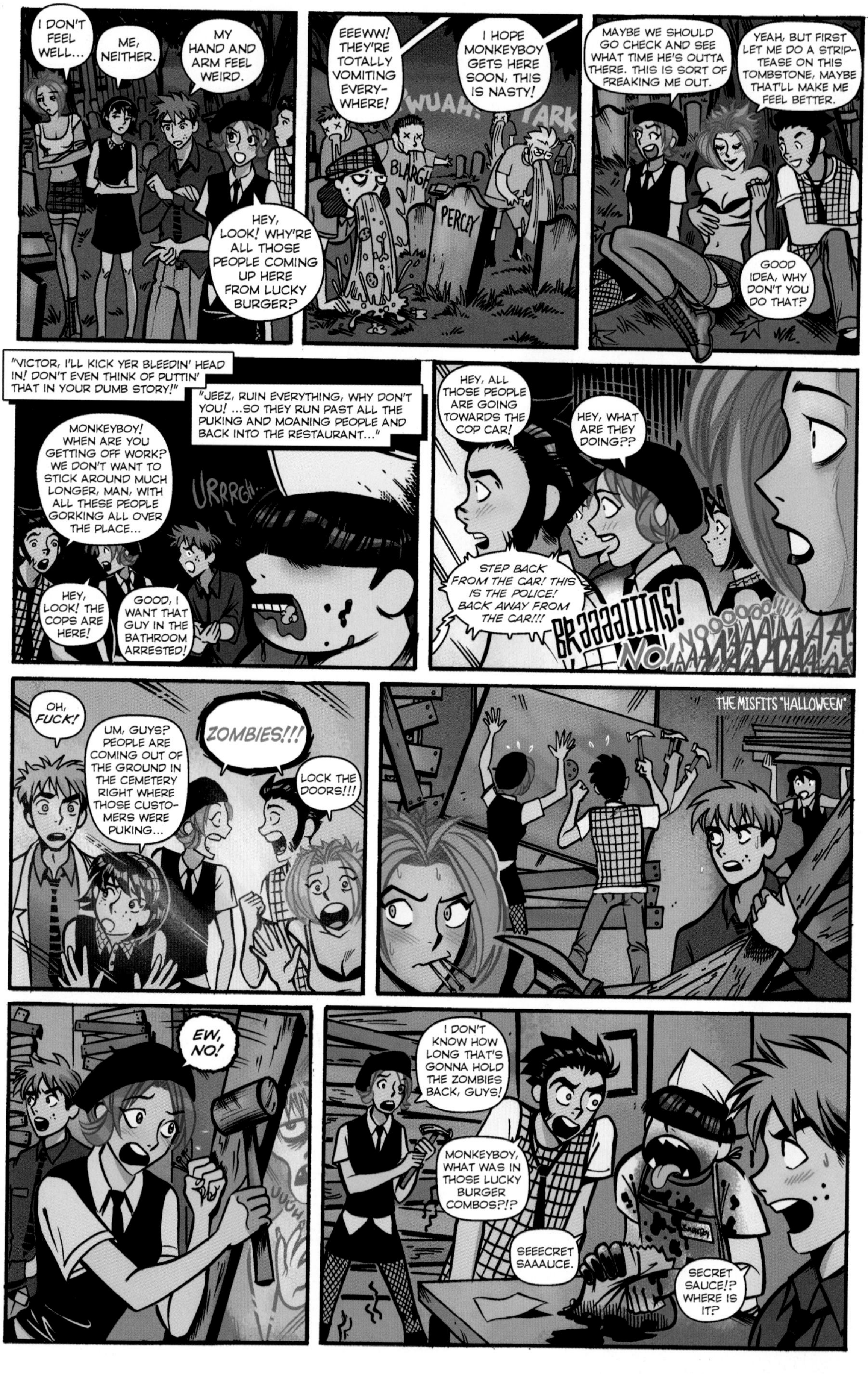

I DON'T FEEL WELL...
ME, NEITHER.
MY HAND AND ARM FEEL WEIRD.
HEY, LOOK! WHY'RE ALL THOSE PEOPLE COMING UP HERE FROM LUCKY BURGER?
EEEWW! THEY'RE TOTALLY VOMITING EVERY-WHERE!
I HOPE MONKEYBOY GETS HERE SOON, THIS IS NASTY!
WUAH!
YARK
BLARGH
PERCEY
MAYBE WE SHOULD GO CHECK AND SEE WHAT TIME HE'S OUTTA THERE. THIS IS SORT OF FREAKING ME OUT.
YEAH, BUT FIRST LET ME DO A STRIP-TEASE ON THIS TOMBSTONE, MAYBE THAT'LL MAKE ME FEEL BETTER.
GOOD IDEA, WHY DON'T YOU DO THAT?
"VICTOR, I'LL KICK YER BLEEDIN' HEAD IN! DON'T EVEN THINK OF PUTTIN' THAT IN YOUR DUMB STORY!"
"JEEZ, RUIN EVERYTHING, WHY DON'T YOU! ...SO THEY RUN PAST ALL THE PUKING AND MOANING PEOPLE AND BACK INTO THE RESTAURANT..."
MONKEYBOY! WHEN ARE YOU GETTING OFF WORK? WE DON'T WANT TO STICK AROUND MUCH LONGER, MAN, WITH ALL THESE PEOPLE GORKING ALL OVER THE PLACE...
URRRGH...
HEY, LOOK! THE COPS ARE HERE!
GOOD, I WANT THAT GUY IN THE BATHROOM ARRESTED!
HEY, ALL THOSE PEOPLE ARE GOING TOWARDS THE COP CAR!
HEY, WHAT ARE THEY DOING??
STEP BACK FROM THE CAR! THIS IS THE POLICE! BACK AWAY FROM THE CAR!!!
BRAAAIIINS!
NO!
NOOOOOO!!!
AAAAAAAAA!
OH, FUCK!
UM, GUYS? PEOPLE ARE COMING OUT OF THE GROUND IN THE CEMETERY RIGHT WHERE THOSE CUSTO-MERS WERE PUKING...
ZOMBIES!!!
LOCK THE DOORS!!!
THE MISFITS "HALLOWEEN"
EW, NO!
I DON'T KNOW HOW LONG THAT'S GONNA HOLD THE ZOMBIES BACK, GUYS!
MONKEYBOY, WHAT WAS IN THOSE LUCKY BURGER COMBOS?!?
SEEECRET SAAAUCE.
SECRET SAUCE!? WHERE IS IT?

"TOP SECRET"? HEY, THAT'S A NUMBER FOR CONTACTING THE ARMY!

AND THIS AIN'T FILLED WITH HAMBURGER SAUCE! LOOK! A CORPSE!

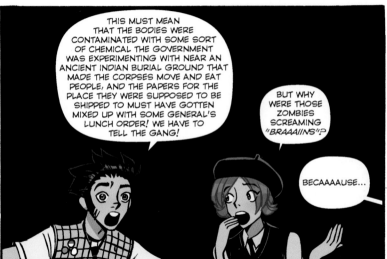

THIS MUST MEAN THAT THE BODIES WERE CONTAMINATED WITH SOME SORT OF CHEMICAL THE GOVERNMENT WAS EXPERIMENTING WITH NEAR AN ANCIENT INDIAN BURIAL GROUND THAT MADE THE CORPSES MOVE AND EAT PEOPLE, AND THE PAPERS FOR THE PLACE THEY WERE SUPPOSED TO BE SHIPPED TO MUST HAVE GOTTEN MIXED UP WITH SOME GENERAL'S LUNCH ORDER! WE HAVE TO TELL THE GANG!

BUT WHY WERE THOSE ZOMBIES SCREAMING "BRAAAIINS"?

BECAAAAUSE...

THAT'S THE ONLY THING THAT MAKES THE PAIN STOP.

WE CAN SEE THAT NOW.

YOU GRAB THAT BASEBALL BAT WITH THE SPIKE THROUGH IT NEXT TO YOU, AND I'LL GRAB THE EMERGENCY AXE! LET'S MUTILATE SOME ZOMBIE ASS!

RIGHT!

I WASN'T GONNA EAT YOUR BRAINS, I JUST WANTED TO GIVE YOU A WET WILLEH!

DIE AGAIN!!!

BUT I DIDN'T EAT MY BURGER! URK!

VIIIICTOR...

UHH!

COME HERE, VICTOR... LET *ME* GIVE YOU A WET WILLY...

SH-SUUUUURE.

GIMME THAT!

TURNING INTO A ZOMBIE DOESN'T MEAN YOU HAVE TO TURN INTO A SKANK!

AW, YOU RUINED A PERFECTLY GOOD ZOMBIE BABE!

SHUT UP! CALL THE NUMBER ON THE SIDE OF THAT TANK!

CHO—

GO, SHE-RA!

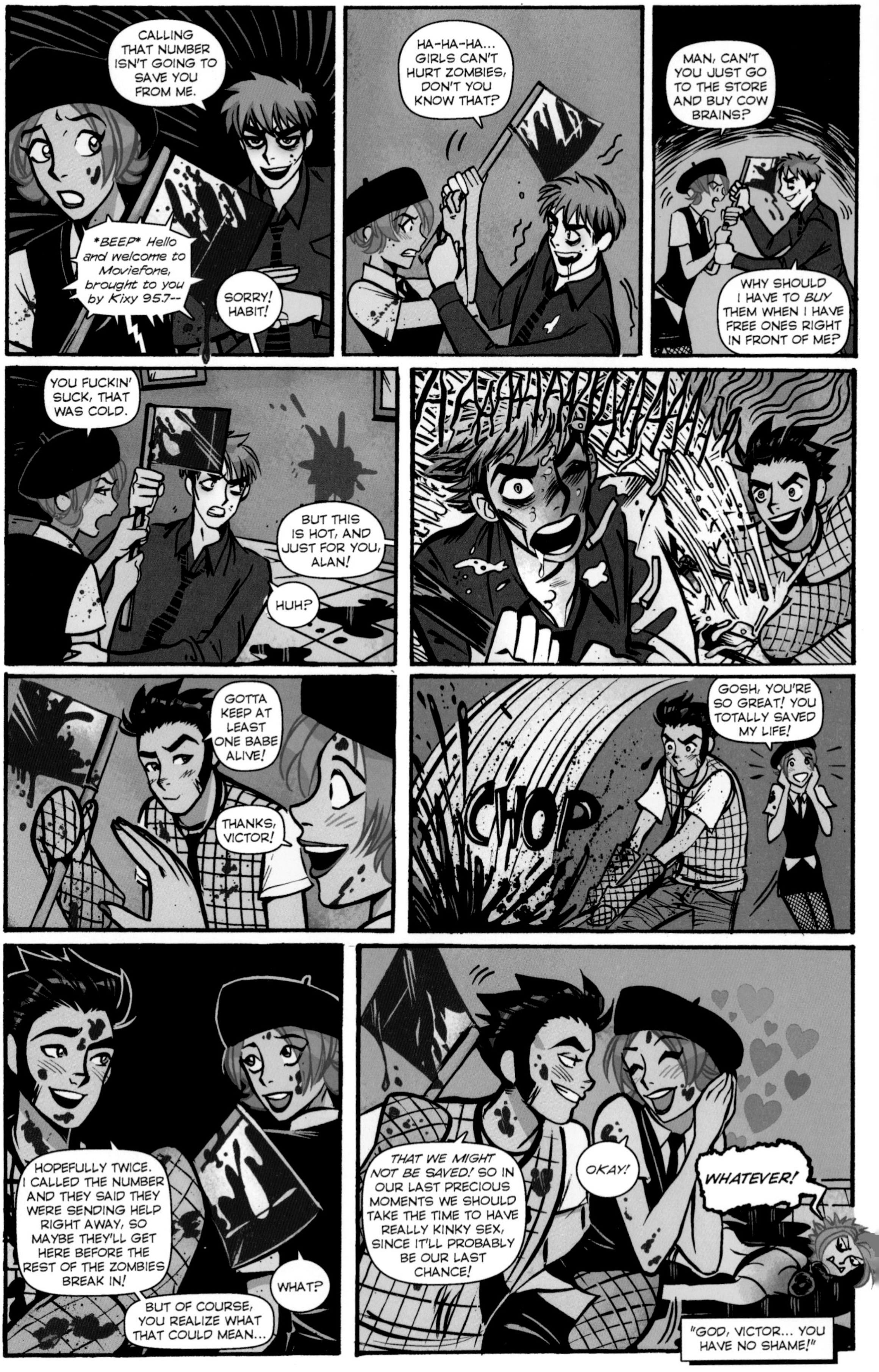
CALLING THAT NUMBER ISN'T GOING TO SAVE YOU FROM ME.
BEEP Hello and welcome to Moviefone, brought to you by Kixy 95.7--
SORRY! HABIT!
HA-HA-HA... GIRLS CAN'T HURT ZOMBIES, DON'T YOU KNOW THAT?
MAN, CAN'T YOU JUST GO TO THE STORE AND BUY COW BRAINS?
WHY SHOULD I HAVE TO BUY THEM WHEN I HAVE FREE ONES RIGHT IN FRONT OF ME?
YOU FUCKIN' SUCK, THAT WAS COLD.
BUT THIS IS HOT, AND JUST FOR YOU, ALAN!
HUH?
GOTTA KEEP AT LEAST ONE BABE ALIVE!
THANKS, VICTOR!
CHOP
GOSH, YOU'RE SO GREAT! YOU TOTALLY SAVED MY LIFE!
HOPEFULLY TWICE. I CALLED THE NUMBER AND THEY SAID THEY WERE SENDING HELP RIGHT AWAY, SO MAYBE THEY'LL GET HERE BEFORE THE REST OF THE ZOMBIES BREAK IN!
WHAT?
BUT OF COURSE, YOU REALIZE WHAT THAT COULD MEAN...
THAT WE MIGHT NOT BE SAVED! SO IN OUR LAST PRECIOUS MOMENTS WE SHOULD TAKE THE TIME TO HAVE REALLY KINKY SEX, SINCE IT'LL PROBABLY BE OUR LAST CHANCE!
OKAY!
WHATEVER!
"GOD, VICTOR... YOU HAVE NO SHAME!"

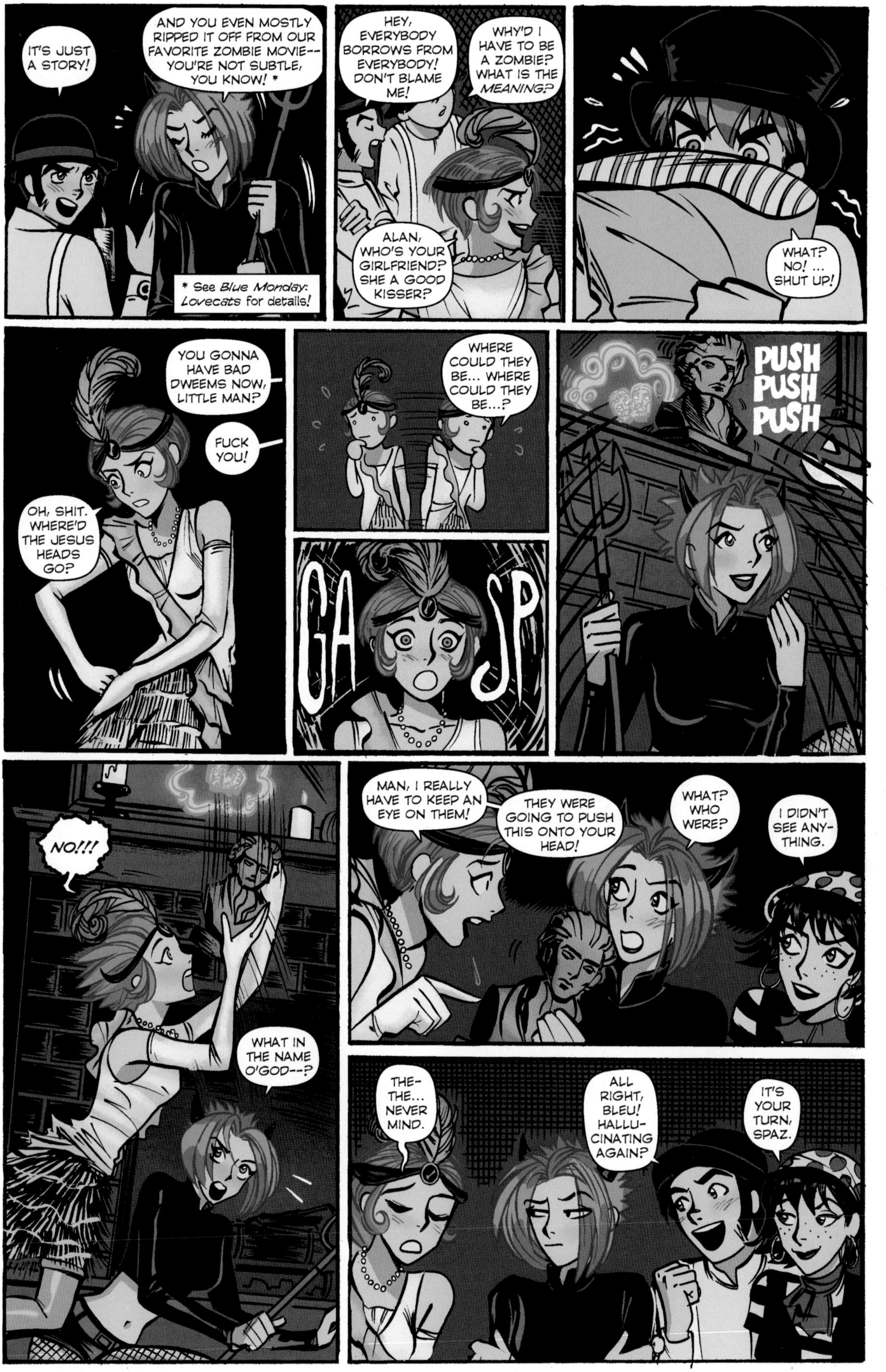
IT'S JUST A STORY!
AND YOU EVEN MOSTLY RIPPED IT OFF FROM OUR FAVORITE ZOMBIE MOVIE-- YOU'RE NOT SUBTLE, YOU KNOW! *
* See *Blue Monday: Lovecats* for details!
HEY, EVERYBODY BORROWS FROM EVERYBODY! DON'T BLAME ME!
WHY'D I HAVE TO BE A ZOMBIE? WHAT IS THE *MEANING?*
ALAN, WHO'S YOUR GIRLFRIEND? SHE A GOOD KISSER?
WHAT? NO! ... SHUT UP!
YOU GONNA HAVE BAD DWEEMS NOW, LITTLE MAN?
FUCK YOU!
OH, SHIT. WHERE'D THE JESUS HEADS GO?
WHERE COULD THEY BE... WHERE COULD THEY BE...?
GASP
PUSH PUSH PUSH
NO!!!
WHAT IN THE NAME O'GOD--?
MAN, I REALLY HAVE TO KEEP AN EYE ON THEM!
THEY WERE GOING TO PUSH THIS ONTO YOUR HEAD!
WHAT? WHO WERE?
I DIDN'T SEE ANYTHING.
THE-THE... NEVER MIND.
ALL RIGHT, BLEU! HALLUCINATING AGAIN?
IT'S YOUR TURN, SPAZ.

"RIGHT, OKAY. SO THE NAME OF MY STORY IS *Dim Silhouettes*."

"OH, NO. PREPARE FOR A TALE OF GOTHIC BORE BY BLEU."

"SHUT YER TRAP, CLOVER!"

"The groundskeeper, Billy, had found and secretly held a diary kept by the great, great, great grand-father of the current Mistress of Colvinwood estates, citing the location of what was thought to be a long lost family treasure.

SNEAK SNEAK

"Though mostly written in complicated riddles, with time Billy finally deciphered them (after he turned the book into the upright position), and had chosen this day as the one when he would make his fortune, running away with what was sure to be more than just semi-precious trinkets."

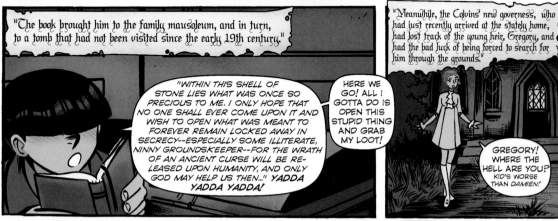

"The book brought him to the family mausoleum, and in turn, to a tomb that had not been visited since the early 19th century."

"WITHIN THIS SHELL OF STONE LIES WHAT WAS ONCE SO PRECIOUS TO ME. I ONLY HOPE THAT NO ONE SHALL EVER COME UPON IT AND WISH TO OPEN WHAT WAS MEANT TO FOREVER REMAIN LOCKED AWAY IN SECRECY--ESPECIALLY SOME ILLITERATE, NINNY GROUNDSKEEPER--FOR THE WRATH OF AN ANCIENT CURSE WILL BE RELEASED UPON HUMANITY, AND ONLY GOD MAY HELP US THEN..." *YADDA YADDA YADDA!*

HERE WE GO! ALL I GOTTA DO IS OPEN THIS STUPID THING AND GRAB MY LOOT!

"Meanwhile, the Colvins' new governess, who had just recently arrived at the stately home, had lost track of the young heir, Gregory, and had the bad luck of being forced to search for him through the grounds."

GREGORY! WHERE THE HELL ARE YOU? KID'S WORSE THAN *DAMIEN!*

"Valerie manages to be locked in the mausoleum by Gregory, who runs off to who-knows-where. Billy insists that she's following him, honing in on his booty."

YOUR *WHAT?*

"Valerie, of course wants nothing to do with his booty, since that's kinda gross, and tells him so, though he believes otherwise. He draws near her, beckoning her to come to him...he won't hurt her too much, he says...and frightened by the behemoth, she shrieks for help."

DON'T SCARE THE BABES, YOU DICK! YOU KNOW WHAT? YOU'RE FUCKIN' FIRED!

SEE IF I CARE!

HE DOESN'T SAY THAT YOU CAN'T SAY "FUCK" IN GOTHIC HORROR!

WELL, I WOULD! IT'S CERTAINLY MORE INTERESTING THAN "I DEMAAAAHND YOH RESIGNATION, SAAAH."

"The two leave Billy alone in the mausoleum again, threatening to call the authorities if he doesn't leave the grounds immediately. Billy scoffs and gets back to searching for his treasure, which appears to be located in an ancient crypt."

PLINK PLINK KRAK

FIRED, SHMIRED.

I'M GONNA BE STINKIN' RICH IN ABOUT TWO MINUTES!

CHRIST ALMIGHTY, WHAT'S THAT SMELL?

IT'S WORSE THAN ANY DEAD BODY I'VE MET BEFORE!

CREEEEAK

AAA!

THANK YOU. IN EXCHANGE FOR ALLOWING YOU TO CONTINUE LIVING, YOU MAY BE MY SERVANT.

NOW BRING ME MINT JULEPS, DAMMIT!

PUT THE FUCKIN' LOTION IN THE CASKET!!!

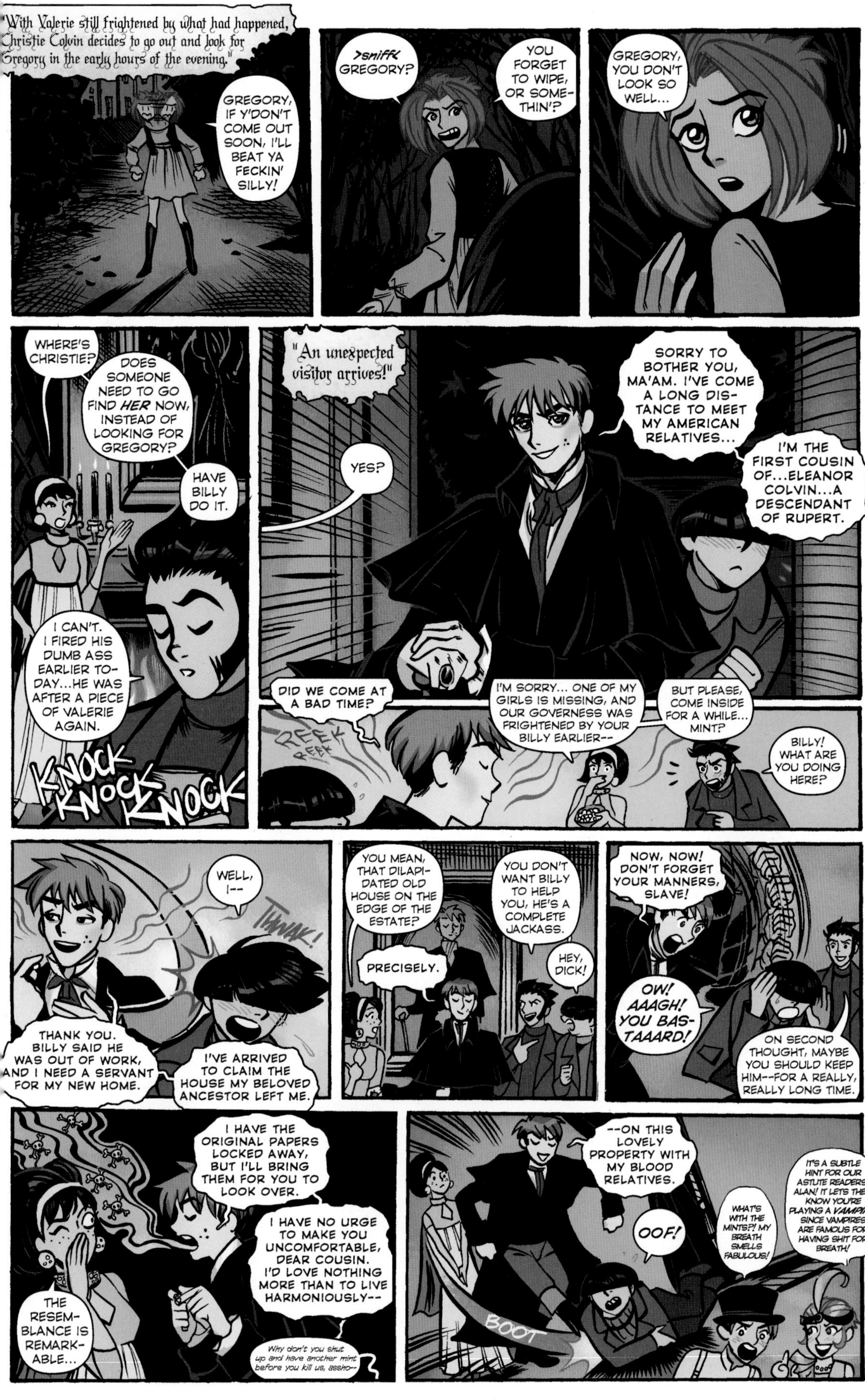
"With Valerie still frightened by what had happened, Christie Colvin decides to go out and look for Gregory in the early hours of the evening."
GREGORY, IF Y'DON'T COME OUT SOON, I'LL BEAT YA FECKIN' SILLY!
>SNIFF< GREGORY?
YOU FORGET TO WIPE, OR SOMETHIN'?
GREGORY, YOU DON'T LOOK SO WELL...
WHERE'S CHRISTIE?
DOES SOMEONE NEED TO GO FIND HER NOW, INSTEAD OF LOOKING FOR GREGORY?
HAVE BILLY DO IT.
I CAN'T. I FIRED HIS DUMB ASS EARLIER TODAY...HE WAS AFTER A PIECE OF VALERIE AGAIN.
KNOCK KNOCK KNOCK
"An unexpected visitor arrives!"
YES?
SORRY TO BOTHER YOU, MA'AM. I'VE COME A LONG DISTANCE TO MEET MY AMERICAN RELATIVES...
I'M THE FIRST COUSIN OF...ELEANOR COLVIN...A DESCENDANT OF RUPERT.
DID WE COME AT A BAD TIME?
REEK REEK
I'M SORRY... ONE OF MY GIRLS IS MISSING, AND OUR GOVERNESS WAS FRIGHTENED BY YOUR BILLY EARLIER--
BUT PLEASE, COME INSIDE FOR A WHILE... MINT?
BILLY! WHAT ARE YOU DOING HERE?
WELL, I--
THWAK!
THANK YOU. BILLY SAID HE WAS OUT OF WORK, AND I NEED A SERVANT FOR MY NEW HOME.
I'VE ARRIVED TO CLAIM THE HOUSE MY BELOVED ANCESTOR LEFT ME.
YOU MEAN, THAT DILAPIDATED OLD HOUSE ON THE EDGE OF THE ESTATE?
PRECISELY.
YOU DON'T WANT BILLY TO HELP YOU, HE'S A COMPLETE JACKASS.
HEY, DICK!
NOW, NOW! DON'T FORGET YOUR MANNERS, SLAVE!
OW! AAAGH! YOU BASTAAARD!
ON SECOND THOUGHT, MAYBE YOU SHOULD KEEP HIM--FOR A REALLY, REALLY LONG TIME.
I HAVE THE ORIGINAL PAPERS LOCKED AWAY, BUT I'LL BRING THEM FOR YOU TO LOOK OVER.
I HAVE NO URGE TO MAKE YOU UNCOMFORTABLE, DEAR COUSIN. I'D LOVE NOTHING MORE THAN TO LIVE HARMONIOUSLY--
THE RESEMBLANCE IS REMARKABLE...
Why don't you shut up and have another mint before you kill us, assho--
--ON THIS LOVELY PROPERTY WITH MY BLOOD RELATIVES.
OOF!
BOOT
WHAT'S WITH THE MINTS?! MY BREATH SMELLS FABULOUS!
IT'S A SUBTLE HINT FOR OUR ASTUTE READERS, ALAN! IT LETS THEM KNOW YOU'RE PLAYING A VAMPIRE, SINCE VAMPIRES ARE FAMOUS FOR HAVING SHIT FOR BREATH!

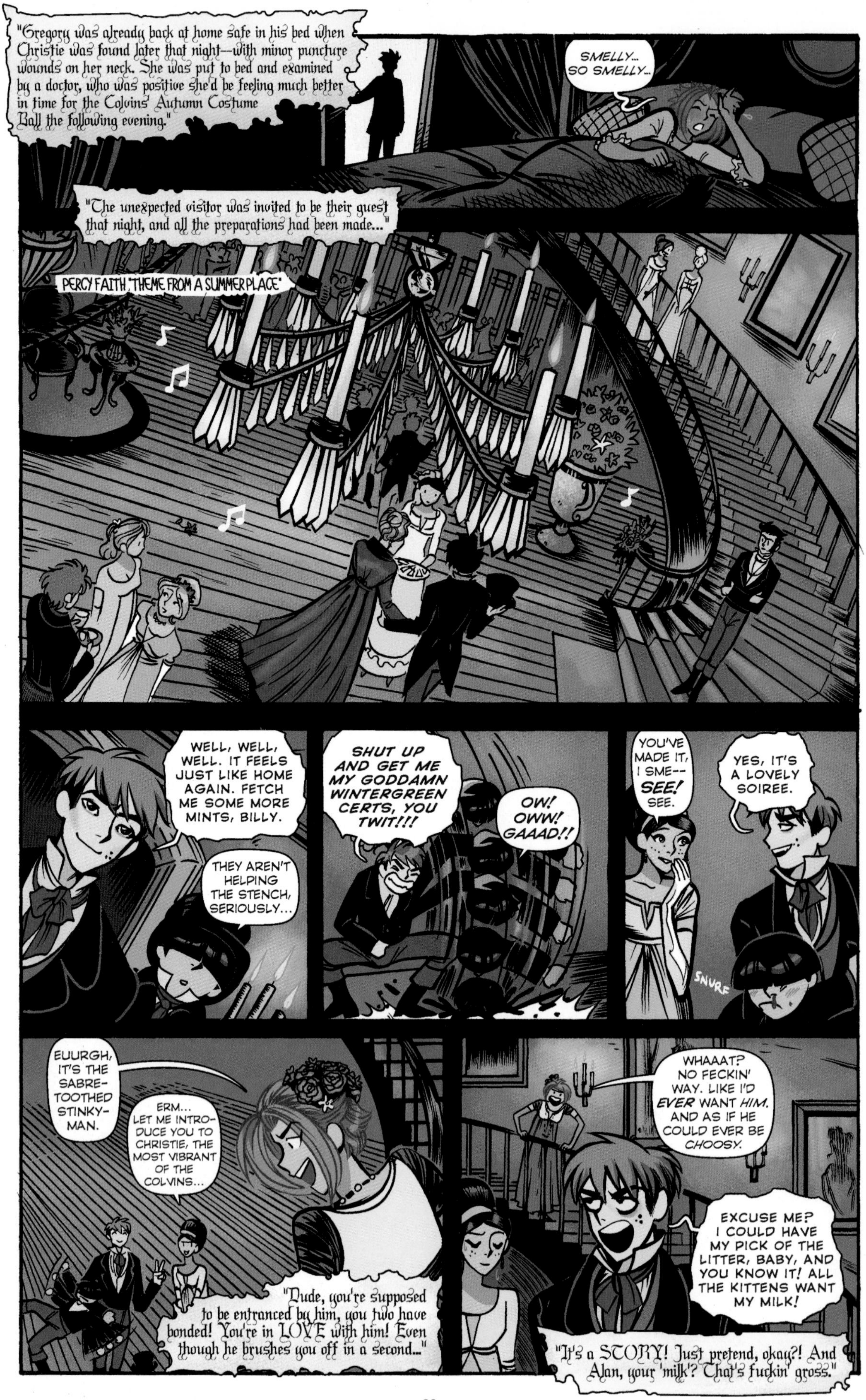
"Gregory was already back at home safe in his bed when Christie was found later that night--with minor puncture wounds on her neck. She was put to bed and examined by a doctor, who was positive she'd be feeling much better in time for the Colvins' Autumn Costume Ball the following evening."
SMELLY... SO SMELLY...
"The unexpected visitor was invited to be their guest that night, and all the preparations had been made..."
PERCY FAITH "THEME FROM A SUMMER PLACE"
WELL, WELL, WELL. IT FEELS JUST LIKE HOME AGAIN. FETCH ME SOME MORE MINTS, BILLY.
THEY AREN'T HELPING THE STENCH, SERIOUSLY...
SHUT UP AND GET ME MY GODDAMN WINTERGREEN CERTS, YOU TWIT!!!
OW! OWW! GAAAD!!
YOU'VE MADE IT, I SME-- SEE! SEE.
YES, IT'S A LOVELY SOIREE.
SNURF
EUURGH, IT'S THE SABRE-TOOTHED STINKY-MAN.
ERM... LET ME INTRODUCE YOU TO CHRISTIE, THE MOST VIBRANT OF THE COLVINS...
"Dude, you're supposed to be entranced by him, you two have bonded! You're in LOVE with him! Even though he brushes you off in a second..."
WHAAAT? NO FECKIN' WAY. LIKE I'D EVER WANT HIM. AND AS IF HE COULD EVER BE CHOOSY.
EXCUSE ME? I COULD HAVE MY PICK OF THE LITTER, BABY, AND YOU KNOW IT! ALL THE KITTENS WANT MY MILK!
"It's a STORY! Just pretend, okay?! And Alan, your 'milk'? That's fuckin' gross."

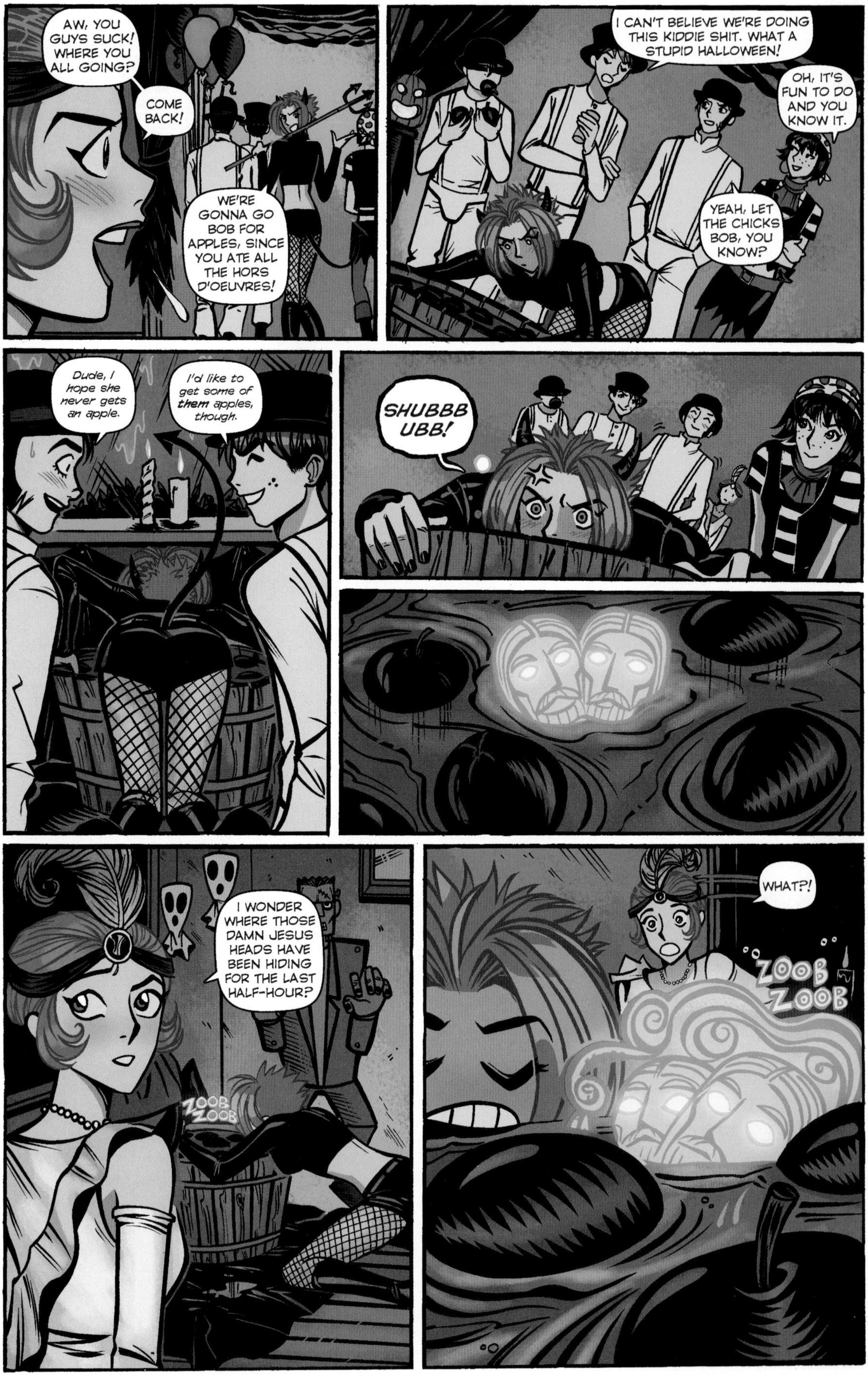
AW, YOU GUYS SUCK! WHERE YOU ALL GOING?
COME BACK!
WE'RE GONNA GO BOB FOR APPLES, SINCE YOU ATE ALL THE HORS D'OEUVRES!
I CAN'T BELIEVE WE'RE DOING THIS KIDDIE SHIT. WHAT A STUPID HALLOWEEN!
OH, IT'S FUN TO DO AND YOU KNOW IT.
YEAH, LET THE CHICKS BOB, YOU KNOW?
Dude, I hope she never gets an apple.
I'd like to get some of *them* apples, though.
SHUBBB UBB!
I WONDER WHERE THOSE DAMN JESUS HEADS HAVE BEEN HIDING FOR THE LAST HALF-HOUR?
ZOOB ZOOB
WHAT?!
ZOOB ZOOB

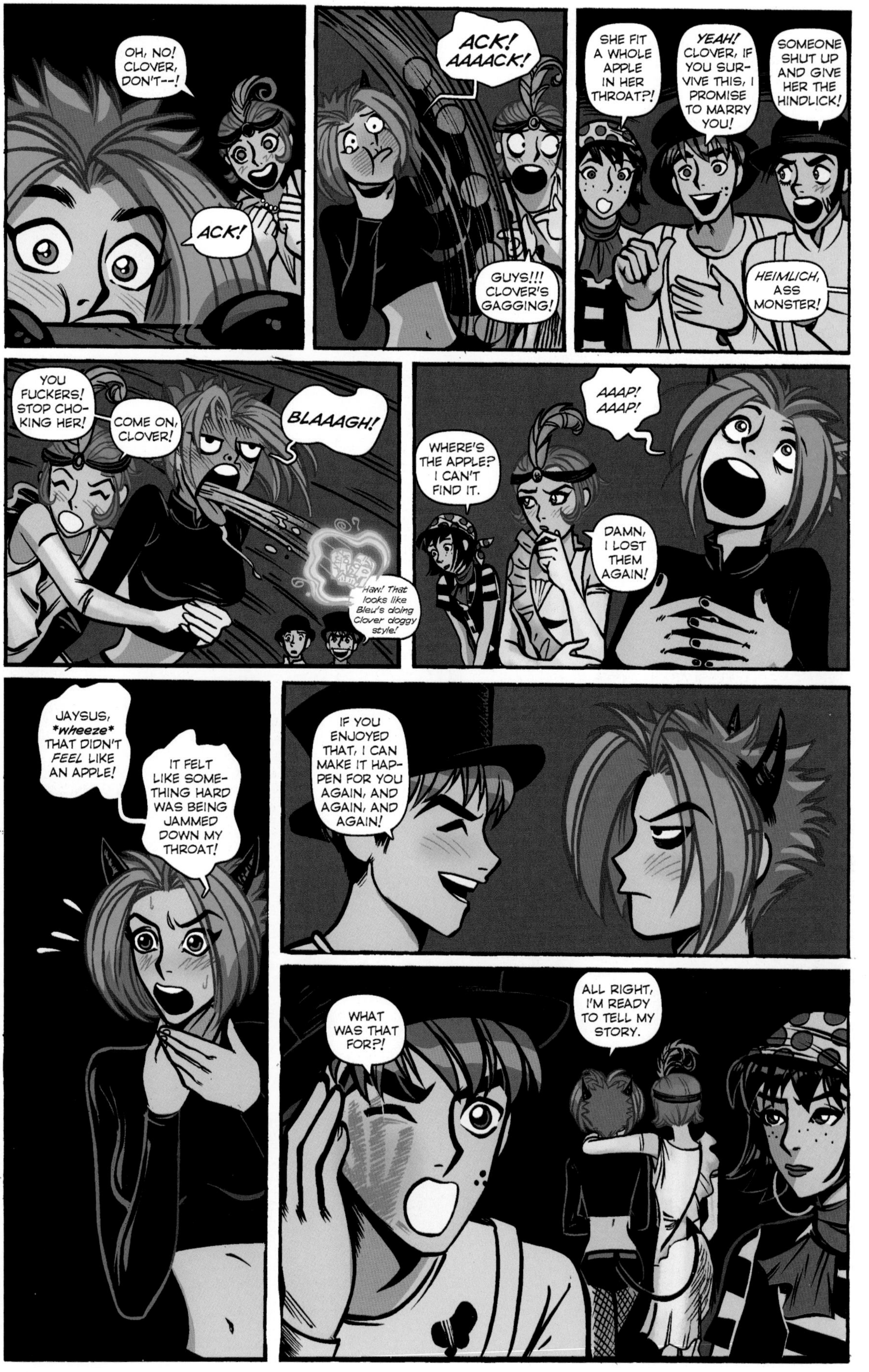
OH, NO! CLOVER, DON'T--!
ACK!
ACK! AAAACK!
GUYS!!! CLOVER'S GAGGING!
SHE FIT A WHOLE APPLE IN HER THROAT?!
YEAH! CLOVER, IF YOU SURVIVE THIS, I PROMISE TO MARRY YOU!
SOMEONE SHUT UP AND GIVE HER THE HINDLICK!
HEIMLICH, ASS MONSTER!
YOU FUCKERS! STOP CHOKING HER!
COME ON, CLOVER!
BLAAAGH!
Haw! That looks like Bleu's doing Clover doggy style!
AAAP! AAAP!
WHERE'S THE APPLE? I CAN'T FIND IT.
DAMN, I LOST THEM AGAIN!
JAYSUS, *wheeze* THAT DIDN'T FEEL LIKE AN APPLE!
IT FELT LIKE SOMETHING HARD WAS BEING JAMMED DOWN MY THROAT!
IF YOU ENJOYED THAT, I CAN MAKE IT HAPPEN FOR YOU AGAIN, AND AGAIN, AND AGAIN!
WHAT WAS THAT FOR?!
ALL RIGHT, I'M READY TO TELL MY STORY.

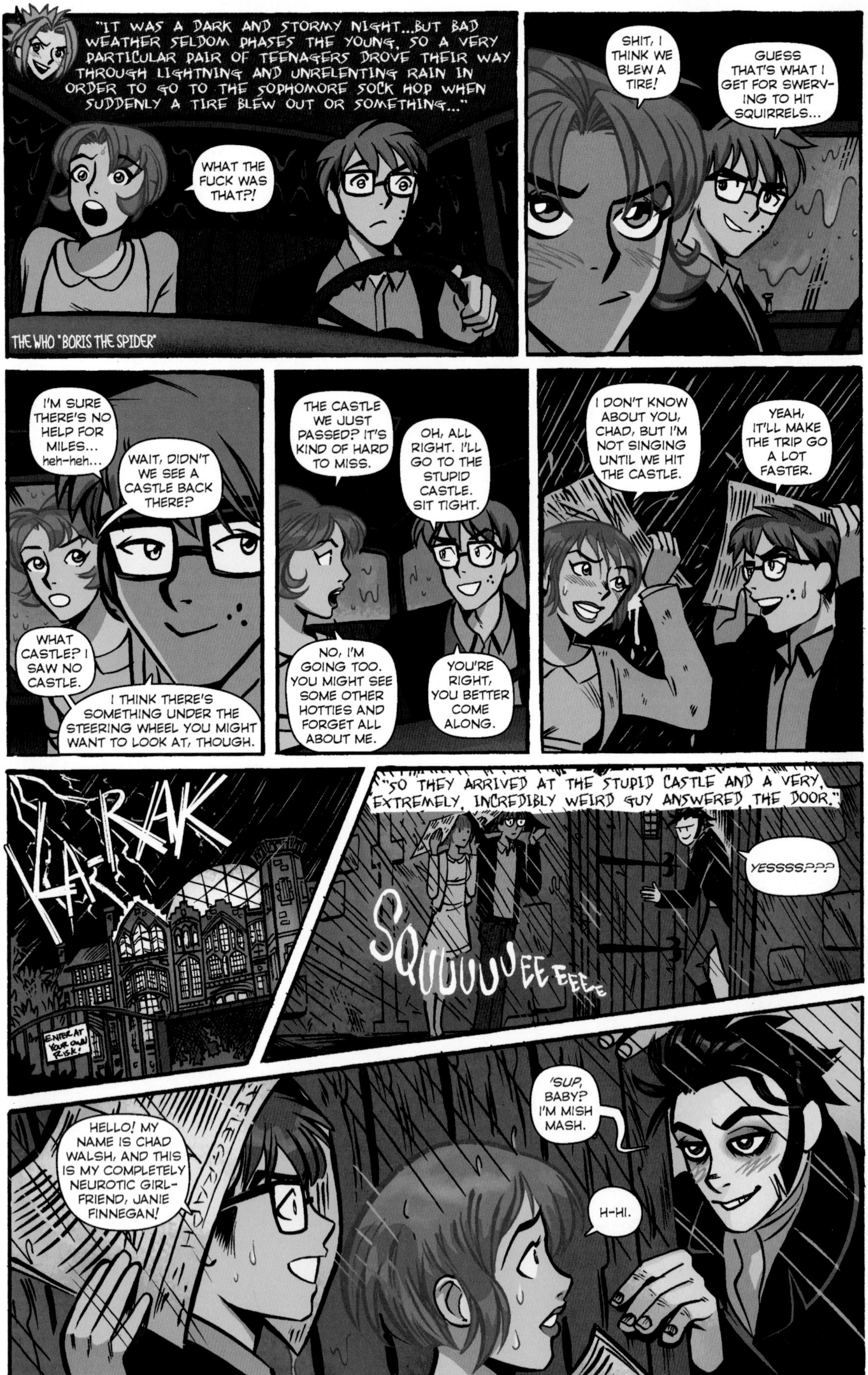
"IT WAS A DARK AND STORMY NIGHT...BUT BAD WEATHER SELDOM PHASES THE YOUNG, SO A VERY PARTICULAR PAIR OF TEENAGERS DROVE THEIR WAY THROUGH LIGHTNING AND UNRELENTING RAIN IN ORDER TO GO TO THE SOPHOMORE SOCK HOP WHEN SUDDENLY A TIRE BLEW OUT OR SOMETHING..."
WHAT THE FUCK WAS THAT?!
THE WHO "BORIS THE SPIDER"
SHIT, I THINK WE BLEW A TIRE!
GUESS THAT'S WHAT I GET FOR SWERVING TO HIT SQUIRRELS...
I'M SURE THERE'S NO HELP FOR MILES... heh-heh...
WAIT, DIDN'T WE SEE A CASTLE BACK THERE?
WHAT CASTLE? I SAW NO CASTLE.
I THINK THERE'S SOMETHING UNDER THE STEERING WHEEL YOU MIGHT WANT TO LOOK AT, THOUGH.
THE CASTLE WE JUST PASSED? IT'S KIND OF HARD TO MISS.
OH, ALL RIGHT. I'LL GO TO THE STUPID CASTLE. SIT TIGHT.
NO, I'M GOING TOO. YOU MIGHT SEE SOME OTHER HOTTIES AND FORGET ALL ABOUT ME.
YOU'RE RIGHT, YOU BETTER COME ALONG.
I DON'T KNOW ABOUT YOU, CHAD, BUT I'M NOT SINGING UNTIL WE HIT THE CASTLE.
YEAH, IT'LL MAKE THE TRIP GO A LOT FASTER.
KA-RAK
ENTER AT YOUR OWN RISK!
"SO THEY ARRIVED AT THE STUPID CASTLE AND A VERY, EXTREMELY, INCREDIBLY WEIRD GUY ANSWERED THE DOOR."
SQUUUUUEEEEE
YESSSS???
HELLO! MY NAME IS CHAD WALSH, AND THIS IS MY COMPLETELY NEUROTIC GIRLFRIEND, JANIE FINNEGAN!
'SUP, BABY? I'M MISH MASH.
H-HI.

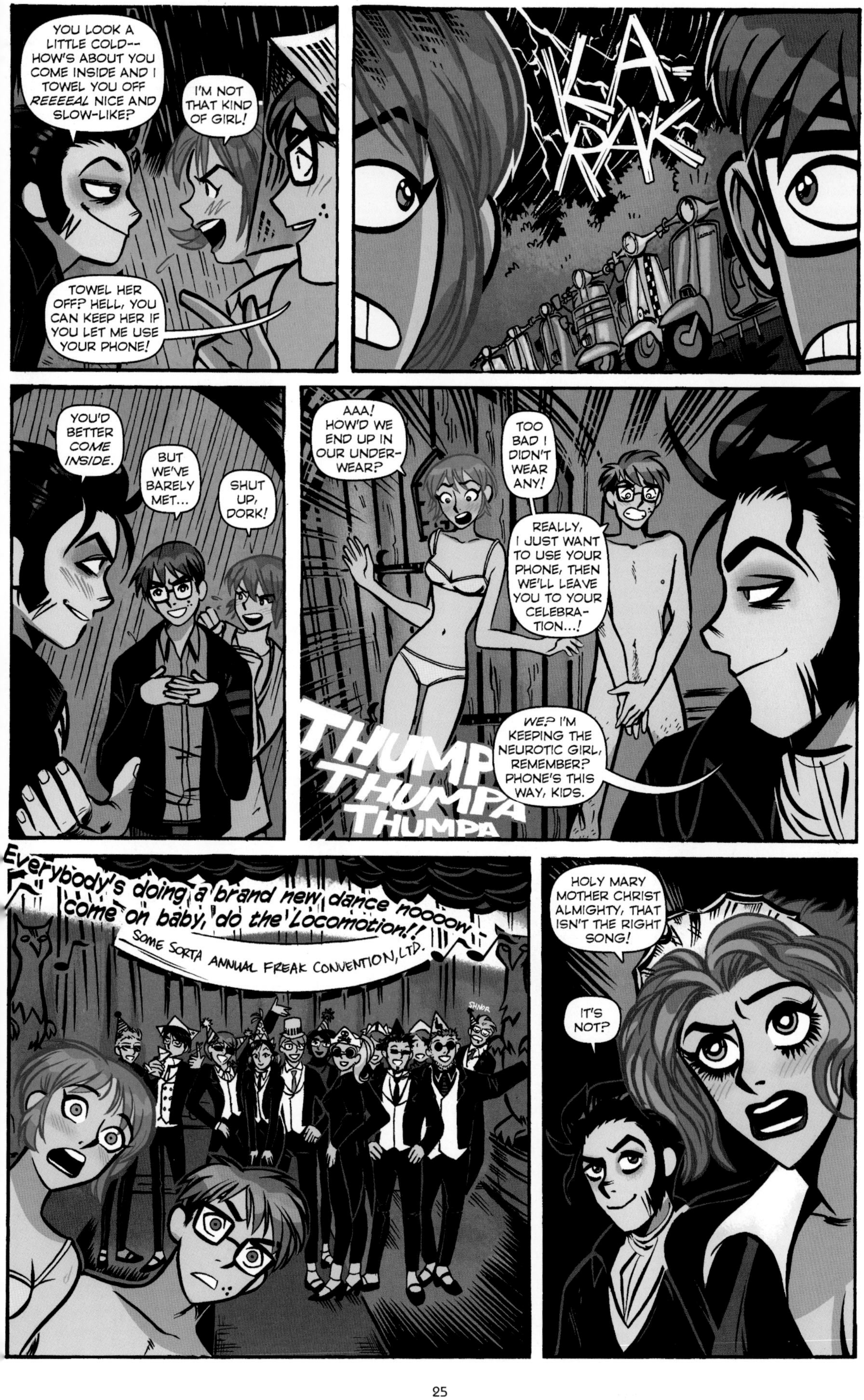

YOU LOOK A LITTLE COLD-- HOW'S ABOUT YOU COME INSIDE AND I TOWEL YOU OFF REEEEAL NICE AND SLOW-LIKE?
I'M NOT THAT KIND OF GIRL!
TOWEL HER OFF? HELL, YOU CAN KEEP HER IF YOU LET ME USE YOUR PHONE!
KA-KRAK
YOU'D BETTER COME INSIDE.
BUT WE'VE BARELY MET...
SHUT UP, DORK!
AAA! HOW'D WE END UP IN OUR UNDER-WEAR?
TOO BAD I DIDN'T WEAR ANY!
REALLY, I JUST WANT TO USE YOUR PHONE, THEN WE'LL LEAVE YOU TO YOUR CELEBRA-TION...!
WE? I'M KEEPING THE NEUROTIC GIRL, REMEMBER? PHONE'S THIS WAY, KIDS.
THUMP THUMPA THUMPA
Everybody's doing a brand new dance noooow, come on baby, do the Locomotion!!
SOME SORTA ANNUAL FREAK CONVENTION, LTD.
SHNOR
HOLY MARY MOTHER CHRIST ALMIGHTY, THAT ISN'T THE RIGHT SONG!
IT'S NOT?

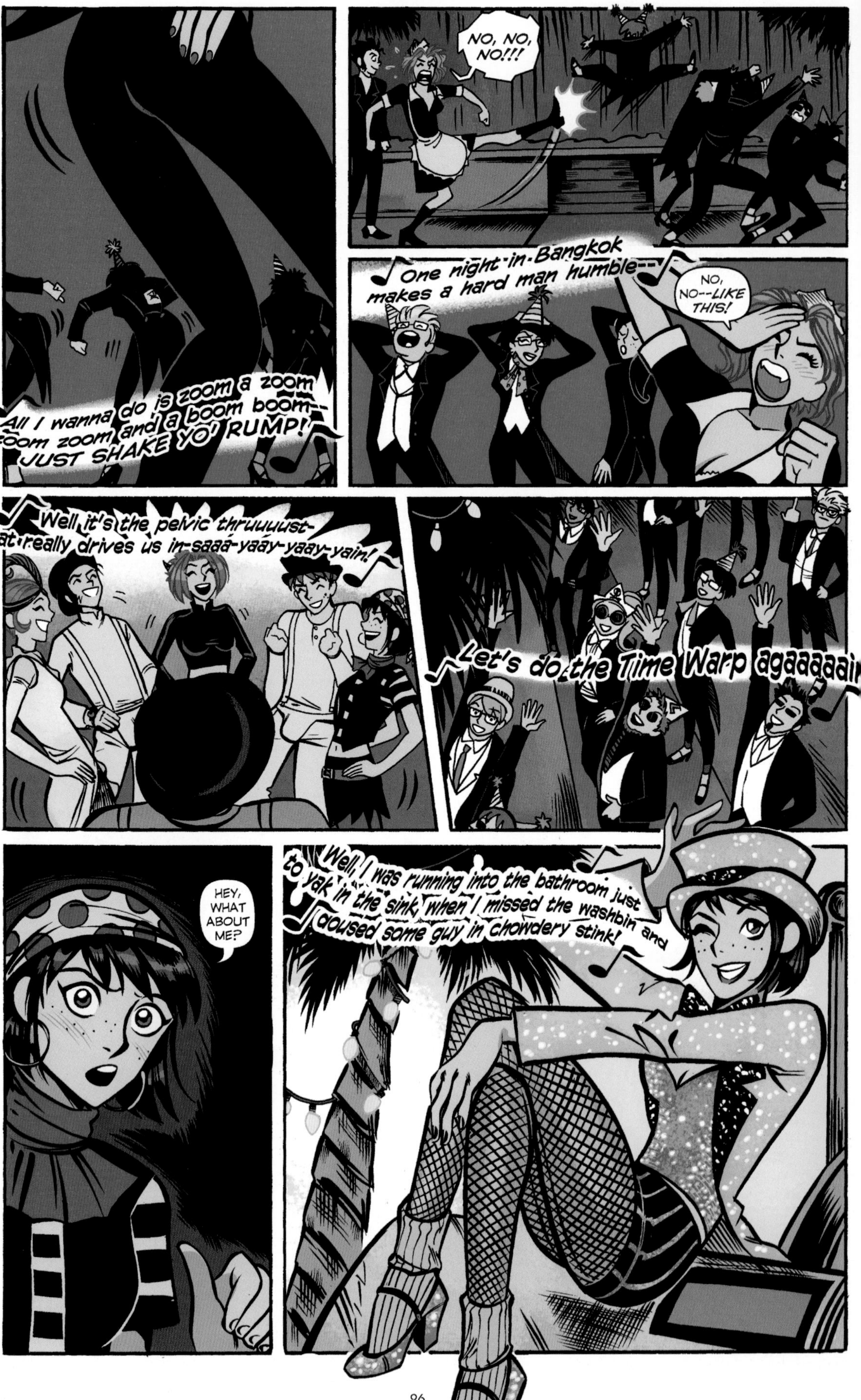
NO, NO, NO!!!
One night in Bangkok makes a hard man humble--
NO, NO--LIKE THIS!
All I wanna do is zoom a zoom zoom zoom and a boom boom-- JUST SHAKE YO' RUMP!
Well it's the pelvic thruuuust- that really drives us in-saaá-yaáy-yaay-yain!
Let's do the Time Warp agaaaaain
HEY, WHAT ABOUT ME?
Well, I was running into the bathroom just to yak in the sink, when I missed the washbin and doused some guy in chowdery stink!

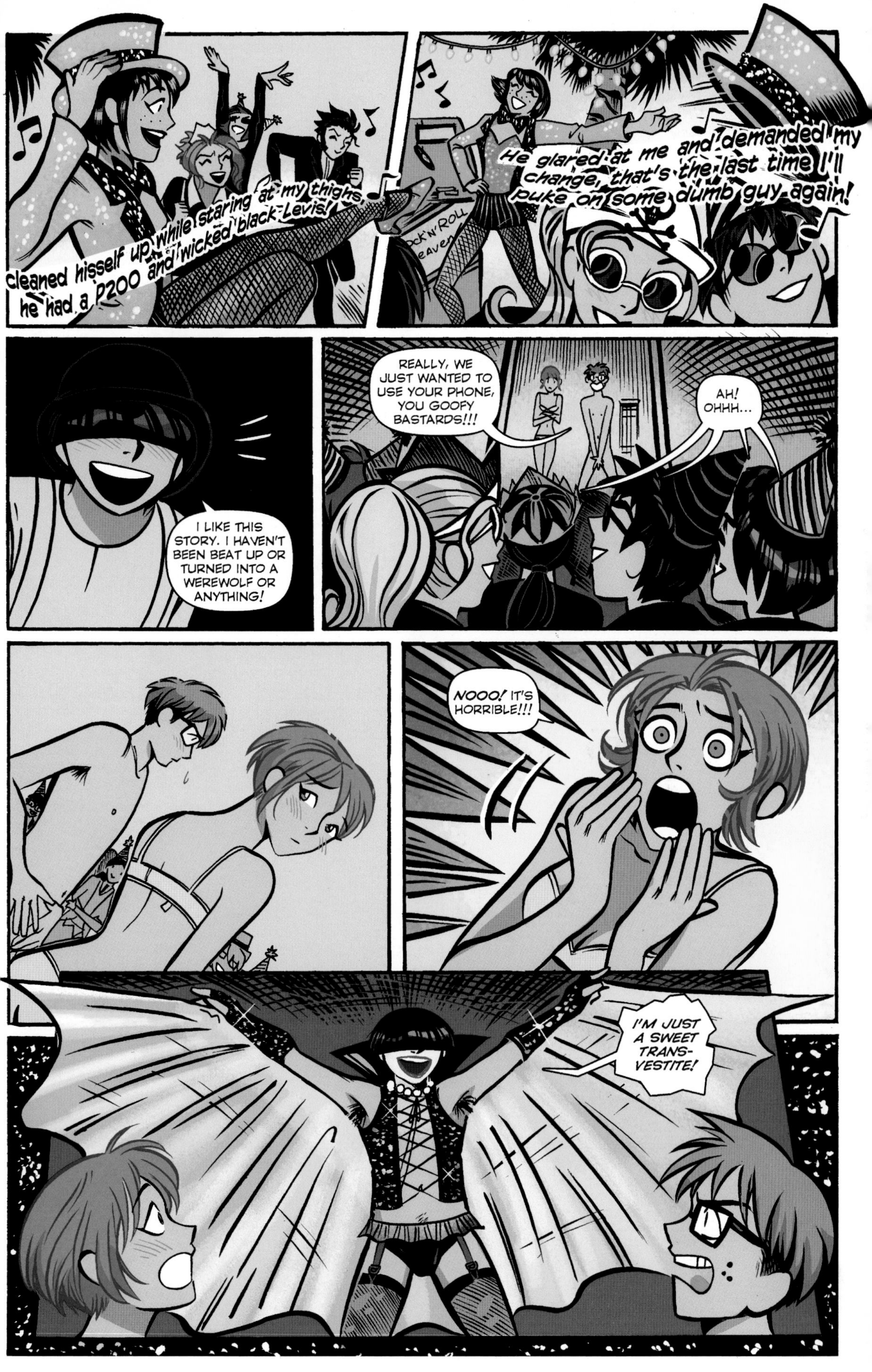
cleaned hisself up while staring at my thighs, he had a P200 and wicked black Levis!
Rock 'n' Roll Heaven
He glared at me and demanded my change, that's the last time I'll puke on some dumb guy again!
I LIKE THIS STORY. I HAVEN'T BEEN BEAT UP OR TURNED INTO A WEREWOLF OR ANYTHING!
REALLY, WE JUST WANTED TO USE YOUR PHONE, YOU GOOFY BASTARDS!!!
AH! OHHH...
NOOO! IT'S HORRIBLE!!!
I'M JUST A SWEET TRANS-VESTITE!

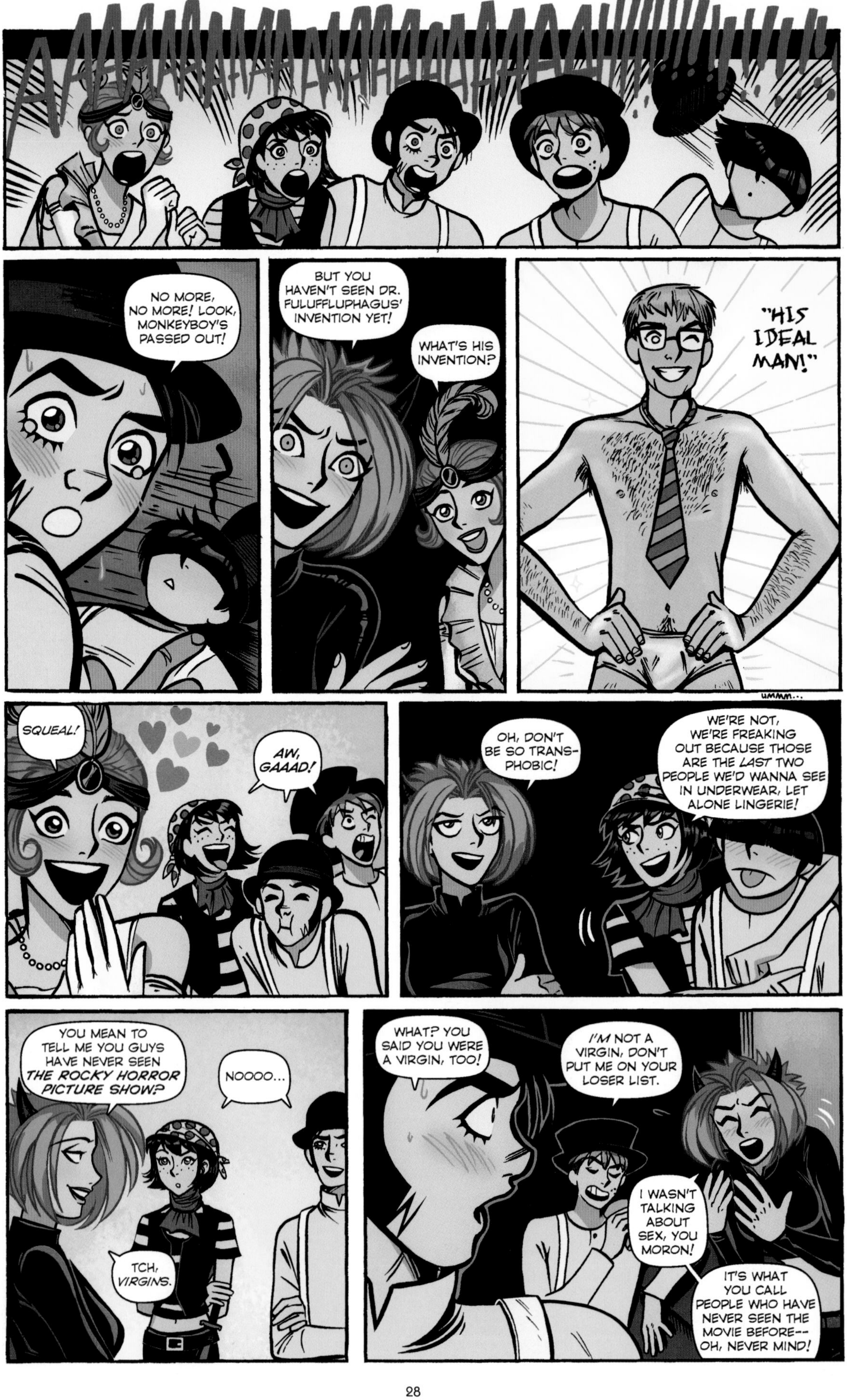
AAAAAAAAAAAAAAAAAAAAAAAAAAAHH!!!!!!!!!!!...
NO MORE, NO MORE! LOOK, MONKEYBOY'S PASSED OUT!
BUT YOU HAVEN'T SEEN DR. FULUFFLUPHAGUS' INVENTION YET!
WHAT'S HIS INVENTION?
"HIS IDEAL MAN!"
ummm...
SQUEAL!
AW, GAAAD!
OH, DON'T BE SO TRANS-PHOBIC!
WE'RE NOT, WE'RE FREAKING OUT BECAUSE THOSE ARE THE LAST TWO PEOPLE WE'D WANNA SEE IN UNDERWEAR, LET ALONE LINGERIE!
YOU MEAN TO TELL ME YOU GUYS HAVE NEVER SEEN THE ROCKY HORROR PICTURE SHOW?
NOOOO...
TCH, VIRGINS.
WHAT? YOU SAID YOU WERE A VIRGIN, TOO!
I'M NOT A VIRGIN, DON'T PUT ME ON YOUR LOSER LIST.
I WASN'T TALKING ABOUT SEX, YOU MORON!
IT'S WHAT YOU CALL PEOPLE WHO HAVE NEVER SEEN THE MOVIE BEFORE-- OH, NEVER MIND!

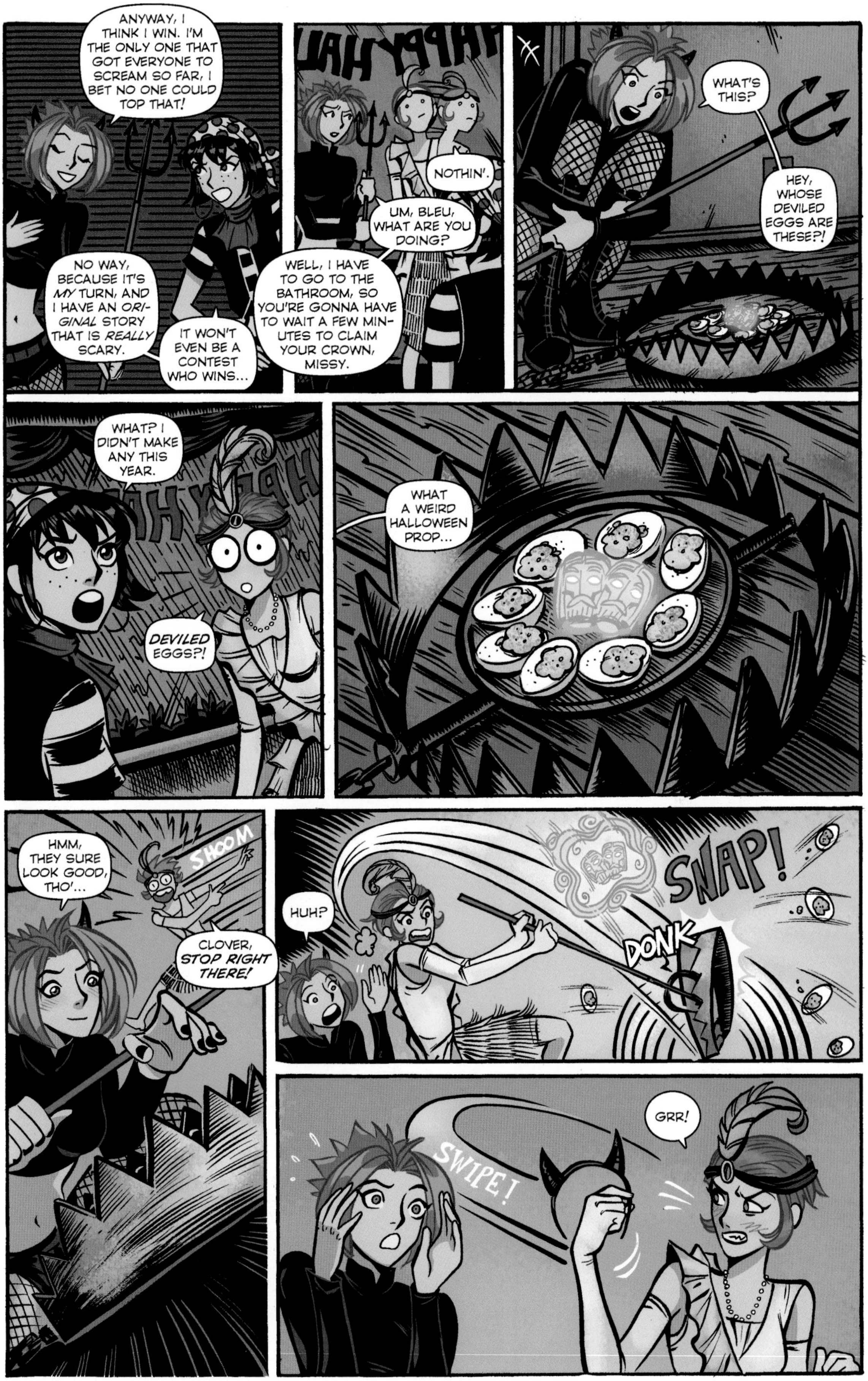
ANYWAY, I THINK I WIN. I'M THE ONLY ONE THAT GOT EVERYONE TO SCREAM SO FAR, I BET NO ONE COULD TOP THAT!
NO WAY, BECAUSE IT'S MY TURN, AND I HAVE AN ORIGINAL STORY THAT IS REALLY SCARY.
IT WON'T EVEN BE A CONTEST WHO WINS...
NOTHIN'.
UM, BLEU, WHAT ARE YOU DOING?
WELL, I HAVE TO GO TO THE BATHROOM, SO YOU'RE GONNA HAVE TO WAIT A FEW MINUTES TO CLAIM YOUR CROWN, MISSY.
WHAT'S THIS?
HEY, WHOSE DEVILED EGGS ARE THESE?!
WHAT? I DIDN'T MAKE ANY THIS YEAR.
DEVILED EGGS?!
WHAT A WEIRD HALLOWEEN PROP...
HMM, THEY SURE LOOK GOOD, THO'...
SHOOM
CLOVER, STOP RIGHT THERE!
HUH?
SNAP!
DONK
GRR!
SWIPE!

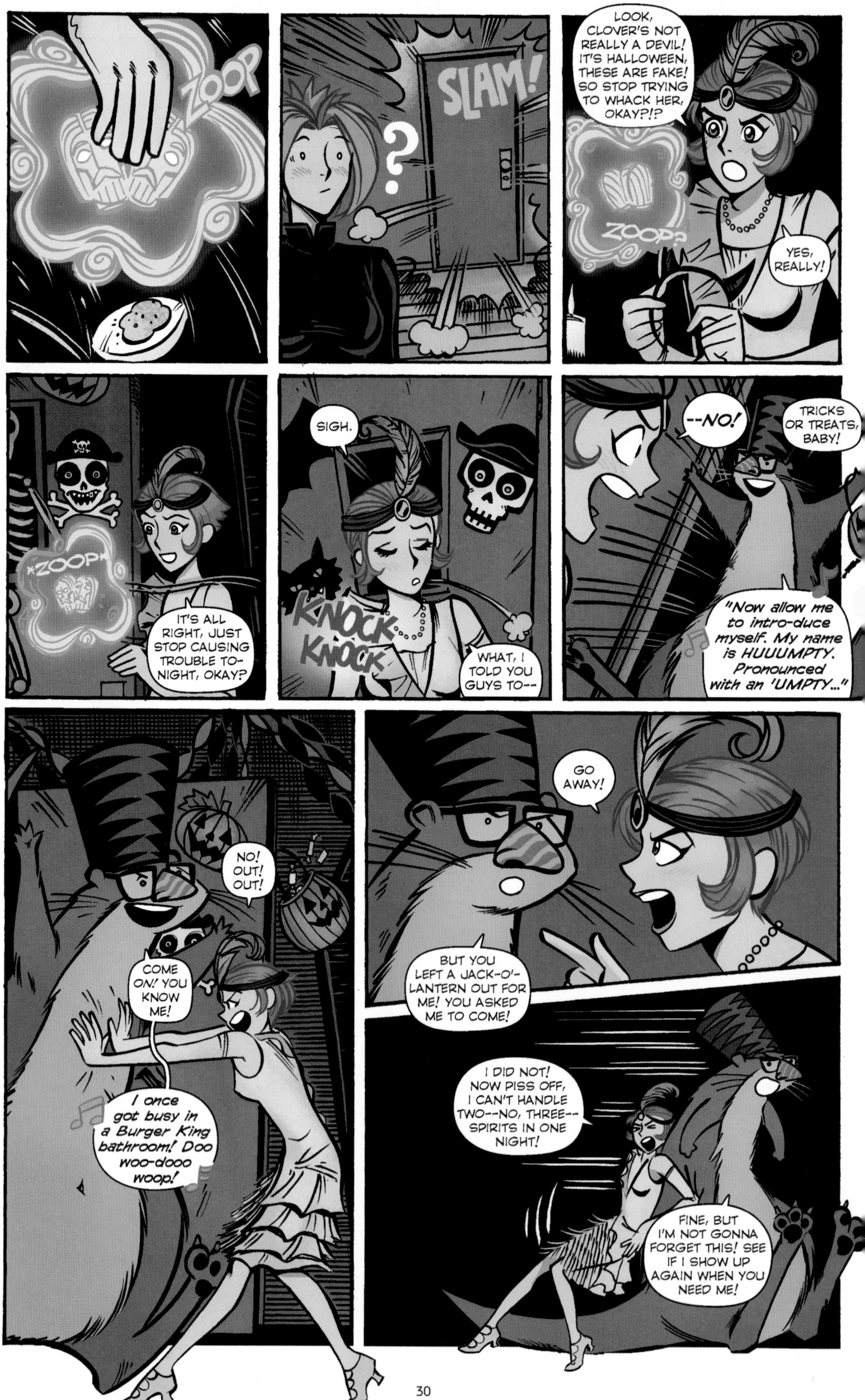
ZOOP
SLAM!
?
LOOK, CLOVER'S NOT REALLY A DEVIL! IT'S HALLOWEEN, THESE ARE FAKE! SO STOP TRYING TO WHACK HER, OKAY?!?
ZOOP?
YES, REALLY!
ZOOP
IT'S ALL RIGHT, JUST STOP CAUSING TROUBLE TO-NIGHT, OKAY?
SIGH.
KNOCK KNOCK
WHAT, I TOLD YOU GUYS TO--
--NO!
TRICKS OR TREATS, BABY!
"Now allow me to intro-duce myself. My name is HUUUMPTY. Pronounced with an 'UMPTY..."
NO! OUT! OUT!
COME ON! YOU KNOW ME!
I once got busy in a Burger King bathroom! Doo woo-dooo woop!
GO AWAY!
BUT YOU LEFT A JACK-O'-LANTERN OUT FOR ME! YOU ASKED ME TO COME!
I DID NOT! NOW PISS OFF, I CAN'T HANDLE TWO--NO, THREE--SPIRITS IN ONE NIGHT!
FINE, BUT I'M NOT GONNA FORGET THIS! SEE IF I SHOW UP AGAIN WHEN YOU NEED ME!

"Blue Belles"

A Special Crossover With Paul Dini's *Jingle Belle*

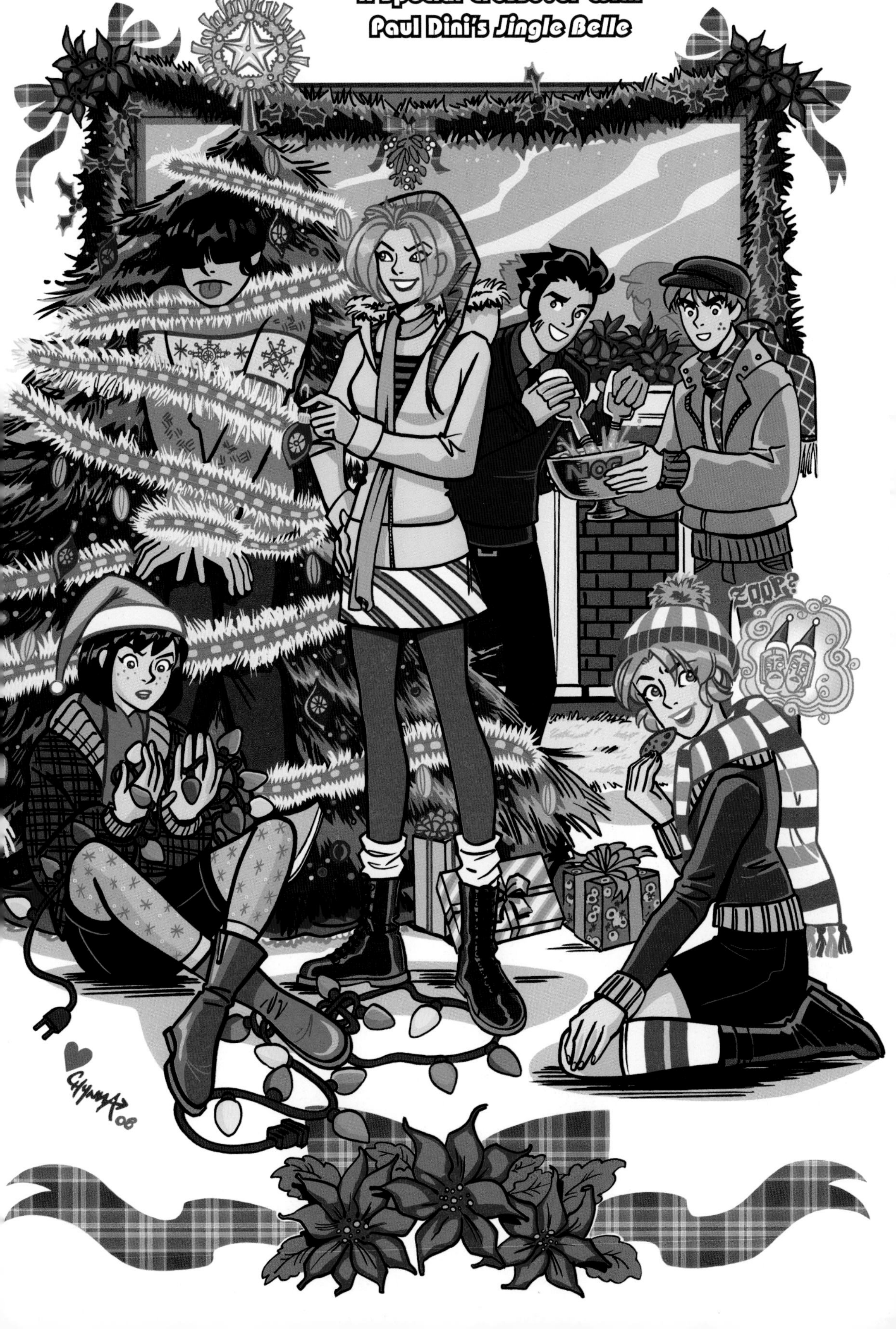
NOG
ZOOP?

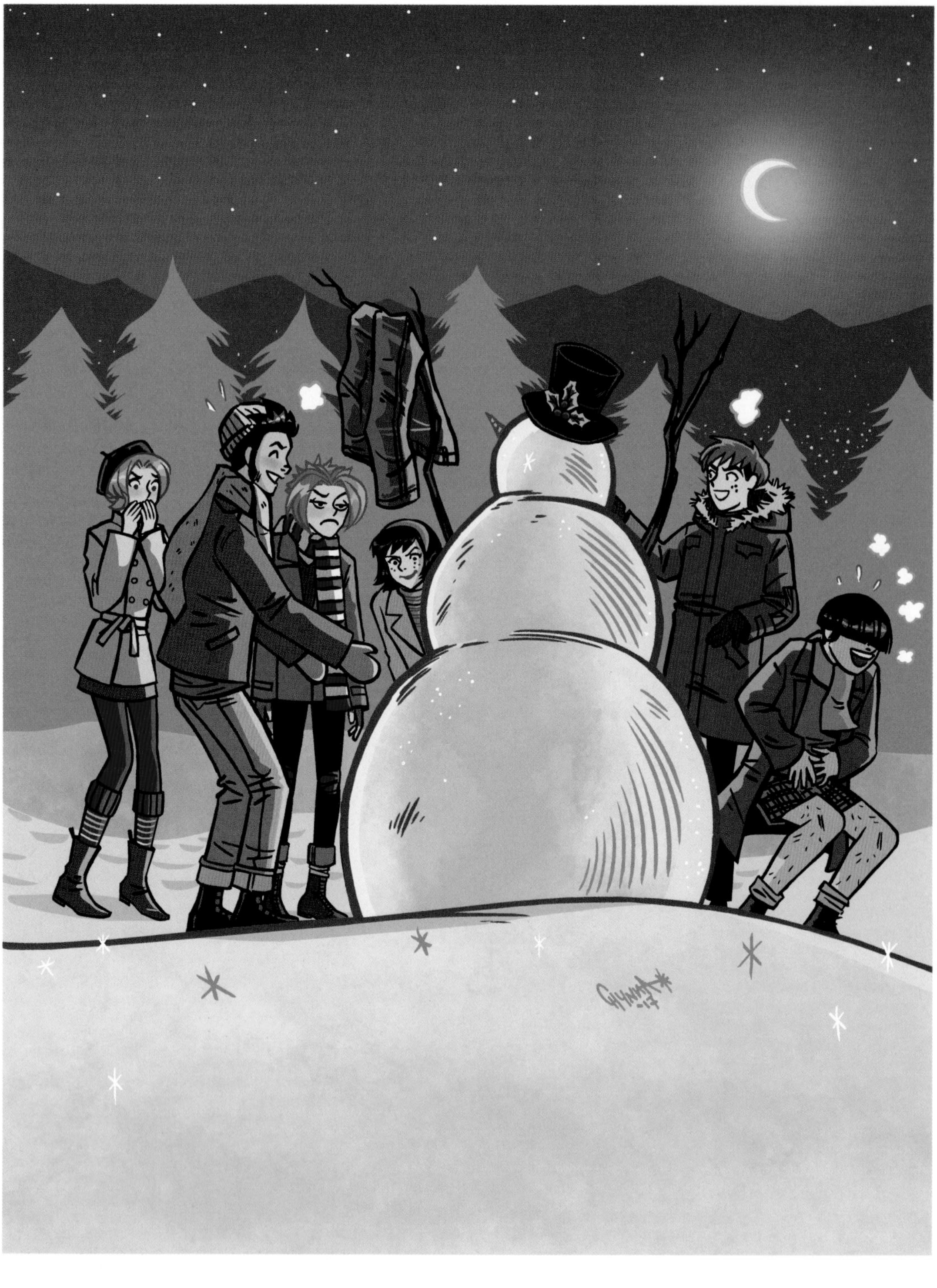

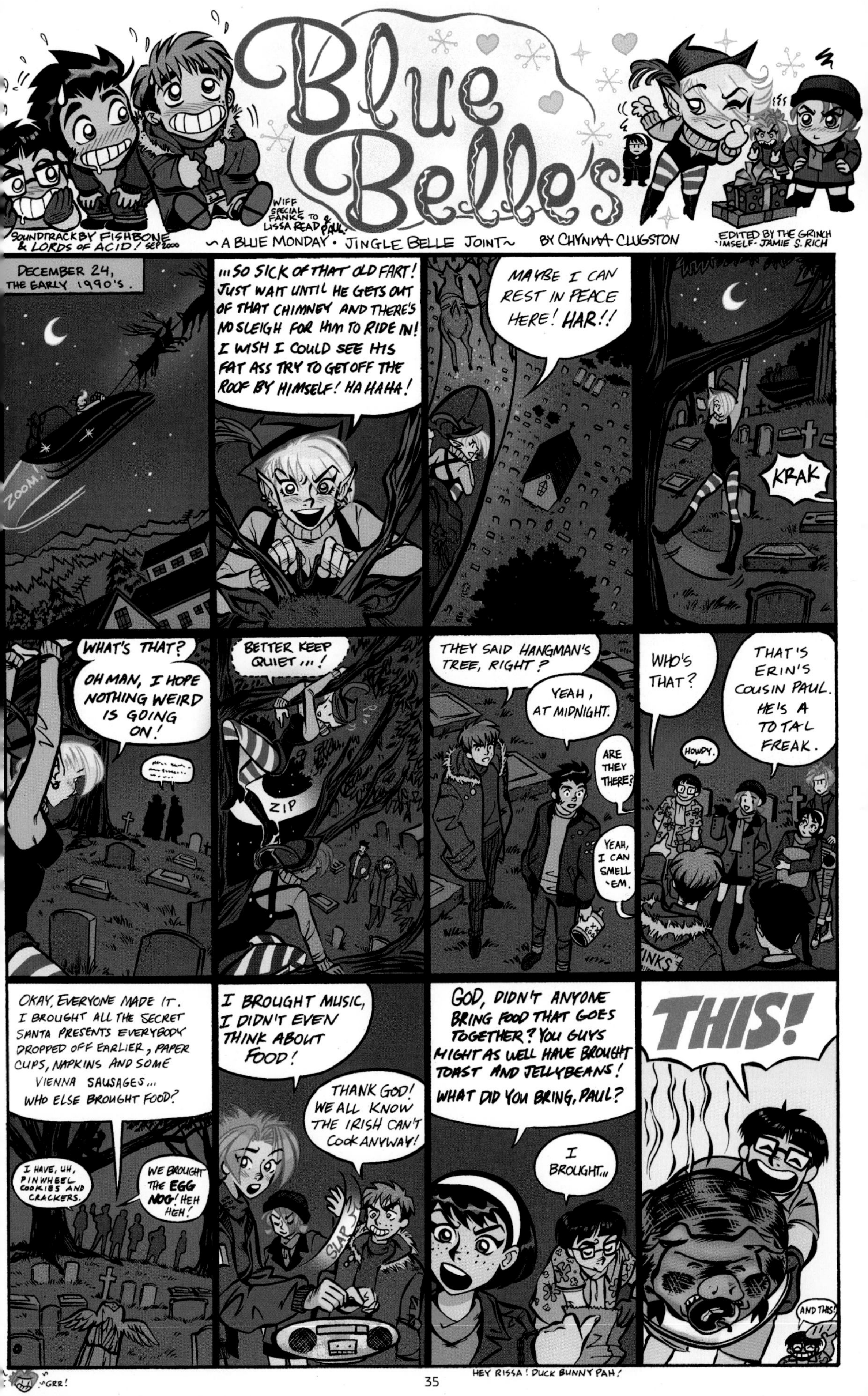
Blue Belle's
WIFF SPECIAL FANKS TO LISSA READ & PAUL!
SOUNDTRACK BY FISHBONE & LORDS OF ACID! SEP 2000
~A BLUE MONDAY • JINGLE BELLE JOINT~
BY CHYNNA CLUGSTON
EDITED BY THE GRINCH 'IMSELF- JAMIE S. RICH
DECEMBER 24, THE EARLY 1990'S.
ZOOM!
...SO SICK OF THAT OLD FART! JUST WAIT UNTIL HE GETS OUT OF THAT CHIMNEY AND THERE'S NO SLEIGH FOR HIM TO RIDE IN! I WISH I COULD SEE HIS FAT ASS TRY TO GET OFF THE ROOF BY HIMSELF! HA HA HA!
MAYBE I CAN REST IN PEACE HERE! HAR!!
KRAK
WHAT'S THAT?
OH MAN, I HOPE NOTHING WEIRD IS GOING ON!
BETTER KEEP QUIET...!
ZIP
THEY SAID HANGMAN'S TREE, RIGHT?
YEAH, AT MIDNIGHT.
ARE THEY THERE?
YEAH, I CAN SMELL 'EM.
WHO'S THAT?
THAT'S ERIN'S COUSIN PAUL. HE'S A TOTAL FREAK.
HOWDY.
OKAY, EVERYONE MADE IT. I BROUGHT ALL THE SECRET SANTA PRESENTS EVERYBODY DROPPED OFF EARLIER, PAPER CUPS, NAPKINS AND SOME VIENNA SAUSAGES... WHO ELSE BROUGHT FOOD?
I HAVE, UH, PINWHEEL COOKIES AND CRACKERS.
WE BROUGHT THE EGG NOG! HEH HEH!
I BROUGHT MUSIC, I DIDN'T EVEN THINK ABOUT FOOD!
THANK GOD! WE ALL KNOW THE IRISH CAN'T COOK ANYWAY!
SLAP
GOD, DIDN'T ANYONE BRING FOOD THAT GOES TOGETHER? YOU GUYS MIGHT AS WELL HAVE BROUGHT TOAST AND JELLYBEANS! WHAT DID YOU BRING, PAUL?
I BROUGHT...
THIS!
AND THIS!
GRR!
HEY RISSA! DUCK BUNNY PAH!

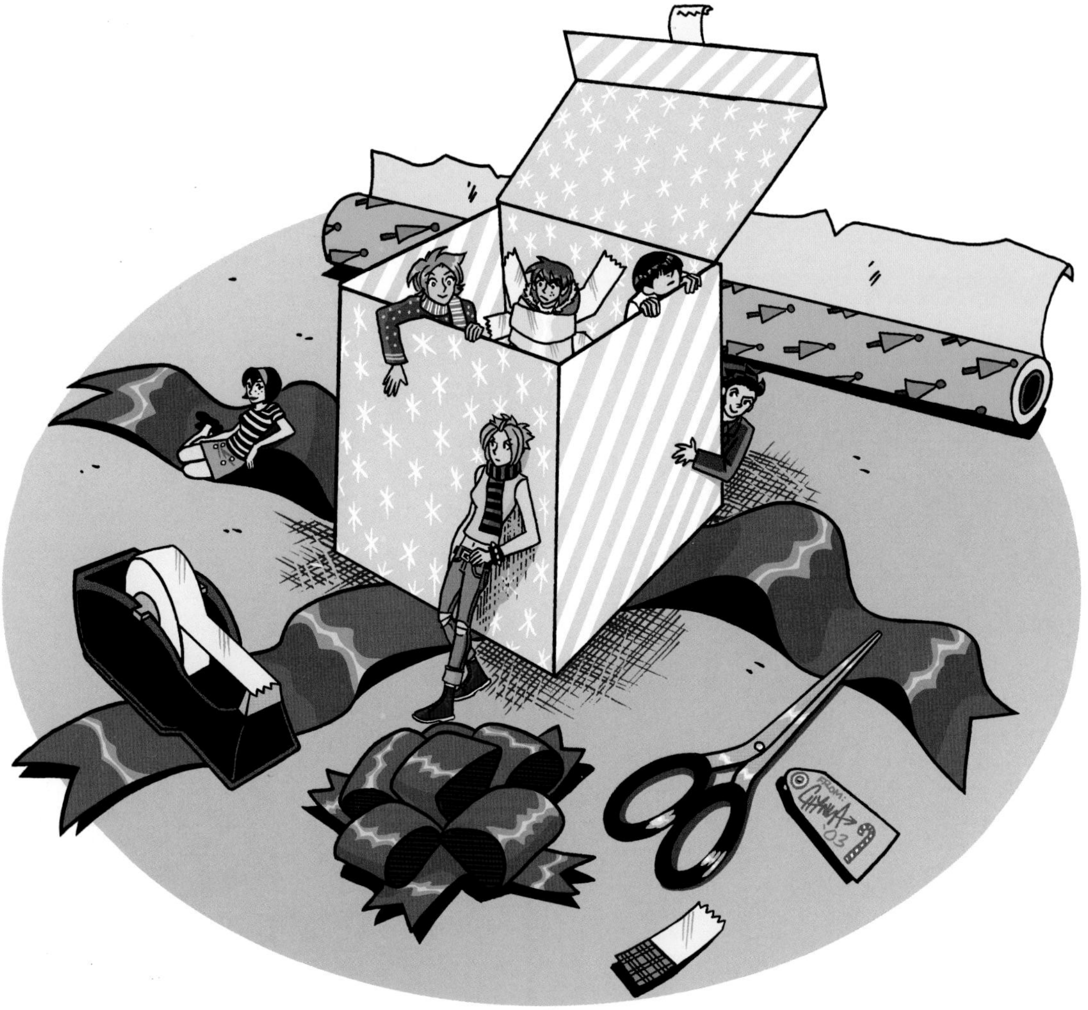
FROM:
'03

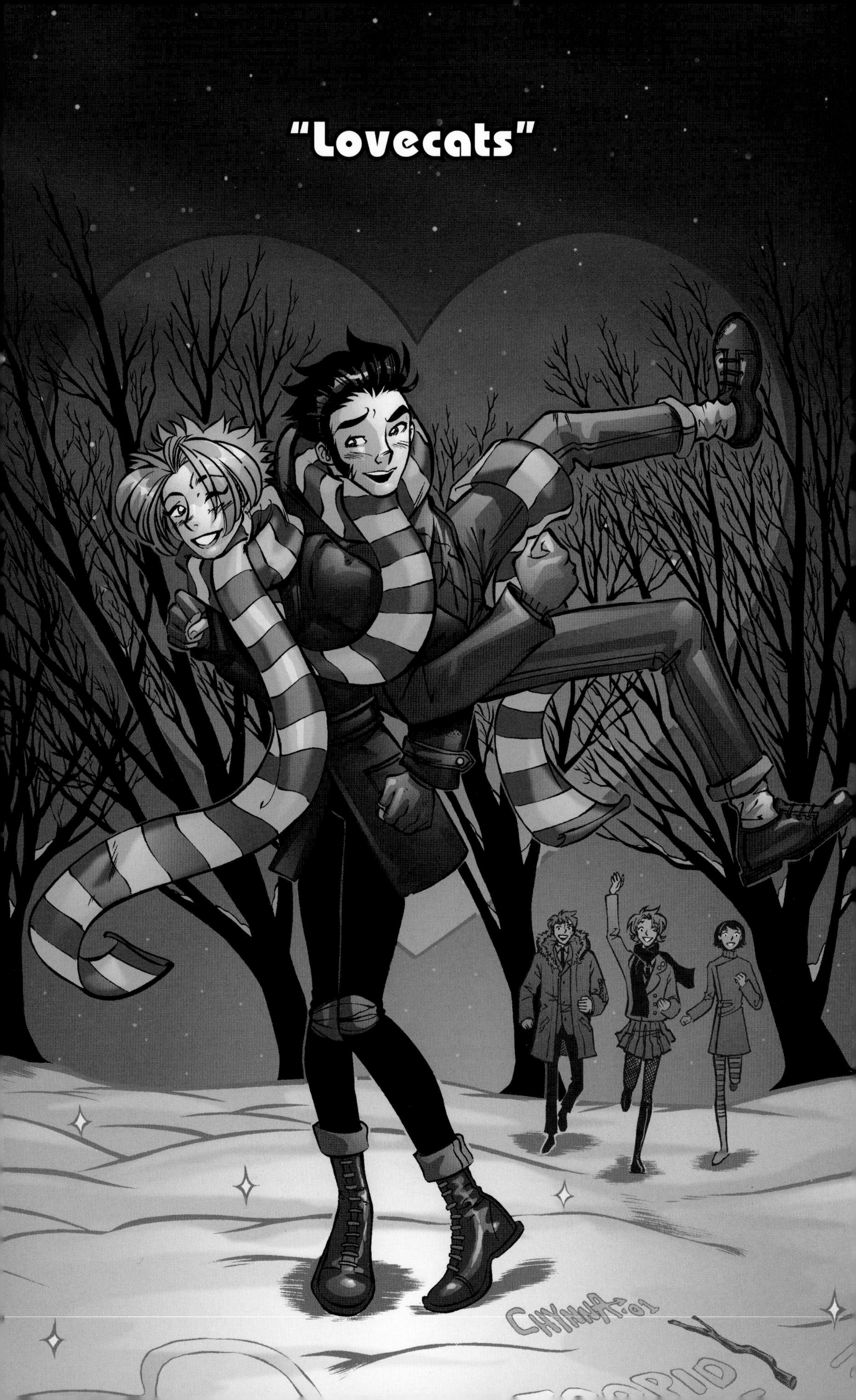
"Lovecats"
CHYNNA '01

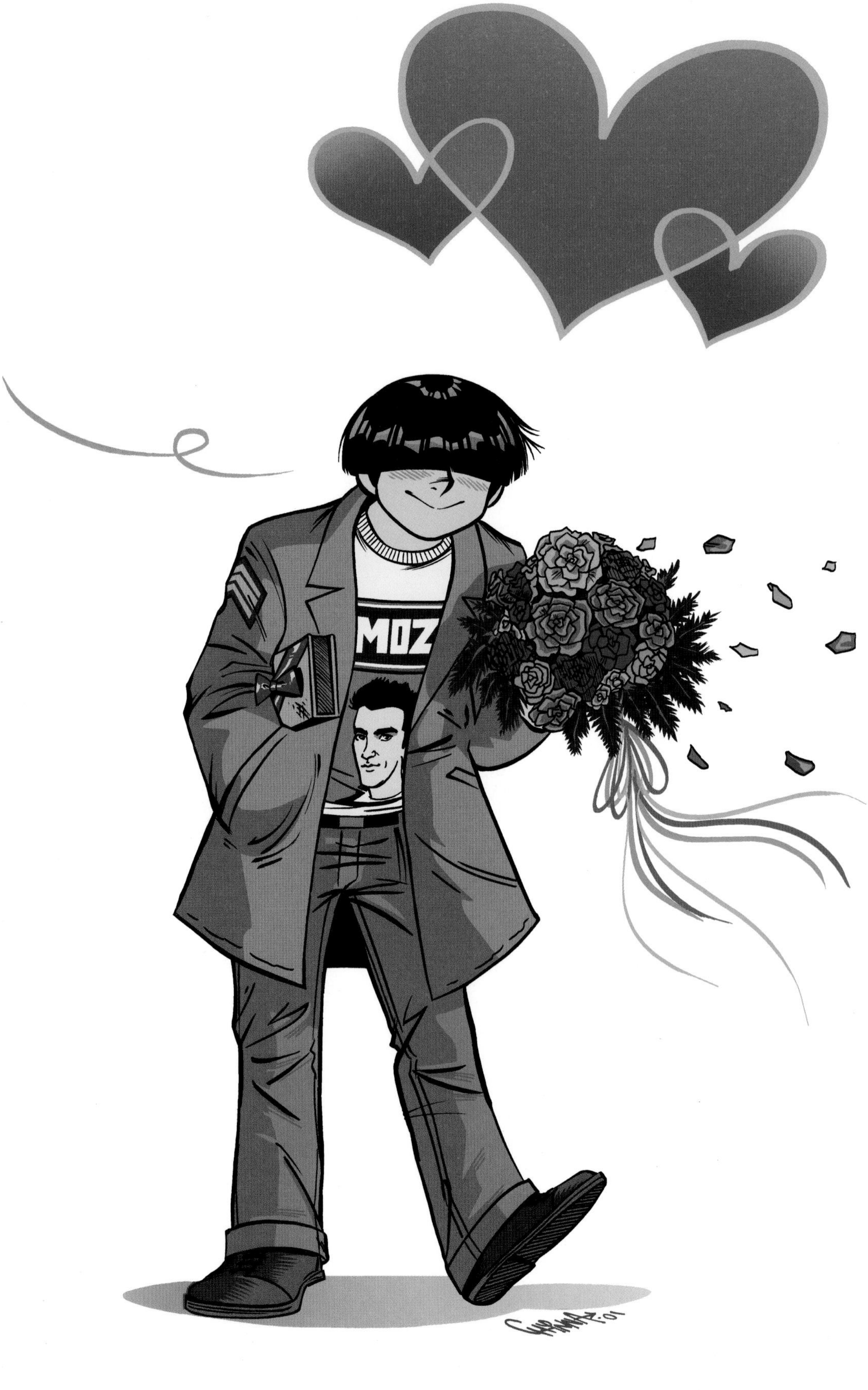
MOZ

HAIRCUT 100, "LOVE PLUS ONE"

...CLEARLY CYNICAL, BUT PERHAPS NOT WITHOUT REASON.

WHAT I WANT YOU TO DO IS WRITE AN ESSAY ON WHAT YOU THINK THE WRITER MEANS. DON'T SNIVEL, YOU HAVE FORTY-FIVE MINUTES TO FINISH IT!

"The worst of having a romance of any kind is that it leaves one so unromantic."

-Oscar Wilde (The Picture of Dorian Gray)

PRETTY SELF-EXPLANATORY, ISN'T IT?

DUDE, I CAN'T BELIEVE WE HAD DETENTION ALL THROUGH LUNCH ON *TODAY* OF ALL DAYS. HOW STUPID!

YEAH, Y'MIGHT HAVE GOTTEN THAT HUGE BOUQUET OF ROSES AND BALLOONS WAITING FOR YOU AT THE TREE AND THE SKY-WRITTEN PROPOSAL FROM MR. BISHOP HAD WE NOT BEEN TOSSED INTO A CUBICLE ALL HOUR.

AW, SHUDDUP. CAN I BORROW SOME PAPER?

THANKS.

AT LEAST THERE'S THE DANCE TONIGHT. DANCES ALWAYS MAKE UP FOR EVERYTHING. I'LL FEEL MUCH BETTER AFTER I GET MY GROOVE ON.

HAVE FUN, THEN.

WHAT? YOU AREN'T GOING?! *WHY*???

IT'S A BLEEDIN' VALENTINE'S DANCE! IT'S A TERRIBLE HOLIDAY, I DON'T LIKE IT, ALL THEY'RE GOING TO PLAY ARE SLOW SONGS, EVERYONE DROOLING ALL OVER EACH OTHER...

AND I THINK IF I HEAR "LOVE HURTS" ONE MORE TIME I'M GOING TO GO FUCKIN' MENTAL!

I CAN'T GO, IT'S UNHEALTHY.

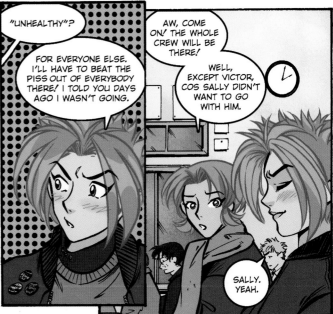

"UNHEALTHY"?

FOR EVERYONE ELSE. I'LL HAVE TO BEAT THE PISS OUT OF EVERYBODY THERE! I TOLD YOU DAYS AGO I WASN'T GOING.

AW, COME ON! THE WHOLE CREW WILL BE THERE!

WELL, EXCEPT VICTOR, COS SALLY DIDN'T WANT TO GO WITH HIM.

SALLY. YEAH.

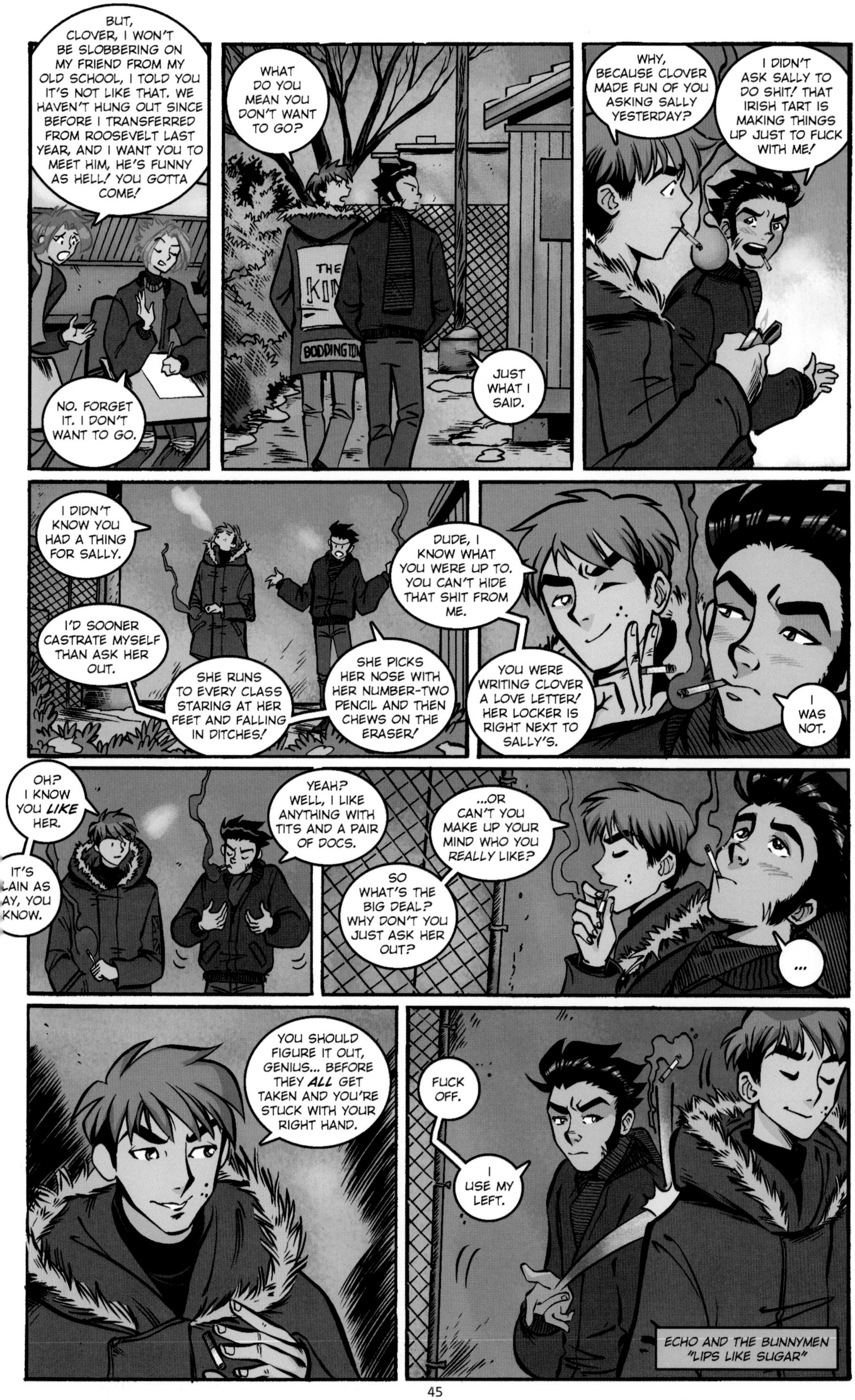

BUT, CLOVER, I WON'T BE SLOBBERING ON MY FRIEND FROM MY OLD SCHOOL, I TOLD YOU IT'S NOT LIKE THAT. WE HAVEN'T HUNG OUT SINCE BEFORE I TRANSFERRED FROM ROOSEVELT LAST YEAR, AND I WANT YOU TO MEET HIM, HE'S FUNNY AS HELL! YOU GOTTA COME!
NO. FORGET IT. I DON'T WANT TO GO.
WHAT DO YOU MEAN YOU DON'T WANT TO GO?
THE KIN
BODDINGTON
JUST WHAT I SAID.
WHY, BECAUSE CLOVER MADE FUN OF YOU ASKING SALLY YESTERDAY?
I DIDN'T ASK SALLY TO DO SHIT! THAT IRISH TART IS MAKING THINGS UP JUST TO FUCK WITH ME!
I DIDN'T KNOW YOU HAD A THING FOR SALLY.
I'D SOONER CASTRATE MYSELF THAN ASK HER OUT.
SHE RUNS TO EVERY CLASS STARING AT HER FEET AND FALLING IN DITCHES!
SHE PICKS HER NOSE WITH HER NUMBER-TWO PENCIL AND THEN CHEWS ON THE ERASER!
DUDE, I KNOW WHAT YOU WERE UP TO. YOU CAN'T HIDE THAT SHIT FROM ME.
YOU WERE WRITING CLOVER A LOVE LETTER! HER LOCKER IS RIGHT NEXT TO SALLY'S.
I WAS NOT.
OH? I KNOW YOU *LIKE* HER.
IT'S
LAIN AS
AY, YOU
KNOW.
YEAH? WELL, I LIKE ANYTHING WITH TITS AND A PAIR OF DOCS.
SO WHAT'S THE BIG DEAL? WHY DON'T YOU JUST ASK HER OUT?
...OR CAN'T YOU MAKE UP YOUR MIND WHO YOU *REALLY* LIKE?
...
YOU SHOULD FIGURE IT OUT, GENIUS... BEFORE THEY *ALL* GET TAKEN AND YOU'RE STUCK WITH YOUR RIGHT HAND.
FUCK OFF.
I USE MY LEFT.
ECHO AND THE BUNNYMEN "LIPS LIKE SUGAR"

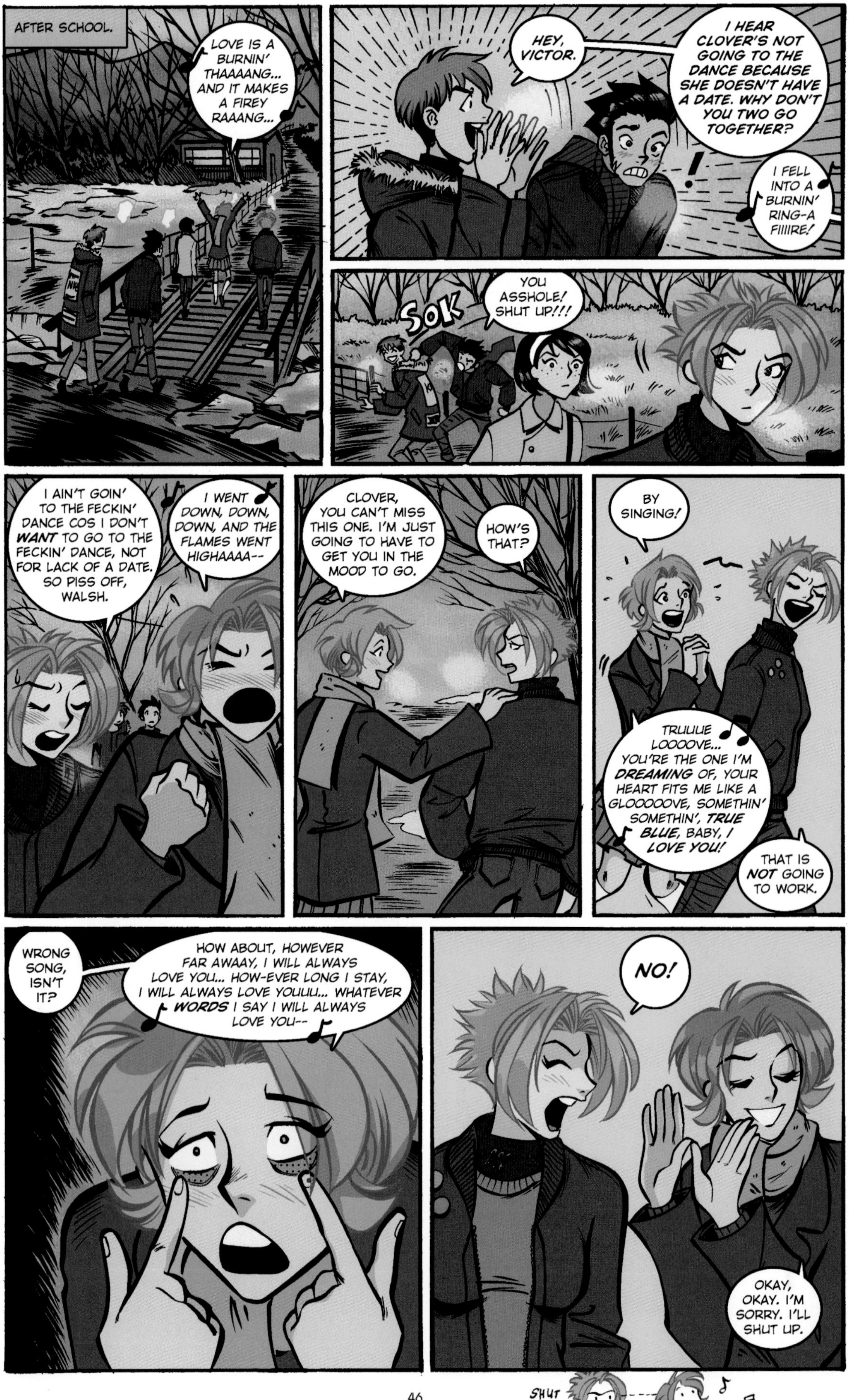
AFTER SCHOOL.
LOVE IS A BURNIN' THAAAANG... AND IT MAKES A FIREY RAAANG...
HEY, VICTOR.
I HEAR CLOVER'S NOT GOING TO THE DANCE BECAUSE SHE DOESN'T HAVE A DATE. WHY DON'T YOU TWO GO TOGETHER?
!
I FELL INTO A BURNIN' RING-A FIIIIRE!
SOK
YOU ASSHOLE! SHUT UP!!!
I AIN'T GOIN' TO THE FECKIN' DANCE COS I DON'T **WANT** TO GO TO THE FECKIN' DANCE, NOT FOR LACK OF A DATE. SO PISS OFF, WALSH.
I WENT DOWN, DOWN, DOWN, AND THE FLAMES WENT HIGHAAAA--
CLOVER, YOU CAN'T MISS THIS ONE. I'M JUST GOING TO HAVE TO GET YOU IN THE MOOD TO GO.
HOW'S THAT?
BY SINGING!
TRUUUE LOOOOVE... YOU'RE THE ONE I'M **DREAMING** OF, YOUR HEART FITS ME LIKE A GLOOOOOVE, SOMETHIN' SOMETHIN', **TRUE BLUE**, BABY, **I LOVE YOU!**
THAT IS **NOT** GOING TO WORK.
WRONG SONG, ISN'T IT?
HOW ABOUT, HOWEVER FAR AWAAY, I WILL ALWAYS LOVE YOU... HOW-EVER LONG I STAY, I WILL ALWAYS LOVE YOUUU... WHATEVER **WORDS** I SAY I WILL ALWAYS LOVE YOU--
NO!
OKAY, OKAY. I'M SORRY. I'LL SHUT UP.
SHUT UP!

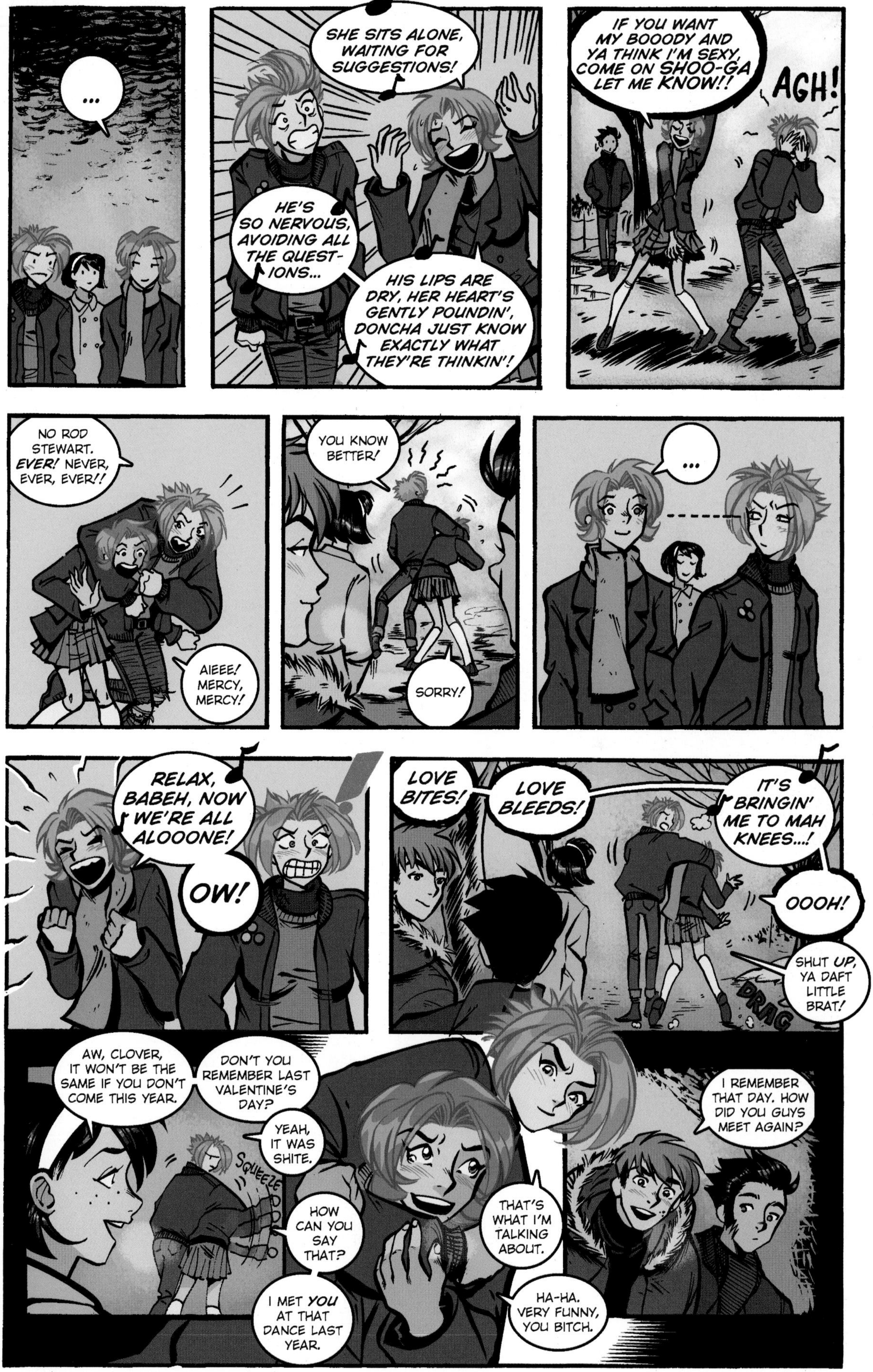
...
SHE SITS ALONE, WAITING FOR SUGGESTIONS!
HE'S SO NERVOUS, AVOIDING ALL THE QUEST-IONS...
HIS LIPS ARE DRY, HER HEART'S GENTLY POUNDIN', DONCHA JUST KNOW EXACTLY WHAT THEY'RE THINKIN'!
IF YOU WANT MY BOOODY AND YA THINK I'M SEXY, COME ON SHOO-GA LET ME KNOW!!
AGH!
NO ROD STEWART. EVER! NEVER, EVER, EVER!!
AIEEE! MERCY, MERCY!
YOU KNOW BETTER!
SORRY!
...
RELAX, BABEH, NOW WE'RE ALL ALOOONE!
OW!
LOVE BITES!
LOVE BLEEDS!
IT'S BRINGIN' ME TO MAH KNEES...!
OOOH!
SHUT UP, YA DAFT LITTLE BRAT!
DRAG
AW, CLOVER, IT WON'T BE THE SAME IF YOU DON'T COME THIS YEAR.
DON'T YOU REMEMBER LAST VALENTINE'S DAY?
YEAH, IT WAS SHITE.
SQUEEZE
HOW CAN YOU SAY THAT?
I MET YOU AT THAT DANCE LAST YEAR.
THAT'S WHAT I'M TALKING ABOUT.
HA-HA. VERY FUNNY, YOU BITCH.
I REMEMBER THAT DAY. HOW DID YOU GUYS MEET AGAIN?

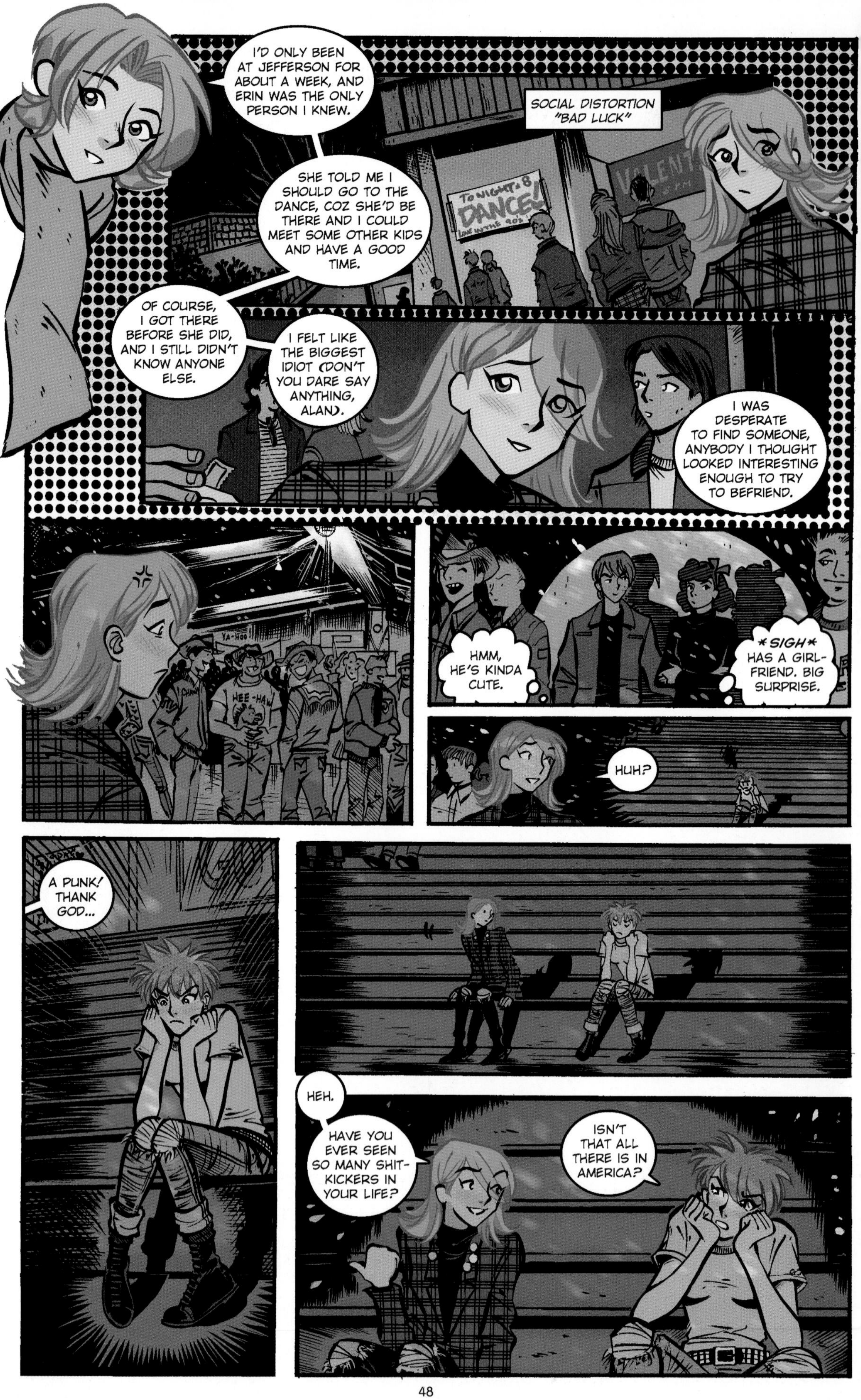
I'D ONLY BEEN AT JEFFERSON FOR ABOUT A WEEK, AND ERIN WAS THE ONLY PERSON I KNEW.
SOCIAL DISTORTION "BAD LUCK"
SHE TOLD ME I SHOULD GO TO THE DANCE, COZ SHE'D BE THERE AND I COULD MEET SOME OTHER KIDS AND HAVE A GOOD TIME.
TONIGHT 8 DANCE!
OF COURSE, I GOT THERE BEFORE SHE DID, AND I STILL DIDN'T KNOW ANYONE ELSE.
I FELT LIKE THE BIGGEST IDIOT (DON'T YOU DARE SAY ANYTHING, ALAN).
I WAS DESPERATE TO FIND SOMEONE, ANYBODY I THOUGHT LOOKED INTERESTING ENOUGH TO TRY TO BEFRIEND.
YA-HOO
HEE-HAW
HMM, HE'S KINDA CUTE.
SIGH HAS A GIRL-FRIEND. BIG SURPRISE.
HUH?
A PUNK! THANK GOD...
HEH.
HAVE YOU EVER SEEN SO MANY SHIT-KICKERS IN YOUR LIFE?
ISN'T THAT ALL THERE IS IN AMERICA?

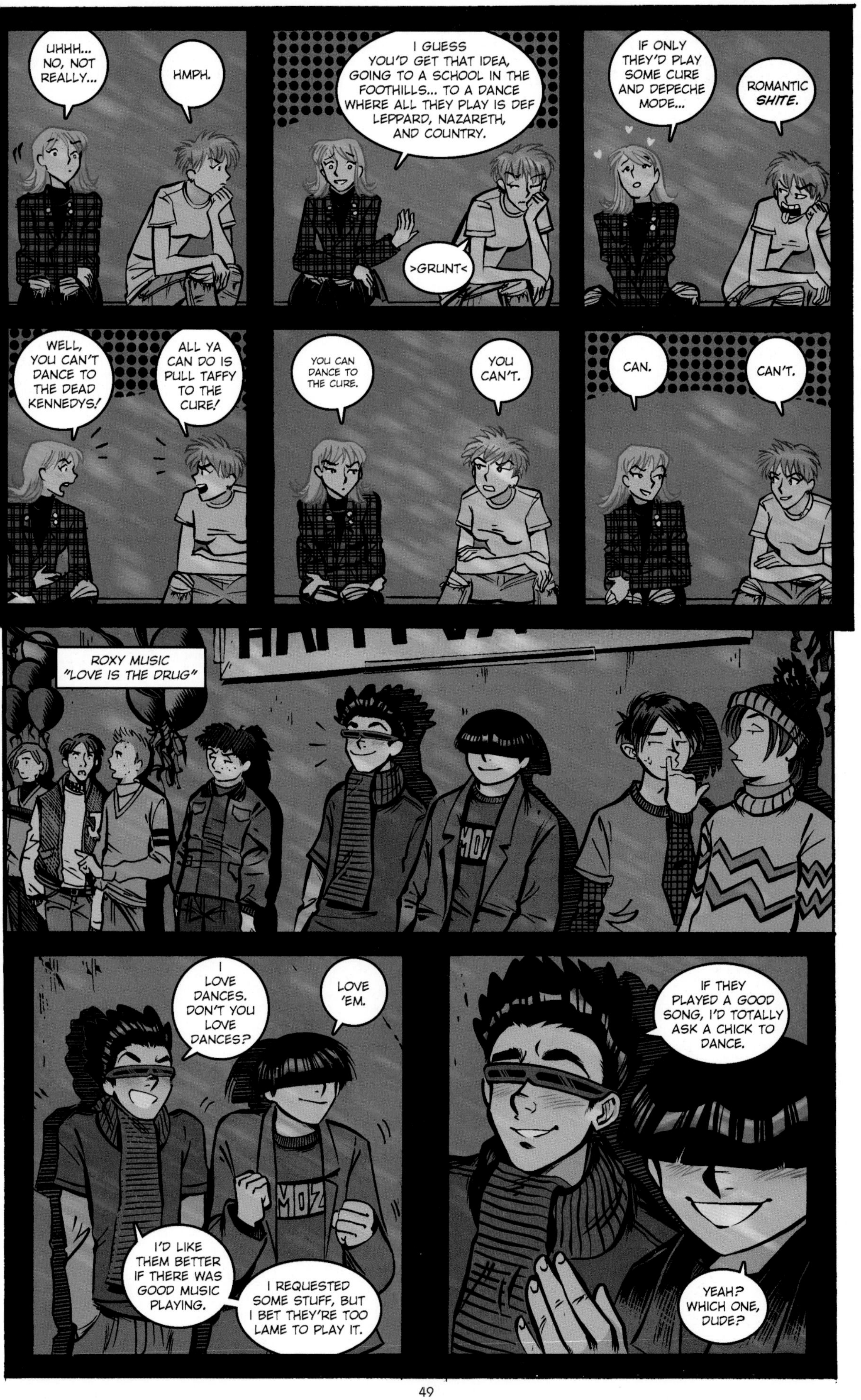
UHHH... NO, NOT REALLY...
HMPH.
I GUESS YOU'D GET THAT IDEA, GOING TO A SCHOOL IN THE FOOTHILLS... TO A DANCE WHERE ALL THEY PLAY IS DEF LEPPARD, NAZARETH, AND COUNTRY.
>GRUNT<
IF ONLY THEY'D PLAY SOME CURE AND DEPECHE MODE...
ROMANTIC *SHITE.*
WELL, YOU CAN'T DANCE TO THE DEAD KENNEDYS!
ALL YA CAN DO IS PULL TAFFY TO THE CURE!
YOU CAN DANCE TO THE CURE.
YOU CAN'T.
CAN.
CAN'T.
ROXY MUSIC "LOVE IS THE DRUG"
MOZ
I LOVE DANCES. DON'T YOU LOVE DANCES?
LOVE 'EM.
I'D LIKE THEM BETTER IF THERE WAS GOOD MUSIC PLAYING.
I REQUESTED SOME STUFF, BUT I BET THEY'RE TOO LAME TO PLAY IT.
IF THEY PLAYED A GOOD SONG, I'D TOTALLY ASK A CHICK TO DANCE.
YEAH? WHICH ONE, DUDE?

HMM... WHO WOULD BE THE LUCKY LADY?

LUCKY LAYDEH, LUCKY LAYDEH...

OH, SHIT! SHE'S HERE!

WHO?

THAT ONE, THE ONE I ALWAYS SEE WALKING PAST DRIVER'S ED! THE PUNK CHICK THAT BEAT UP THAT DICK WESLEY STEIN-HOSER! SHE SAID "HI" TO ME ONCE!

OH, THAT'S THE GIRL THAT TURNED AROUND AND SAID "HI" TO YOU BECAUSE YOU KEPT STARING AT HER EVERY TIME SHE PASSED BY AND YOU DIDN'T SAY ANYTHING BACK BECAUSE YOU WERE SO FREAKED OUT SHE TALKED TO YOU?

THAT ONE?

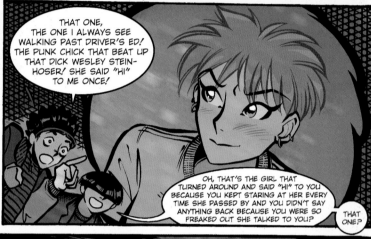

I DON'T KNOW WHERE YOU HEARD *THAT*, BUT...

WHO'S THAT WITH HER?

I DUNNO, BUT SHE'S PRETTY CUTE TOO, MAN!

TARGETS ACQUIRED!

WHAT'S YOUR SHIRT SAY? "STAY SICK." HOLY SHIT, YOU LISTEN TO THE CRAMPS?!

YOU'RE THE ONLY ONE AT THIS SCHOOL THAT I BET LIKES THEM BESIDES ME!

WHAT, YOU LIKE THEM TOO?

YOU?

I *LOVE* THE CRAMPS.

"CREATURE FROM THE BLACK LEATHER LAGOON" IS MY FAVORITE SONG OF THEIRS.

PLUS, "SURFIN' DEAD," 'CAUSE IT WAS IN *RETURN OF THE LIVING DEAD*, MY FAVORITE ZOMBIE MOVIE.

GOOD FILM.

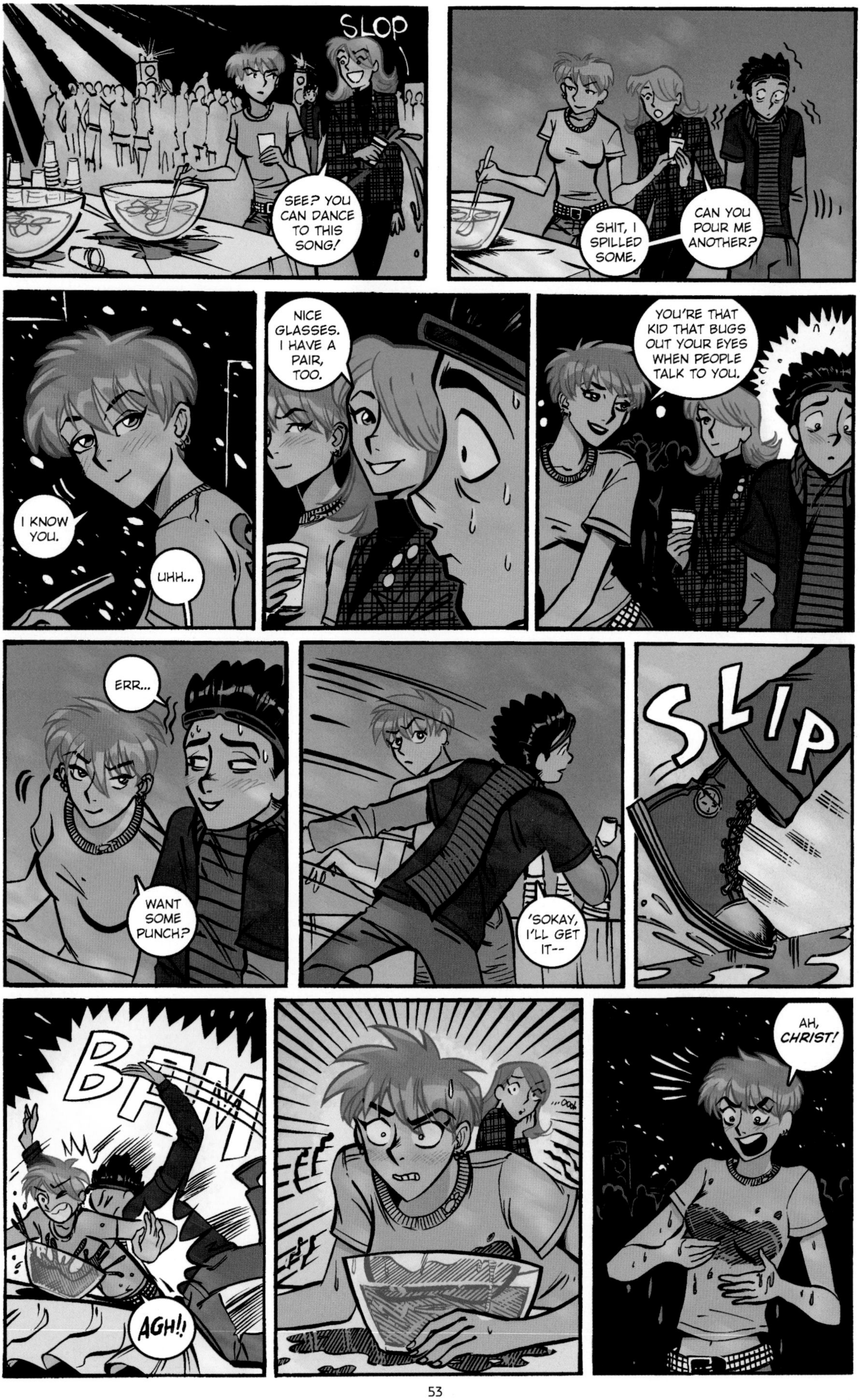
SLOP
SEE? YOU CAN DANCE TO THIS SONG!
CAN YOU POUR ME ANOTHER?
SHIT, I SPILLED SOME.
I KNOW YOU.
UHH...
NICE GLASSES. I HAVE A PAIR, TOO.
YOU'RE THAT KID THAT BUGS OUT YOUR EYES WHEN PEOPLE TALK TO YOU.
ERR...
WANT SOME PUNCH?
'SOKAY, I'LL GET IT--
SLIP
BAM
AGH!!
AH, CHRIST!

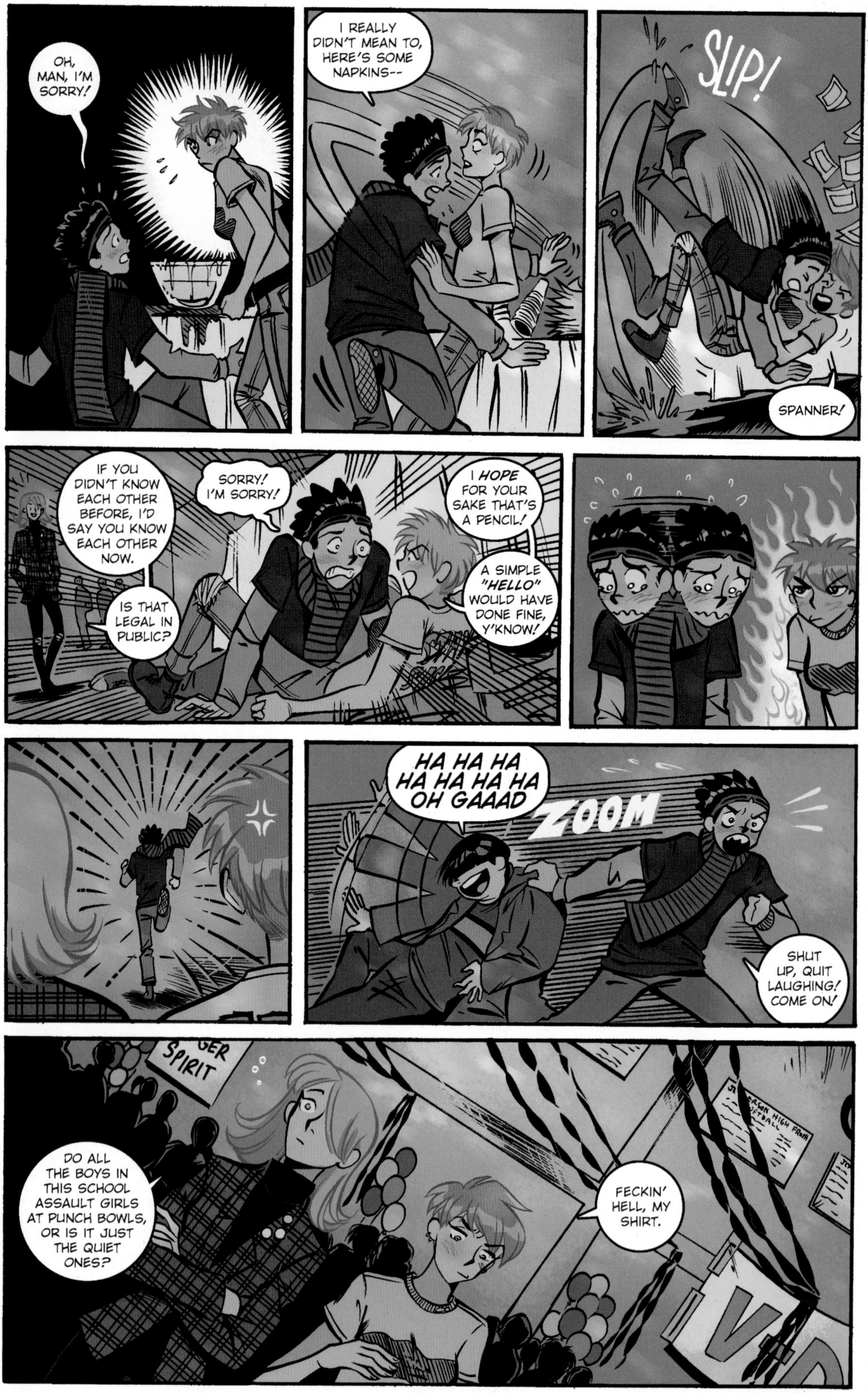
OH, MAN, I'M SORRY!
I REALLY DIDN'T MEAN TO, HERE'S SOME NAPKINS--
SLIP!
SPANNER!
IF YOU DIDN'T KNOW EACH OTHER BEFORE, I'D SAY YOU KNOW EACH OTHER NOW.
IS THAT LEGAL IN PUBLIC?
SORRY! I'M SORRY!
I HOPE FOR YOUR SAKE THAT'S A PENCIL!
A SIMPLE "HELLO" WOULD HAVE DONE FINE, Y'KNOW!
HA HA HA HA HA HA HA OH GAAAD
ZOOM
SHUT UP, QUIT LAUGHING! COME ON!
SPIRIT
DO ALL THE BOYS IN THIS SCHOOL ASSAULT GIRLS AT PUNCH BOWLS, OR IS IT JUST THE QUIET ONES?
FECKIN' HELL, MY SHIRT.

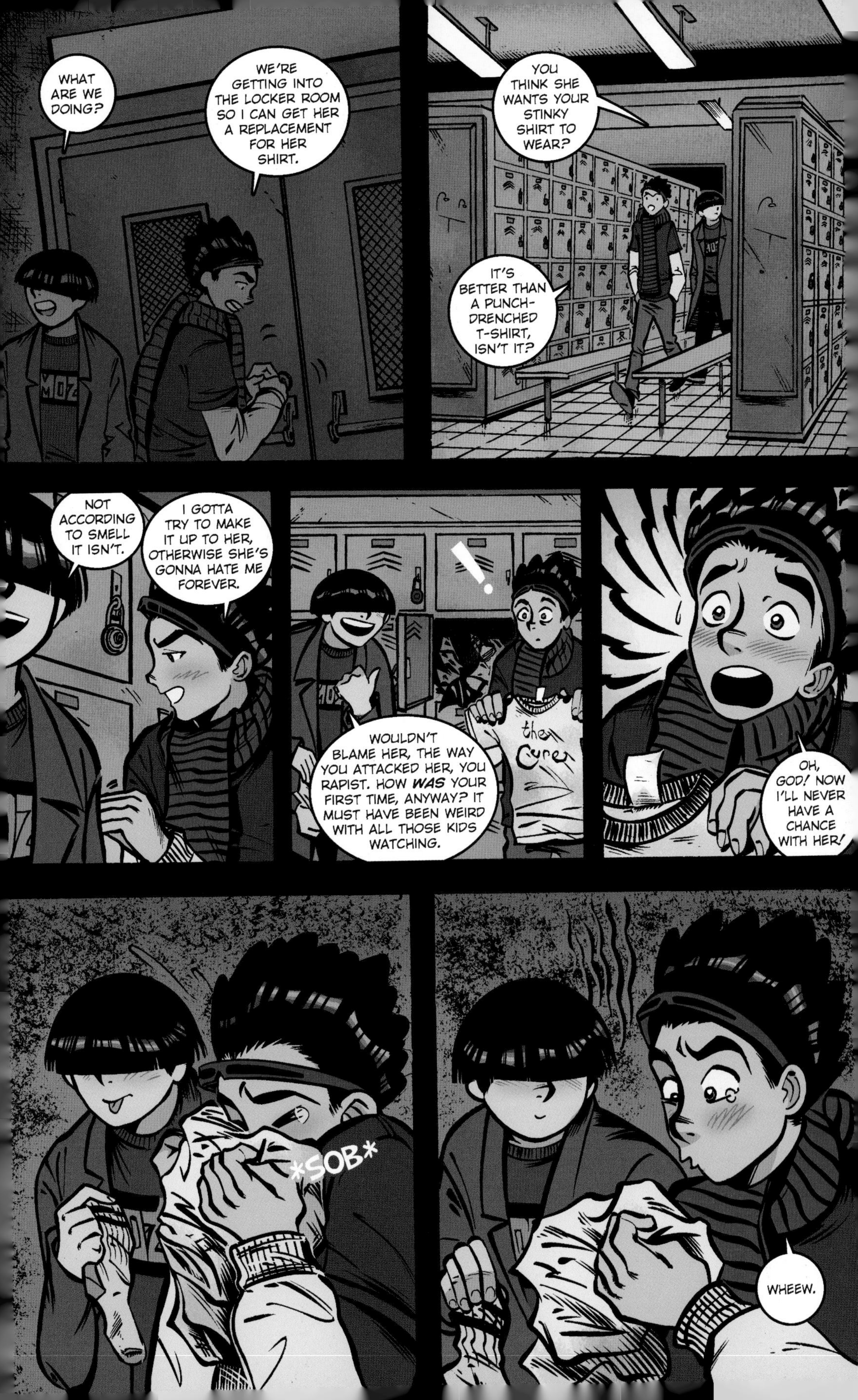
WHAT ARE WE DOING?
WE'RE GETTING INTO THE LOCKER ROOM SO I CAN GET HER A REPLACEMENT FOR HER SHIRT.
YOU THINK SHE WANTS YOUR STINKY SHIRT TO WEAR?
IT'S BETTER THAN A PUNCH-DRENCHED T-SHIRT, ISN'T IT?
NOT ACCORDING TO SMELL IT ISN'T.
I GOTTA TRY TO MAKE IT UP TO HER, OTHERWISE SHE'S GONNA HATE ME FOREVER.
!
the Cure
WOULDN'T BLAME HER, THE WAY YOU ATTACKED HER, YOU RAPIST. HOW **WAS** YOUR FIRST TIME, ANYWAY? IT MUST HAVE BEEN WEIRD WITH ALL THOSE KIDS WATCHING.
OH, GOD! NOW I'LL NEVER HAVE A CHANCE WITH HER!
SOB
WHEEW.

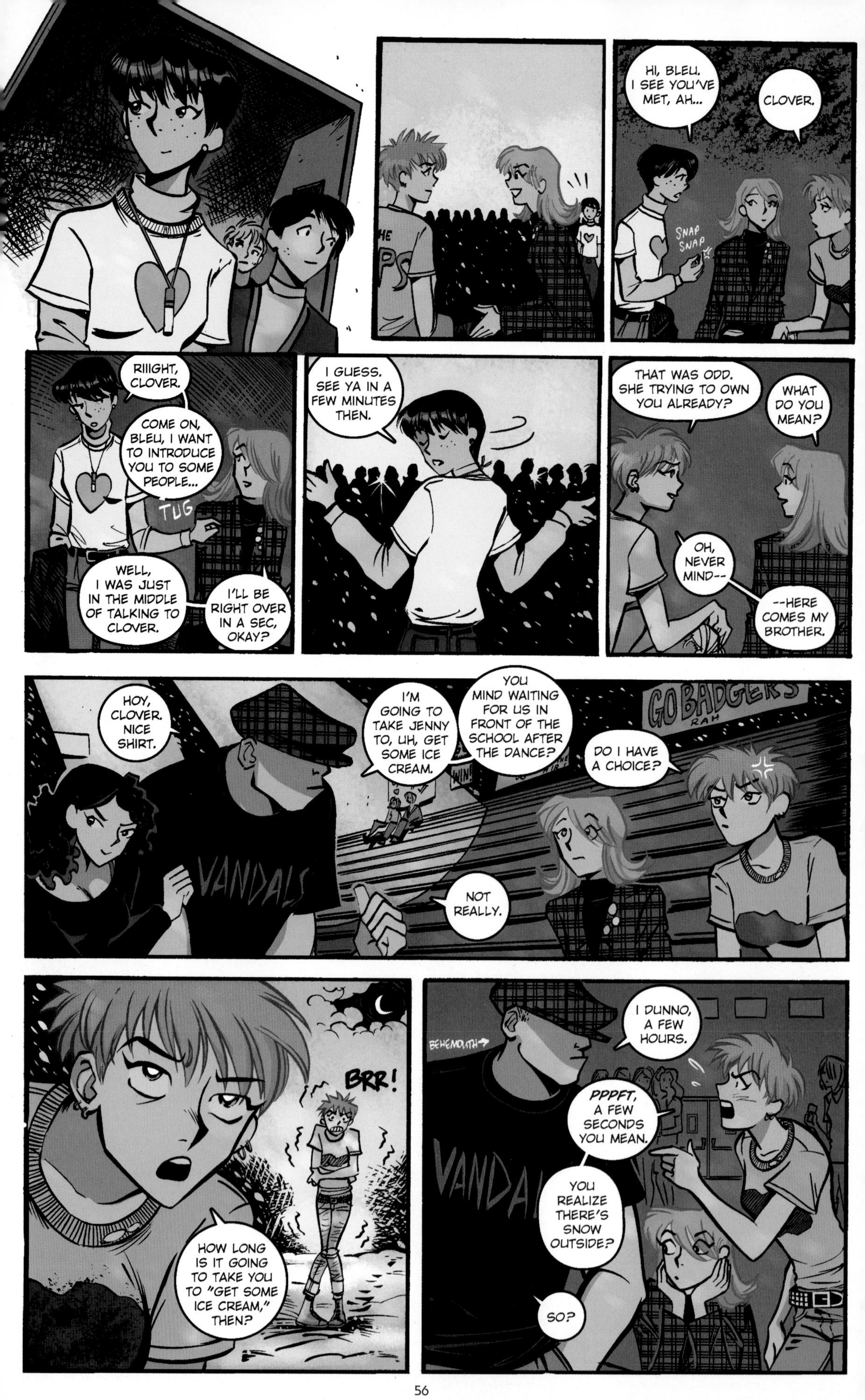
HI, BLEU. I SEE YOU'VE MET, AH...
CLOVER.
SNAP SNAP
RIIIGHT, CLOVER.
COME ON, BLEU, I WANT TO INTRODUCE YOU TO SOME PEOPLE...
TUG
WELL, I WAS JUST IN THE MIDDLE OF TALKING TO CLOVER.
I'LL BE RIGHT OVER IN A SEC, OKAY?
I GUESS. SEE YA IN A FEW MINUTES THEN.
THAT WAS ODD. SHE TRYING TO OWN YOU ALREADY?
WHAT DO YOU MEAN?
OH, NEVER MIND--
--HERE COMES MY BROTHER.
HOY, CLOVER. NICE SHIRT.
VANDALS
I'M GOING TO TAKE JENNY TO, UH, GET SOME ICE CREAM.
YOU MIND WAITING FOR US IN FRONT OF THE SCHOOL AFTER THE DANCE?
GO BADGERS
RAH
DO I HAVE A CHOICE?
NOT REALLY.
BRR!
HOW LONG IS IT GOING TO TAKE YOU TO "GET SOME ICE CREAM," THEN?
BEHEMOUTH
I DUNNO, A FEW HOURS.
PPPFT, A FEW SECONDS YOU MEAN.
YOU REALIZE THERE'S SNOW OUTSIDE?
SO?

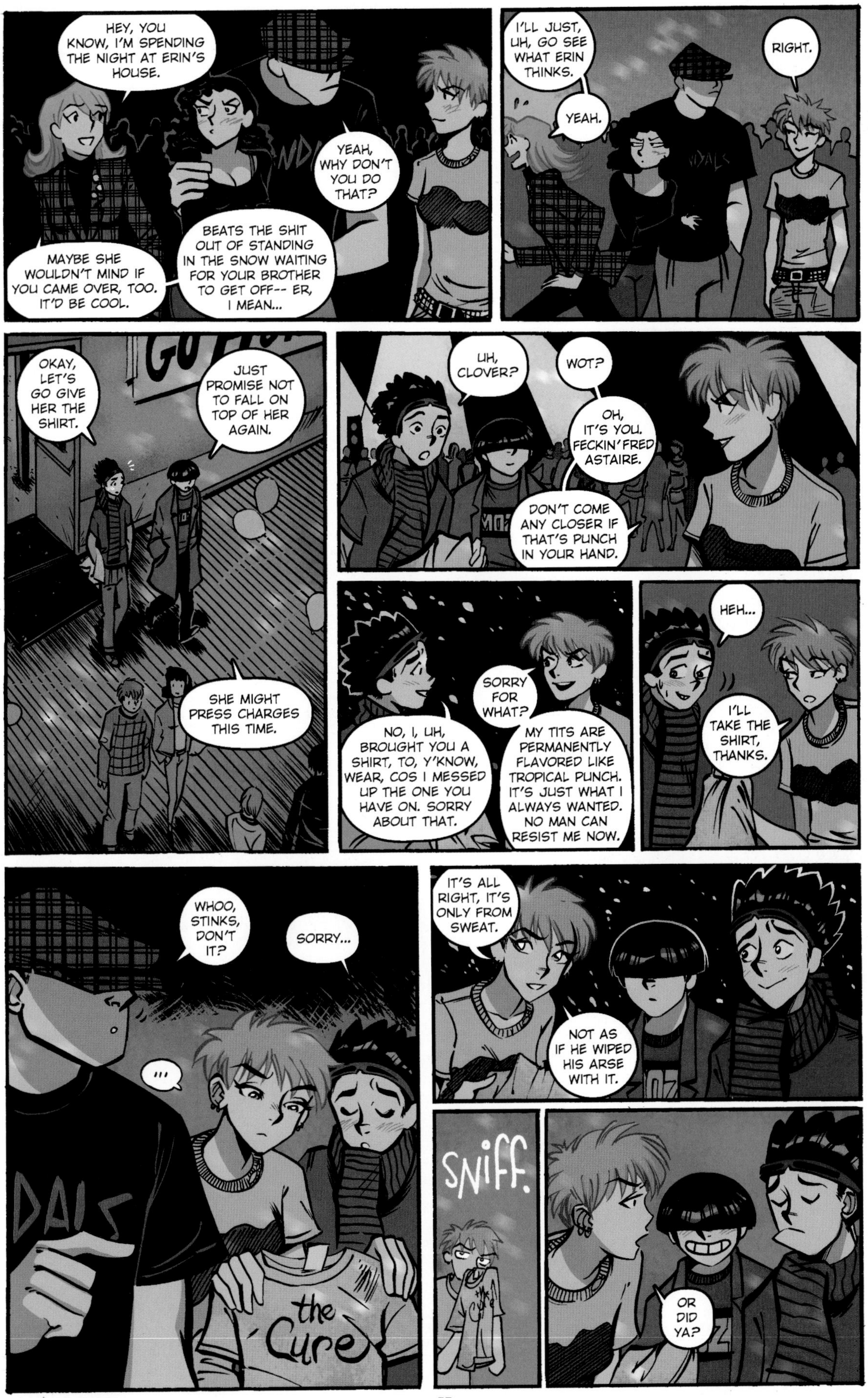
HEY, YOU KNOW, I'M SPENDING THE NIGHT AT ERIN'S HOUSE.
MAYBE SHE WOULDN'T MIND IF YOU CAME OVER, TOO. IT'D BE COOL.
BEATS THE SHIT OUT OF STANDING IN THE SNOW WAITING FOR YOUR BROTHER TO GET OFF-- ER, I MEAN...
YEAH, WHY DON'T YOU DO THAT?
I'LL JUST, UH, GO SEE WHAT ERIN THINKS.
YEAH.
RIGHT.
OKAY, LET'S GO GIVE HER THE SHIRT.
JUST PROMISE NOT TO FALL ON TOP OF HER AGAIN.
SHE MIGHT PRESS CHARGES THIS TIME.
UH, CLOVER?
WOT?
OH, IT'S YOU. FECKIN' FRED ASTAIRE.
DON'T COME ANY CLOSER IF THAT'S PUNCH IN YOUR HAND.
SORRY FOR WHAT?
NO, I, UH, BROUGHT YOU A SHIRT, TO, Y'KNOW, WEAR, COS I MESSED UP THE ONE YOU HAVE ON. SORRY ABOUT THAT.
MY TITS ARE PERMANENTLY FLAVORED LIKE TROPICAL PUNCH. IT'S JUST WHAT I ALWAYS WANTED. NO MAN CAN RESIST ME NOW.
HEH...
I'LL TAKE THE SHIRT, THANKS.
WHOO, STINKS, DON'T IT?
SORRY...
...
the Cure
IT'S ALL RIGHT, IT'S ONLY FROM SWEAT.
NOT AS IF HE WIPED HIS ARSE WITH IT.
SNIFF.
OR DID YA?

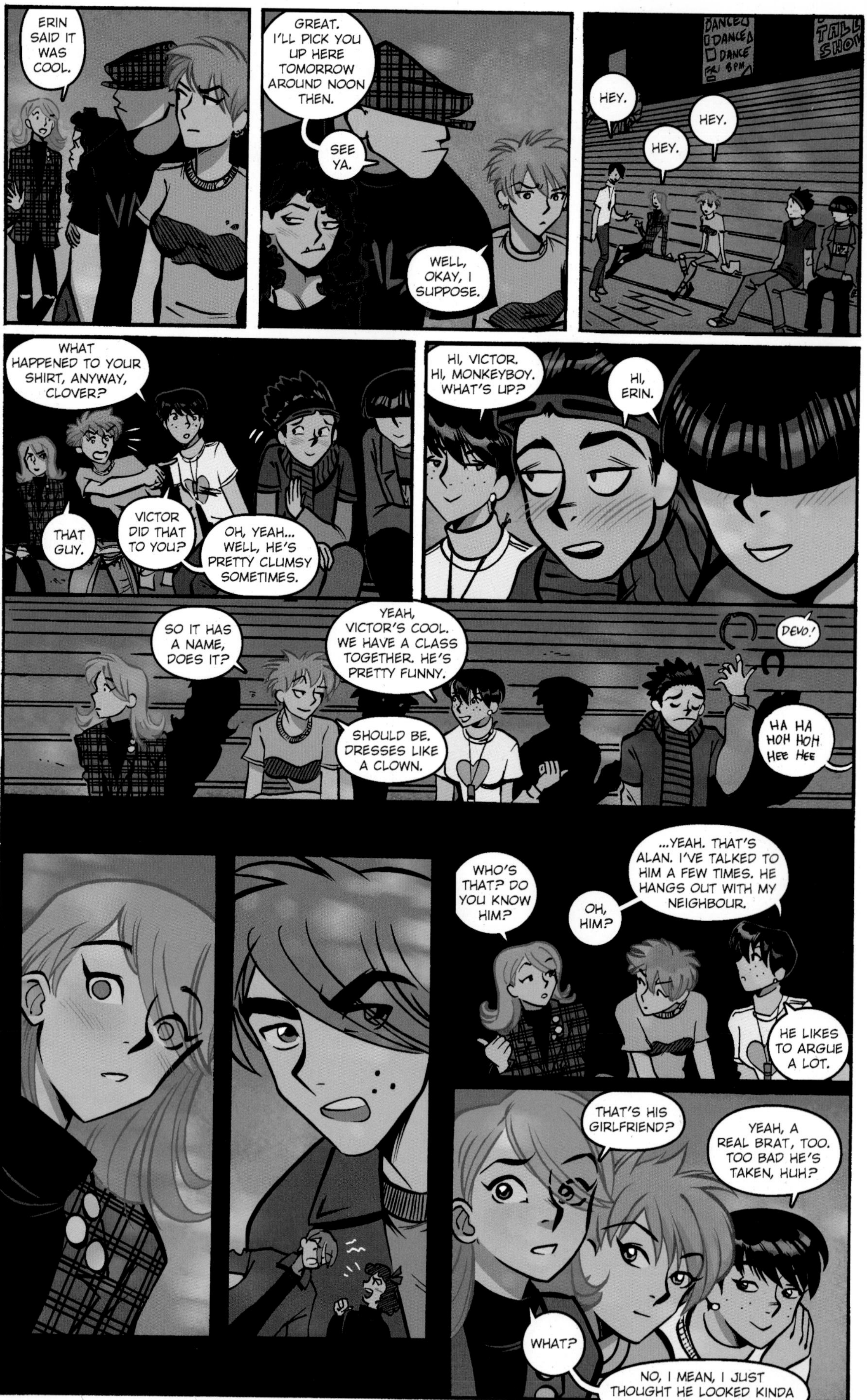
ERIN SAID IT WAS COOL.
GREAT. I'LL PICK YOU UP HERE TOMORROW AROUND NOON THEN.
SEE YA.
WELL, OKAY, I SUPPOSE.
DANCE DANCE DANCE FRI 8PM
HEY.
HEY.
HEY.
WHAT HAPPENED TO YOUR SHIRT, ANYWAY, CLOVER?
THAT GUY.
VICTOR DID THAT TO YOU?
OH, YEAH... WELL, HE'S PRETTY CLUMSY SOMETIMES.
HI, VICTOR. HI, MONKEYBOY. WHAT'S UP?
HI, ERIN.
SO IT HAS A NAME, DOES IT?
YEAH, VICTOR'S COOL. WE HAVE A CLASS TOGETHER. HE'S PRETTY FUNNY.
SHOULD BE. DRESSES LIKE A CLOWN.
DEVO!
HA HA HOH HOH HEE HEE
WHO'S THAT? DO YOU KNOW HIM?
OH, HIM?
...YEAH. THAT'S ALAN. I'VE TALKED TO HIM A FEW TIMES. HE HANGS OUT WITH MY NEIGHBOUR.
HE LIKES TO ARGUE A LOT.
THAT'S HIS GIRLFRIEND?
YEAH, A REAL BRAT, TOO. TOO BAD HE'S TAKEN, HUH?
WHAT?
NO, I MEAN, I JUST THOUGHT HE LOOKED KINDA INTERESTING IS ALL.

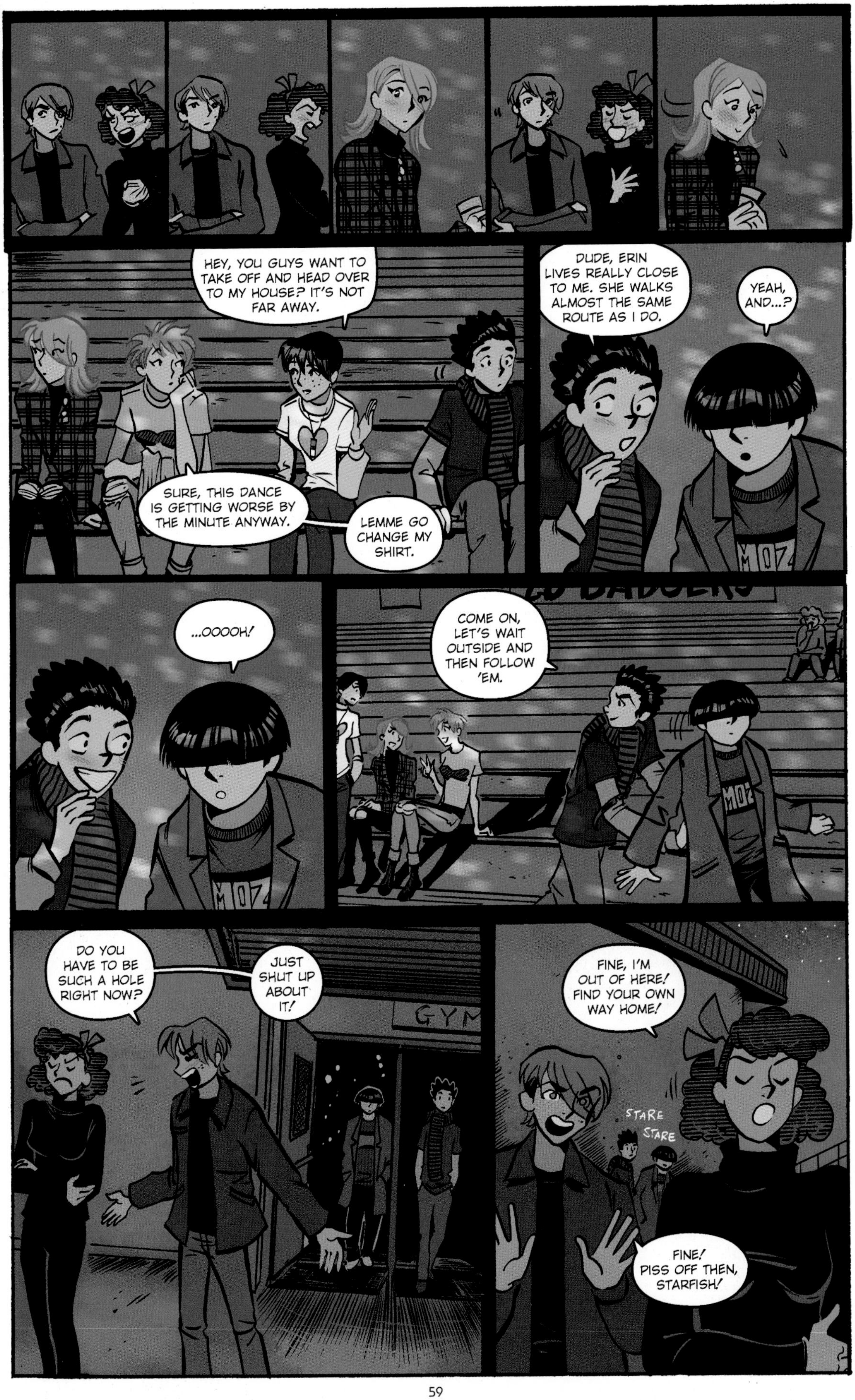
HEY, YOU GUYS WANT TO TAKE OFF AND HEAD OVER TO MY HOUSE? IT'S NOT FAR AWAY.
SURE, THIS DANCE IS GETTING WORSE BY THE MINUTE ANYWAY.
LEMME GO CHANGE MY SHIRT.
DUDE, ERIN LIVES REALLY CLOSE TO ME. SHE WALKS ALMOST THE SAME ROUTE AS I DO.
YEAH, AND...?
MOZ
...OOOOH!
MOZ
COME ON, LET'S WAIT OUTSIDE AND THEN FOLLOW 'EM.
MOZ
DO YOU HAVE TO BE SUCH A HOLE RIGHT NOW?
JUST SHUT UP ABOUT IT!
GYM
FINE, I'M OUT OF HERE! FIND YOUR OWN WAY HOME!
STARE
STARE
FINE! PISS OFF THEN, STARFISH!

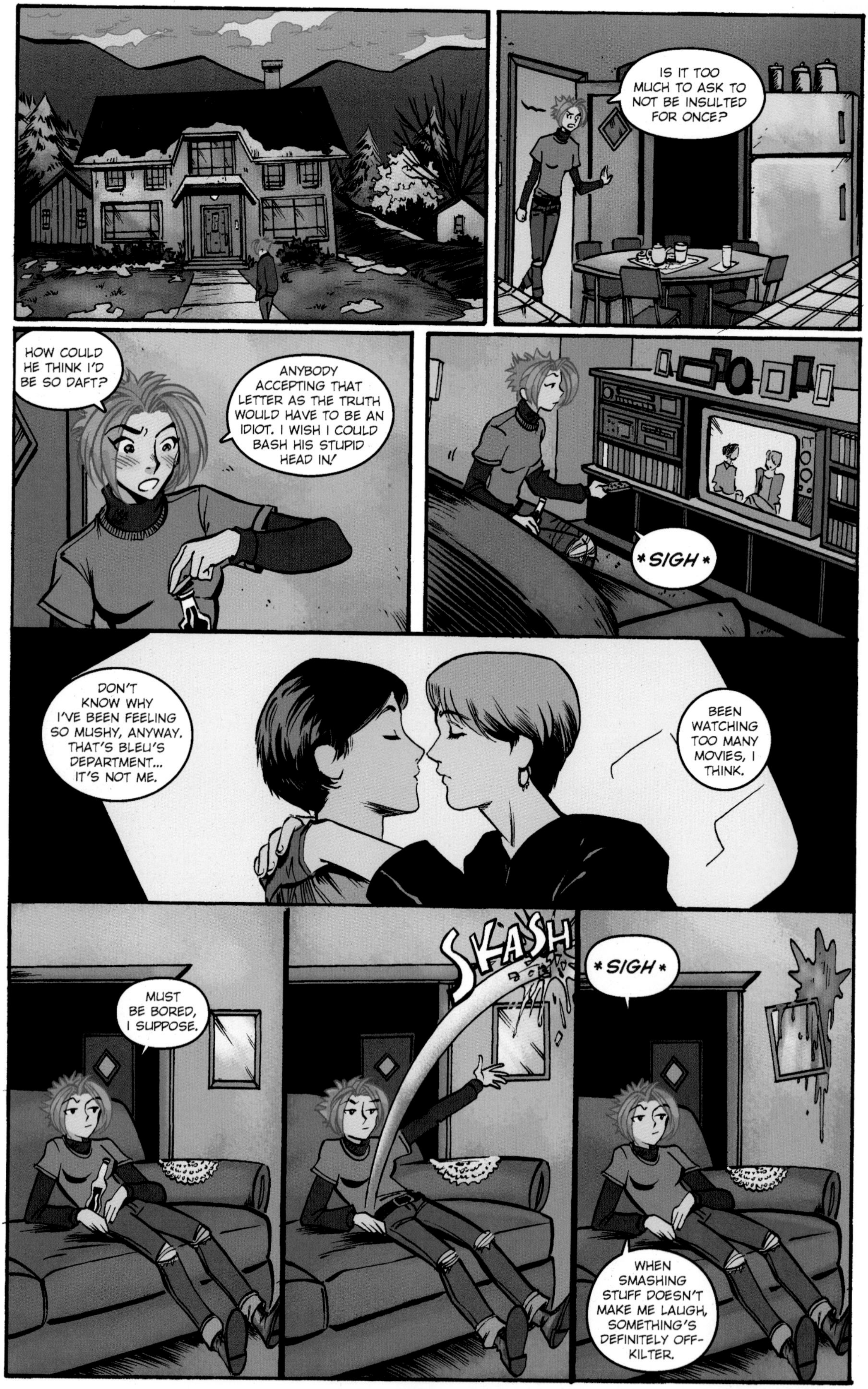
IS IT TOO MUCH TO ASK TO NOT BE INSULTED FOR ONCE?
HOW COULD HE THINK I'D BE SO DAFT?
ANYBODY ACCEPTING THAT LETTER AS THE TRUTH WOULD HAVE TO BE AN IDIOT. I WISH I COULD BASH HIS STUPID HEAD IN!
SIGH
DON'T KNOW WHY I'VE BEEN FEELING SO MUSHY, ANYWAY. THAT'S BLEU'S DEPARTMENT... IT'S NOT ME.
BEEN WATCHING TOO MANY MOVIES, I THINK.
MUST BE BORED, I SUPPOSE.
SKASH
SIGH
WHEN SMASHING STUFF DOESN'T MAKE ME LAUGH, SOMETHING'S DEFINITELY OFF-KILTER.

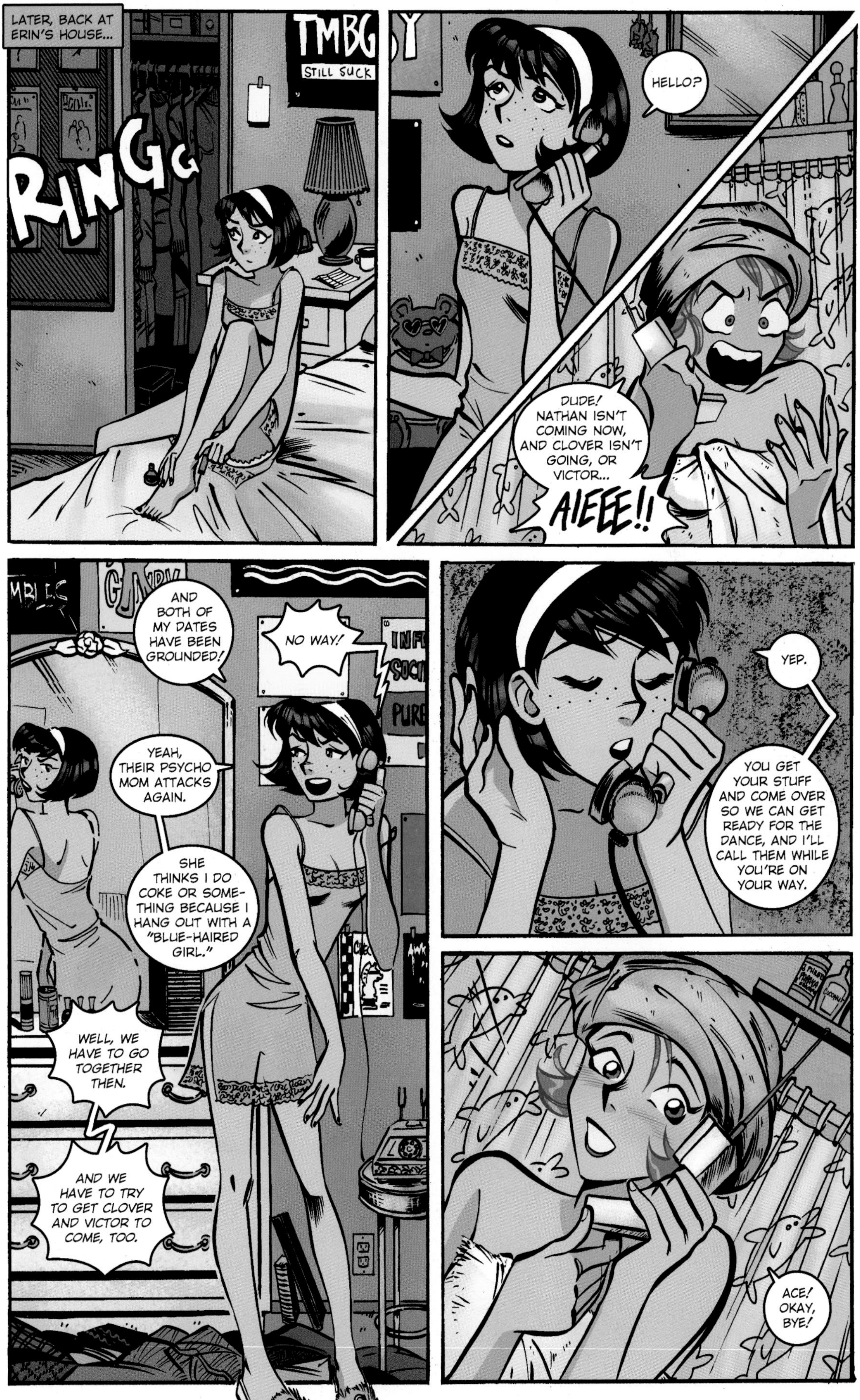
LATER, BACK AT ERIN'S HOUSE...
TMBG
STILL SUCK
RINGG
HELLO?
DUDE! NATHAN ISN'T COMING NOW, AND CLOVER ISN'T GOING, OR VICTOR...
AIEEE!!
AND BOTH OF MY DATES HAVE BEEN GROUNDED!
NO WAY!
YEAH, THEIR PSYCHO MOM ATTACKS AGAIN.
SHE THINKS I DO COKE OR SOMETHING BECAUSE I HANG OUT WITH A "BLUE-HAIRED GIRL."
WELL, WE HAVE TO GO TOGETHER THEN.
AND WE HAVE TO TRY TO GET CLOVER AND VICTOR TO COME, TOO.
YEP.
YOU GET YOUR STUFF AND COME OVER SO WE CAN GET READY FOR THE DANCE, AND I'LL CALL THEM WHILE YOU'RE ON YOUR WAY.
ACE! OKAY, BYE!

HEY, WATTS. NOTHING VENTURED, NOTHING GAINED, RIGHT?

KEITH, ONCE A FOOL, ALWAYS A FOOL, RIGHT?

> GRUNT <

television

I GOTTA GET OUT OF HERE. I AM *NOT* STAYING HOME ON VALENTINE'S DAY.

I'D NEVER HEAR THE END OF IT FROM THOSE USELESS BROTHERS OF MINE, AND THAT'D MAKE ME HAVE TO KILL 'EM.

RRIIIING!

VWIP!

I GOT IT!

HELLO?!?

HEY, VICTOR, EVERYBODY'S DATES ARE FLAKING ON THEM FOR THE DANCE...

...SO WE WERE WONDERING IF YOU WANTED TO COME WITH US AS A GROUP.

WELLIDON'TKNOWOKAYYES!

COOL, SEE YOU AT EIGHT!

YES!!! SAVED!

NO DATES MEANS I CAN DANCE WITH *ALL* THE CHICKS TONIGHT!

ALTHOUGH...

...MAYBE JUST ONE WOULD BE BETTER...

poit

(Theme from A Summer Place)

VICTOR...?

YES, CLOVER?

AH... I WAS WONDERIN'... COULD YOU POSSIBLY...

YES??

GRAB ME FECKIN' ARSE ANY HARDER?

WHAT, ARE YOU TRYING TO DRAW BLOOD OR SOMETHIN', YA PERVERT?!?

SQUISH!

GRR

OH, SORRY...

YEAH, EXACTLY.

LIKE I COULD EVER PIERCE THAT ROCK SHE HAS FOR A HEART! HA!

AND SO...

PRIMAL
AM
LOADED

DID YOU GET A HOLD OF THEM?

I GOT VICTOR, BUT CLOVER WASN'T HOME.

HER DAD SAID SHE WAS GONE WHEN HE GOT THERE AND HAS NO IDEA WHERE SHE'S OFF TO...

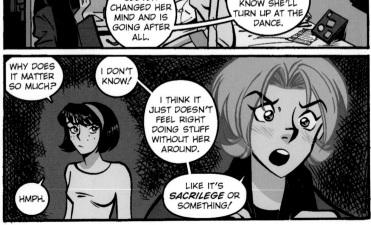

SHIT! IS VICTOR COMING?

YEAH, HE'LL BE THERE.

MAYBE CLOVER CHANGED HER MIND AND IS GOING AFTER ALL.

IF SHE DOESN'T MEET US HERE, I KNOW SHE'LL TURN UP AT THE DANCE.

SHE HAS TO!

WHY DOES IT MATTER SO MUCH?

I DON'T KNOW!

I THINK IT JUST DOESN'T FEEL RIGHT DOING STUFF WITHOUT HER AROUND.

LIKE IT'S *SACRILEGE* OR SOMETHING!

HMPH.

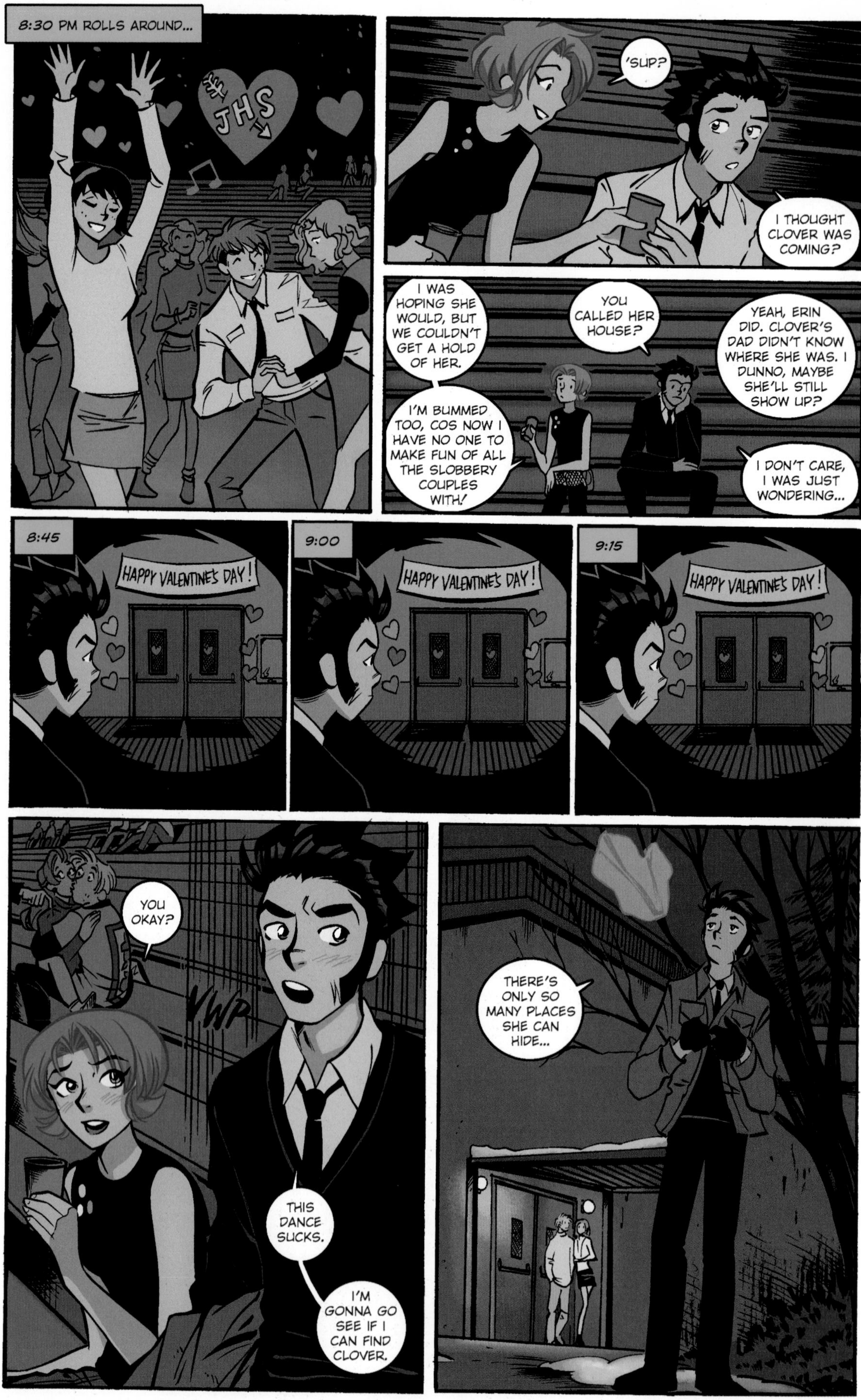
8:30 PM ROLLS AROUND...
JHS
'SUP?
I THOUGHT CLOVER WAS COMING?
I WAS HOPING SHE WOULD, BUT WE COULDN'T GET A HOLD OF HER.
I'M BUMMED TOO, COS NOW I HAVE NO ONE TO MAKE FUN OF ALL THE SLOBBERY COUPLES WITH!
YOU CALLED HER HOUSE?
YEAH, ERIN DID. CLOVER'S DAD DIDN'T KNOW WHERE SHE WAS. I DUNNO, MAYBE SHE'LL STILL SHOW UP?
I DON'T CARE, I WAS JUST WONDERING...
8:45
HAPPY VALENTINE'S DAY!
9:00
HAPPY VALENTINE'S DAY!
9:15
HAPPY VALENTINE'S DAY!
YOU OKAY?
VWP
THIS DANCE SUCKS.
I'M GONNA GO SEE IF I CAN FIND CLOVER.
THERE'S ONLY SO MANY PLACES SHE CAN HIDE...

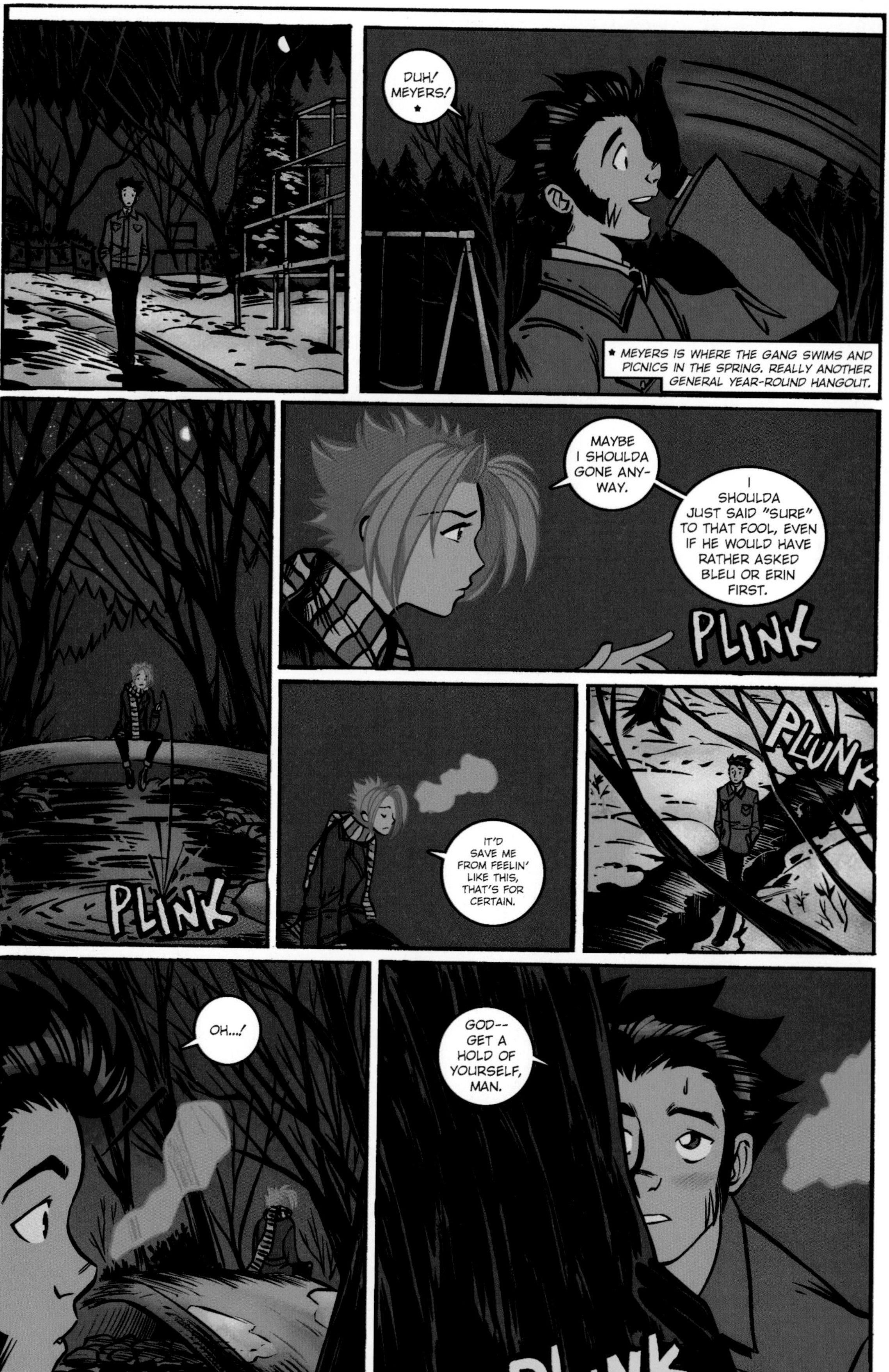

DUH! MEYERS! *
* MEYERS IS WHERE THE GANG SWIMS AND PICNICS IN THE SPRING. REALLY ANOTHER GENERAL YEAR-ROUND HANGOUT.
MAYBE I SHOULDA GONE ANY-WAY.
I SHOULDA JUST SAID "SURE" TO THAT FOOL, EVEN IF HE WOULD HAVE RATHER ASKED BLEU OR ERIN FIRST.
PLINK
PLINK
IT'D SAVE ME FROM FEELIN' LIKE THIS, THAT'S FOR CERTAIN.
PLUNK
OH...!
GOD-- GET A HOLD OF YOURSELF, MAN.
PLINK

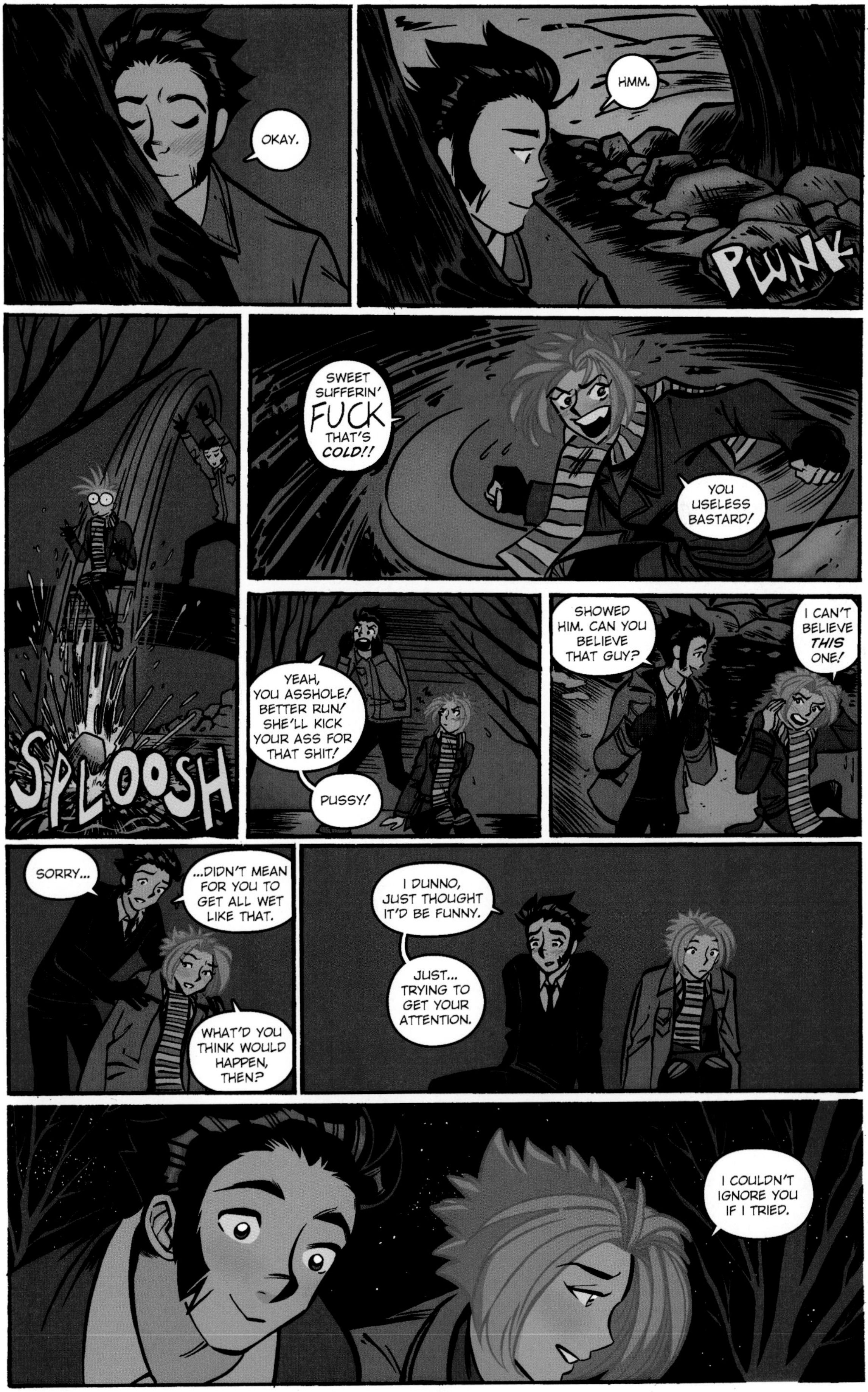
OKAY.
HMM.
PLUNK
SPLOOSH
SWEET SUFFERIN' FUCK THAT'S COLD!!
YOU USELESS BASTARD!
YEAH, YOU ASSHOLE! BETTER RUN! SHE'LL KICK YOUR ASS FOR THAT SHIT!
PUSSY!
SHOWED HIM. CAN YOU BELIEVE THAT GUY?
I CAN'T BELIEVE THIS ONE!
SORRY...
...DIDN'T MEAN FOR YOU TO GET ALL WET LIKE THAT.
WHAT'D YOU THINK WOULD HAPPEN, THEN?
I DUNNO, JUST THOUGHT IT'D BE FUNNY.
JUST... TRYING TO GET YOUR ATTENTION.
I COULDN'T IGNORE YOU IF I TRIED.

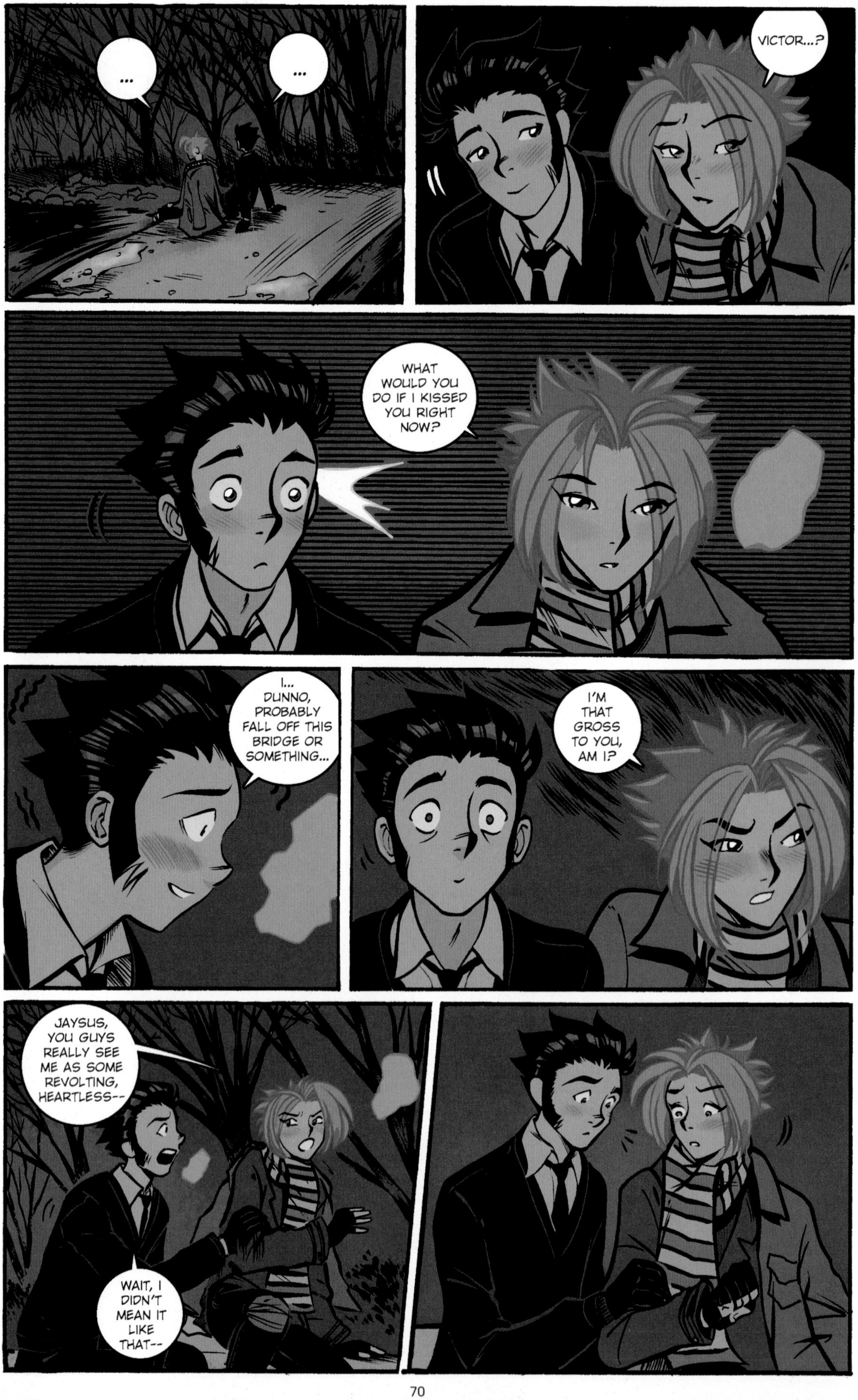
...
...
VICTOR...?
WHAT WOULD YOU DO IF I KISSED YOU RIGHT NOW?
I... DUNNO, PROBABLY FALL OFF THIS BRIDGE OR SOMETHING...
I'M THAT GROSS TO YOU, AM I?
JAYSUS, YOU GUYS REALLY SEE ME AS SOME REVOLTING, HEARTLESS--
WAIT, I DIDN'T MEAN IT LIKE THAT--

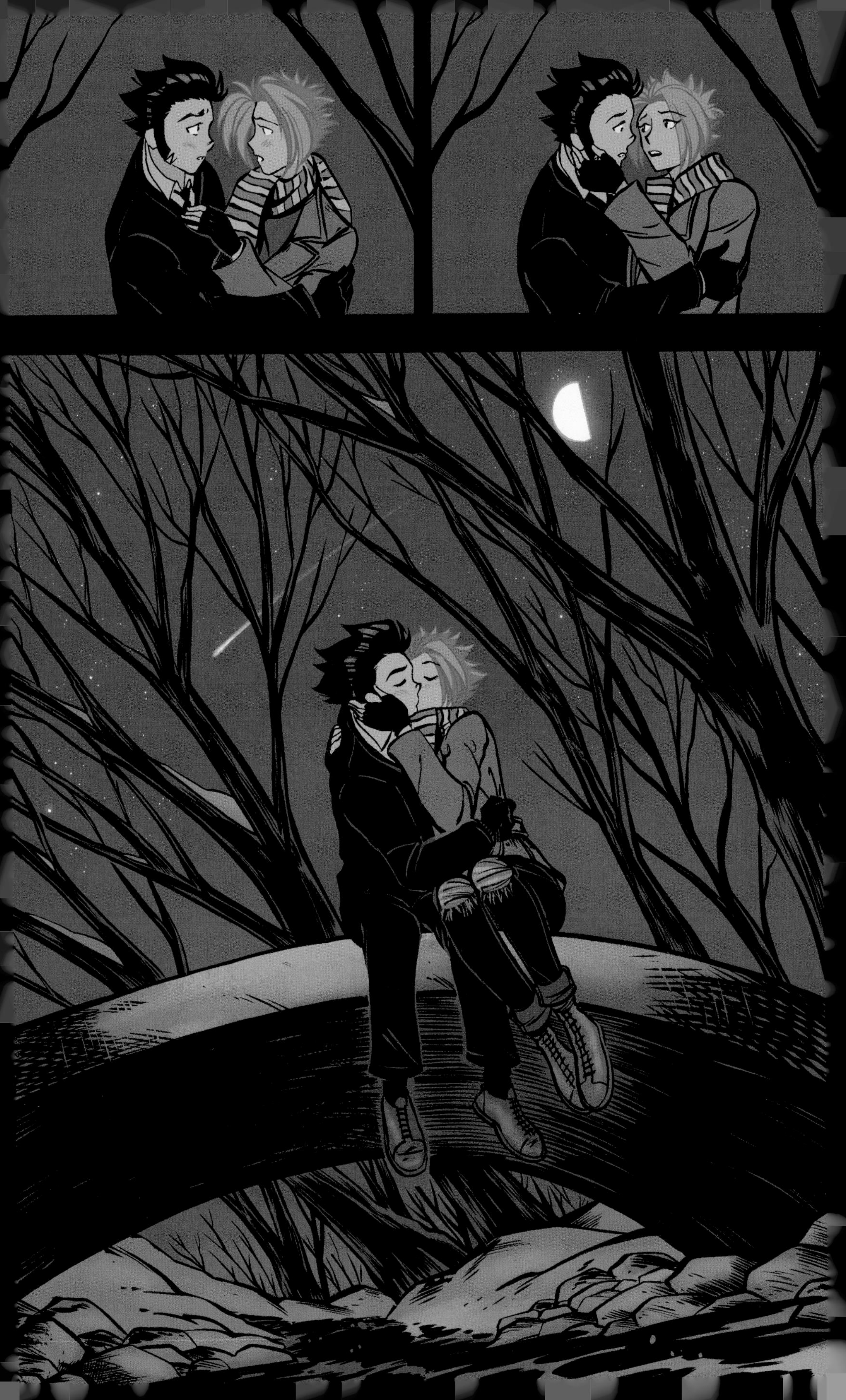

.02 NANOSECONDS LATER.

I THINK I SEE THEM UP AHEAD!

ZOOM

JESUS, IT'S COLD AS HELL OUT HERE, YOU GUYS!

WH- WHAT ARE YOU DOING HERE?

ERIN THOUGHT WE SHOULD HELP VICTOR FIND YOU.

YEAH, IT'S WAY TOO FREEZING TO BE OUT HERE ALL NIGHT.

WE SHOULD GO SOMEWHERE WARM TO HANG OUT.

Y-YEAH, UH, WASN'T THERE A DANCE TONIGHT?

UHH, SURE...

YAY! 'BOUT TIME YOU CAME TO YOUR SENSES!

COME ON, CHICKIE BABY, LET'S GO SHAKE IT!

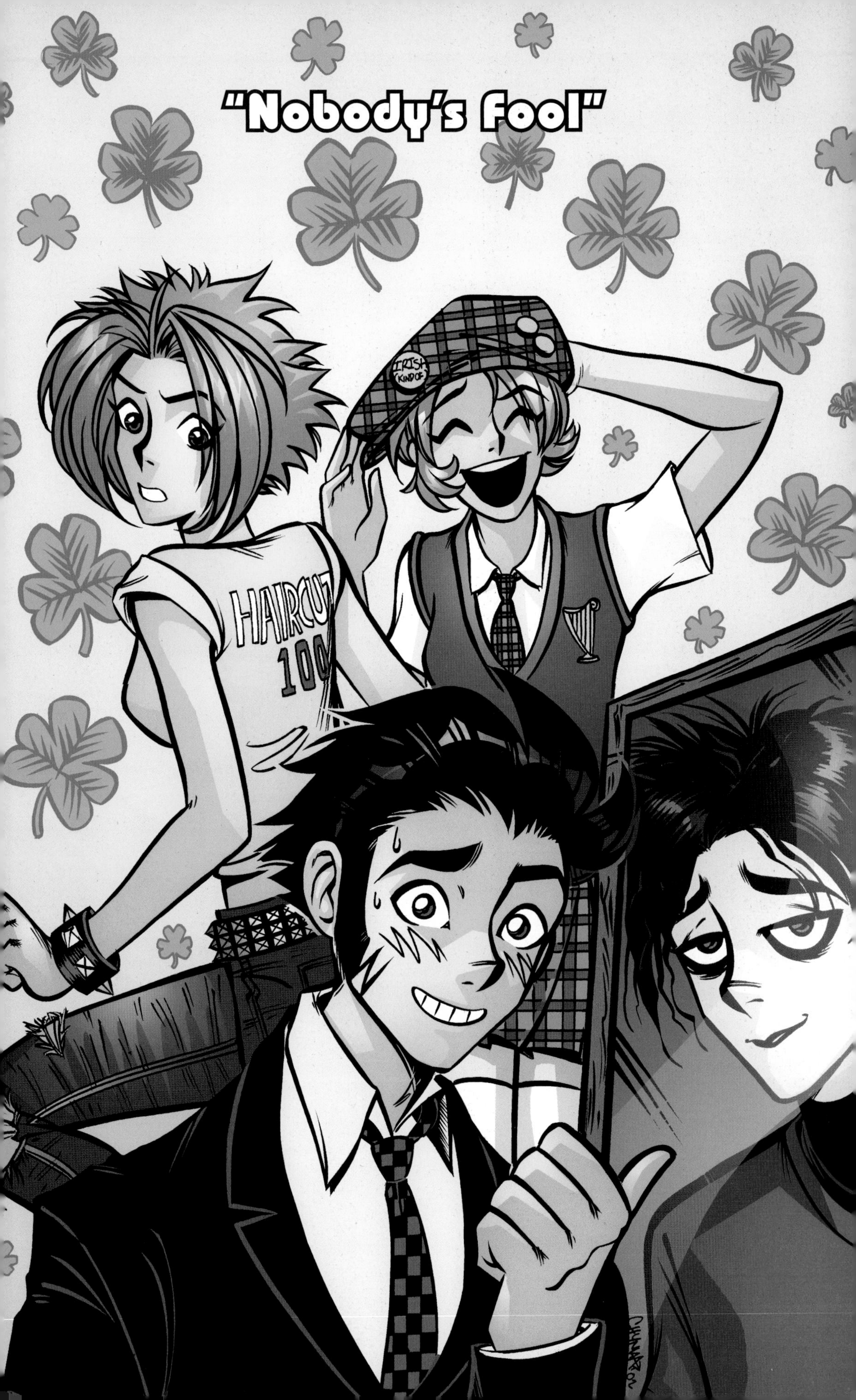
"Nobody's Fool"
IRISH KIND OF
HAIRCUT
100

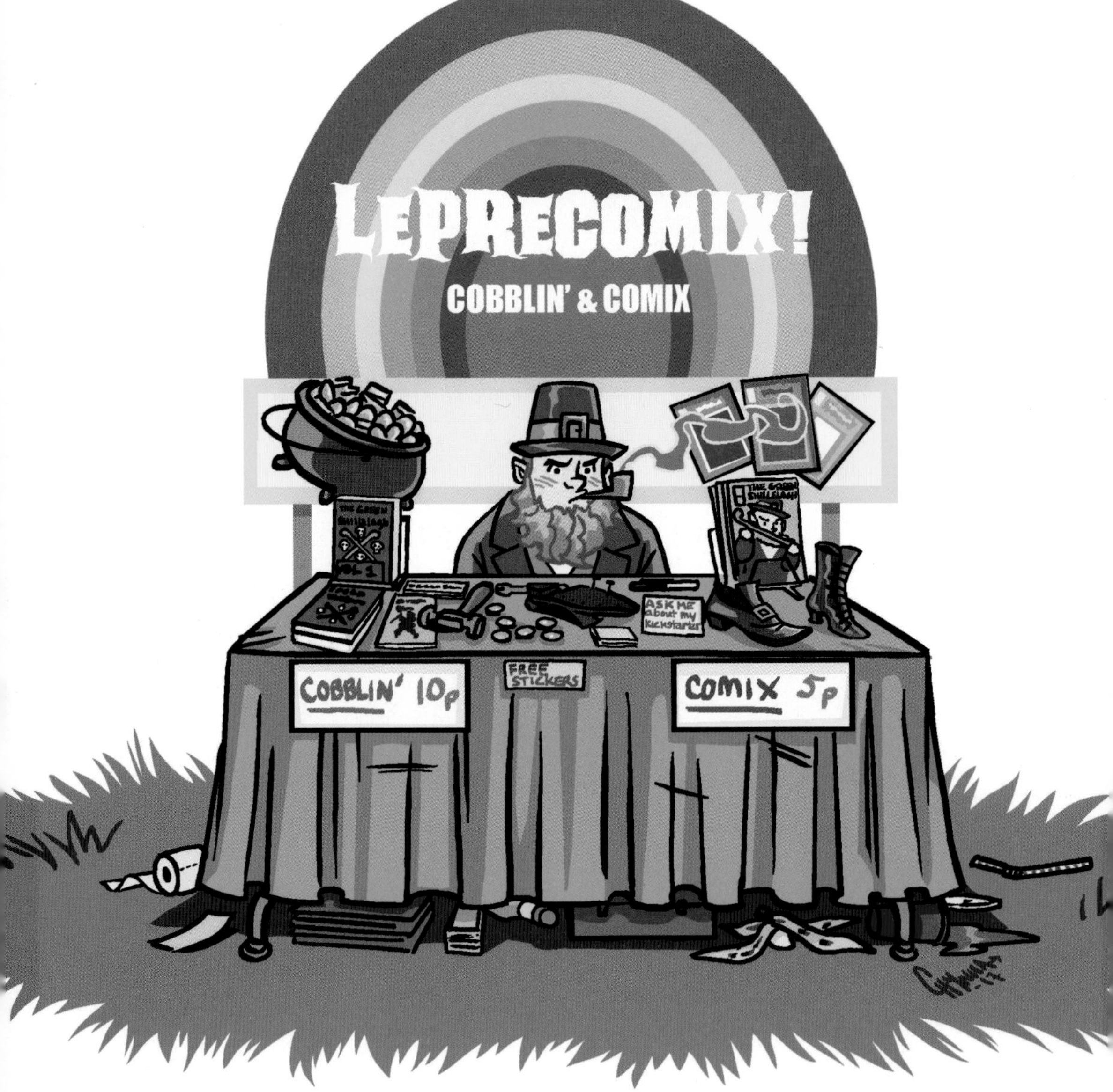
LEPRECOMIX!
COBBLIN' & COMIX
THE GREEN SHILLELAGH
VOL 1
ASK ME about my kickstarter
COBBLIN' 10p
FREE STICKERS
COMIX 5p

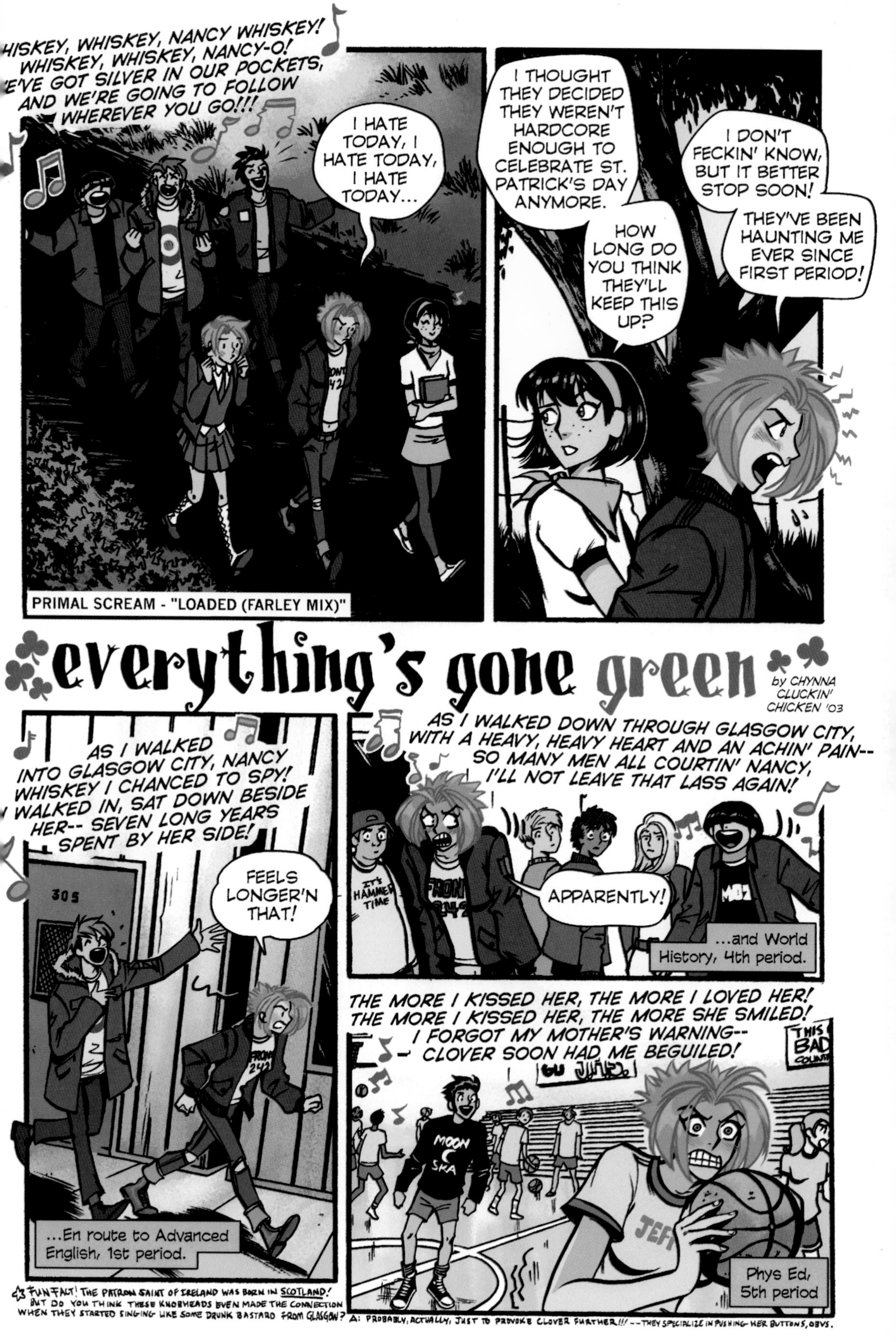
HISKEY, WHISKEY, NANCY WHISKEY! WHISKEY, WHISKEY, NANCY-O! 'E'VE GOT SILVER IN OUR POCKETS, AND WE'RE GOING TO FOLLOW WHEREVER YOU GO!!!
I HATE TODAY, I HATE TODAY, I HATE TODAY...
PRIMAL SCREAM - "LOADED (FARLEY MIX)"
I THOUGHT THEY DECIDED THEY WEREN'T HARDCORE ENOUGH TO CELEBRATE ST. PATRICK'S DAY ANYMORE.
HOW LONG DO YOU THINK THEY'LL KEEP THIS UP?
I DON'T FECKIN' KNOW, BUT IT BETTER STOP SOON!
THEY'VE BEEN HAUNTING ME EVER SINCE FIRST PERIOD!
everything's gone green
by CHYNNA CLUCKIN' CHICKEN '03
AS I WALKED INTO GLASGOW CITY, NANCY WHISKEY I CHANCED TO SPY! WALKED IN, SAT DOWN BESIDE HER-- SEVEN LONG YEARS SPENT BY HER SIDE!
305
FEELS LONGER'N THAT!
...En route to Advanced English, 1st period.
AS I WALKED DOWN THROUGH GLASGOW CITY, WITH A HEAVY, HEAVY HEART AND AN ACHIN' PAIN-- SO MANY MEN ALL COURTIN' NANCY, I'LL NOT LEAVE THAT LASS AGAIN!
IT'S HAMMER TIME
APPARENTLY!
...and World History, 4th period.
THE MORE I KISSED HER, THE MORE I LOVED HER! THE MORE I KISSED HER, THE MORE SHE SMILED! I FORGOT MY MOTHER'S WARNING-- CLOVER SOON HAD ME BEGUILED!
MOON SKA
JEFF
Phys Ed, 5th period
FUN FACT! THE PATRON SAINT OF IRELAND WAS BORN IN SCOTLAND! BUT DO YOU THINK THESE KNOBHEADS EVEN MADE THE CONNECTION WHEN THEY STARTED SINGING LIKE SOME DRUNK BASTARD FROM GLASGOW?
A: PROBABLY, ACTUALLY, JUST TO PROVOKE CLOVER FURTHER!!! --THEY SPECIALIZE IN PUSHING HER BUTTONS, OBVS.

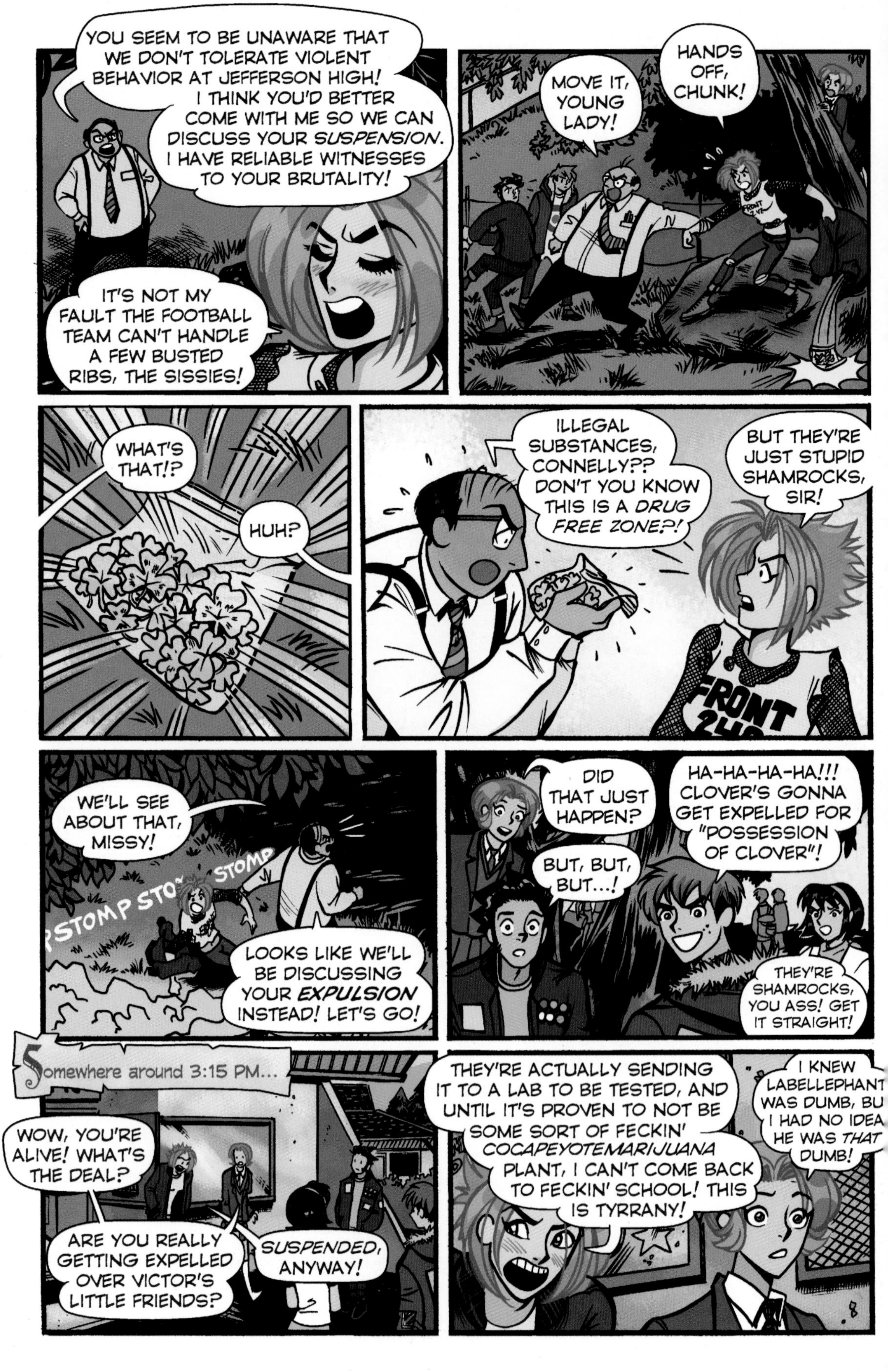
YOU SEEM TO BE UNAWARE THAT WE DON'T TOLERATE VIOLENT BEHAVIOR AT JEFFERSON HIGH! I THINK YOU'D BETTER COME WITH ME SO WE CAN DISCUSS YOUR SUSPENSION. I HAVE RELIABLE WITNESSES TO YOUR BRUTALITY!
IT'S NOT MY FAULT THE FOOTBALL TEAM CAN'T HANDLE A FEW BUSTED RIBS, THE SISSIES!
MOVE IT, YOUNG LADY!
HANDS OFF, CHUNK!
WHAT'S THAT!?
HUH?
ILLEGAL SUBSTANCES, CONNELLY?? DON'T YOU KNOW THIS IS A DRUG FREE ZONE?!
BUT THEY'RE JUST STUPID SHAMROCKS, SIR!
FRONT 242
WE'LL SEE ABOUT THAT, MISSY!
STOMP STOMP STOMP
LOOKS LIKE WE'LL BE DISCUSSING YOUR EXPULSION INSTEAD! LET'S GO!
DID THAT JUST HAPPEN?
BUT, BUT, BUT...!
HA-HA-HA-HA!!! CLOVER'S GONNA GET EXPELLED FOR "POSSESSION OF CLOVER"!
THEY'RE SHAMROCKS, YOU ASS! GET IT STRAIGHT!
Somewhere around 3:15 PM...
WOW, YOU'RE ALIVE! WHAT'S THE DEAL?
ARE YOU REALLY GETTING EXPELLED OVER VICTOR'S LITTLE FRIENDS?
SUSPENDED, ANYWAY!
THEY'RE ACTUALLY SENDING IT TO A LAB TO BE TESTED, AND UNTIL IT'S PROVEN TO NOT BE SOME SORT OF FECKIN' COCAPEYOTEMARIJUANA PLANT, I CAN'T COME BACK TO FECKIN' SCHOOL! THIS IS TYRRANY!
I KNEW LABELLEPHANT WAS DUMB, BU I HAD NO IDEA HE WAS THAT DUMB!

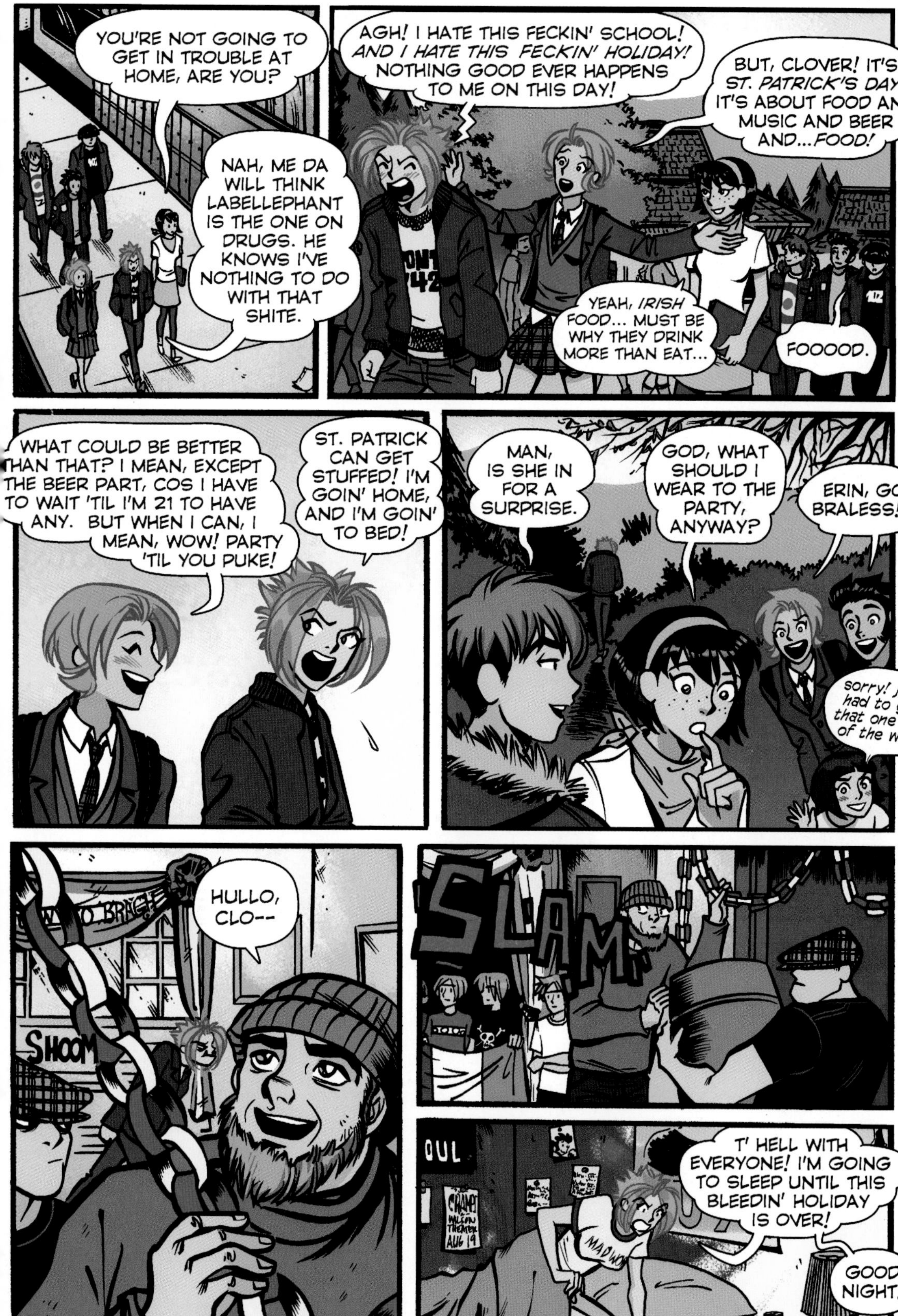
YOU'RE NOT GOING TO GET IN TROUBLE AT HOME, ARE YOU?
NAH, ME DA WILL THINK LABELLEPHANT IS THE ONE ON DRUGS. HE KNOWS I'VE NOTHING TO DO WITH THAT SHITE.
AGH! I HATE THIS FECKIN' SCHOOL! *AND I HATE THIS FECKIN' HOLIDAY!* NOTHING GOOD EVER HAPPENS TO ME ON THIS DAY!
BUT, CLOVER! IT'S *ST. PATRICK'S DAY!* IT'S ABOUT FOOD AND MUSIC AND BEER AND...*FOOD!*
YEAH, *IRISH* FOOD... MUST BE WHY THEY DRINK MORE THAN EAT...
FOOOOD.
WHAT COULD BE BETTER THAN THAT? I MEAN, EXCEPT THE BEER PART, COS I HAVE TO WAIT 'TIL I'M 21 TO HAVE ANY. BUT WHEN I CAN, I MEAN, WOW! PARTY 'TIL YOU PUKE!
ST. PATRICK CAN GET STUFFED! I'M GOIN' HOME, AND I'M GOIN' TO BED!
MAN, IS SHE IN FOR A SURPRISE.
GOD, WHAT SHOULD I WEAR TO THE PARTY, ANYWAY?
ERIN, GO BRALESS!!!
sorry! just had to get that one out of the way!
HULLO, CLO--
SHOOM
SLAM
T' HELL WITH EVERYONE! I'M GOING TO SLEEP UNTIL THIS BLEEDIN' HOLIDAY IS OVER!
GOOD NIGHT!

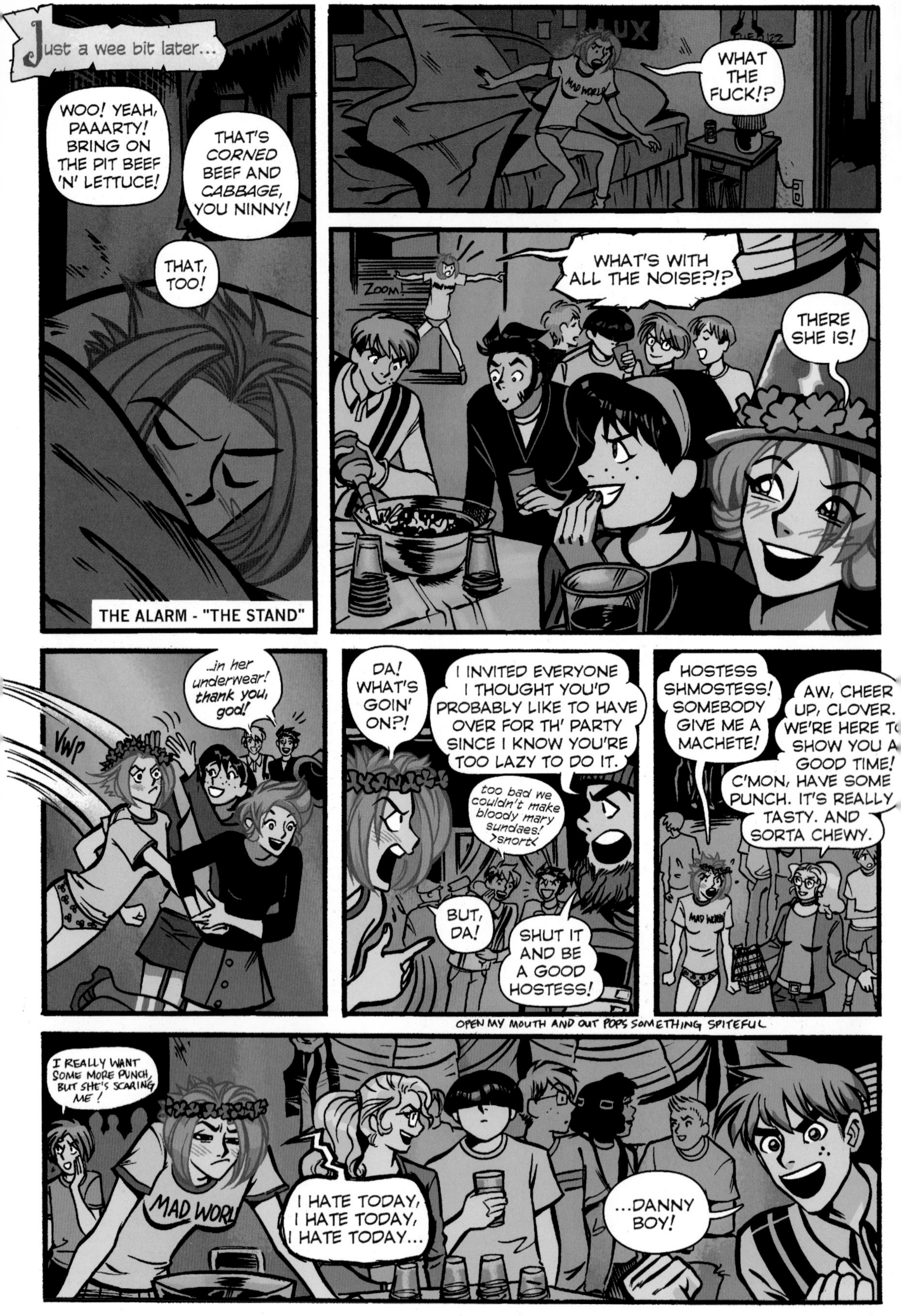

Just a wee bit later...
WOO! YEAH, PAAARTY! BRING ON THE PIT BEEF 'N' LETTUCE!
THAT'S CORNED BEEF AND CABBAGE, YOU NINNY!
THAT, TOO!
THE ALARM - "THE STAND"
WHAT THE FUCK!?
WHAT'S WITH ALL THE NOISE?!?
ZOOM!
THERE SHE IS!
VWP
..in her underwear! thank you, god!
DA! WHAT'S GOIN' ON?!
I INVITED EVERYONE I THOUGHT YOU'D PROBABLY LIKE TO HAVE OVER FOR TH' PARTY SINCE I KNOW YOU'RE TOO LAZY TO DO IT.
too bad we couldn't make bloody mary sundaes! >snort<
BUT, DA!
SHUT IT AND BE A GOOD HOSTESS!
HOSTESS SHMOSTESS! SOMEBODY GIVE ME A MACHETE!
AW, CHEER UP, CLOVER. WE'RE HERE TO SHOW YOU A GOOD TIME! C'MON, HAVE SOME PUNCH. IT'S REALLY TASTY. AND SORTA CHEWY.
OPEN MY MOUTH AND OUT POPS SOMETHING SPITEFUL
I REALLY WANT SOME MORE PUNCH, BUT SHE'S SCARING ME!
I HATE TODAY, I HATE TODAY, I HATE TODAY...
...DANNY BOY!

h danny booooy, the pipes, the pipes are caaaaaallling...!

NO, NO, NO, NO!

from glen to glennnnn, and dooooown the mountain siiiiide!

Give me back me Lucky Charms!

GOD ABOVE, KILL ME NOW...

!!!

SHLURP

MAD WORLD

the summer's gooooooone and all the leaves are faaaalling...

WHOA, CLOVER, SAVE SOME PUNCH FOR US! YOU ALMOST DOWNED THE WHOLE THING!

URRGH... I'M GONNA BE SICK...

WIPE 'EM

BLEEEAAGH

ZIP! ZIP!

UGGGH.

HOY! Y'VOMITED IN ME CASHBOX!

ME POT O' GOLD!

HUH?

YOUR *WHAT?*

SHOO, SHOO! OFF WITH YE, BEHEMOTH!

POP!

ME POT O' GOLD!

ACH, *LEPRECHAUNS?!* I DON'T EVEN BELIEVE IN YOU BASTARDS!

WHAT THE HELL IS GOING ON??

It's very practical.

Yes, very practical.

YOU SHOULD KNOW THAT BY NOW! IT'S WHAT WE DO EVERY ST. PATRICK'S DAY IN THESE PARTS! WE GROUP TOGETHER FOR PROTECTION FROM ROVING, GOLD-HUNTIN' HUMANS AND SELL OUR WARES AT THE SAME TIME...

IT'S THE Northern California Annual Leprechaun Convention!

A.K.A. *LEPRECON!*

HUAAARCH

AGH! NOT AGAIN! GO AWAY!

PTOO... PTOO! GOD... WHY ME?

MUS**SHOVE** LOSING MVM

THERE YOU ARE! YOU'RE LATE! COME WITH US!

MAD WORLD

SHOVE

YICK! DON'T FECKIN' TOUCH ME, YOU WADDLING BOOGER!

ACH, SHE'S DRUNK!

SO? WE LIKE 'EM THAT WAY!

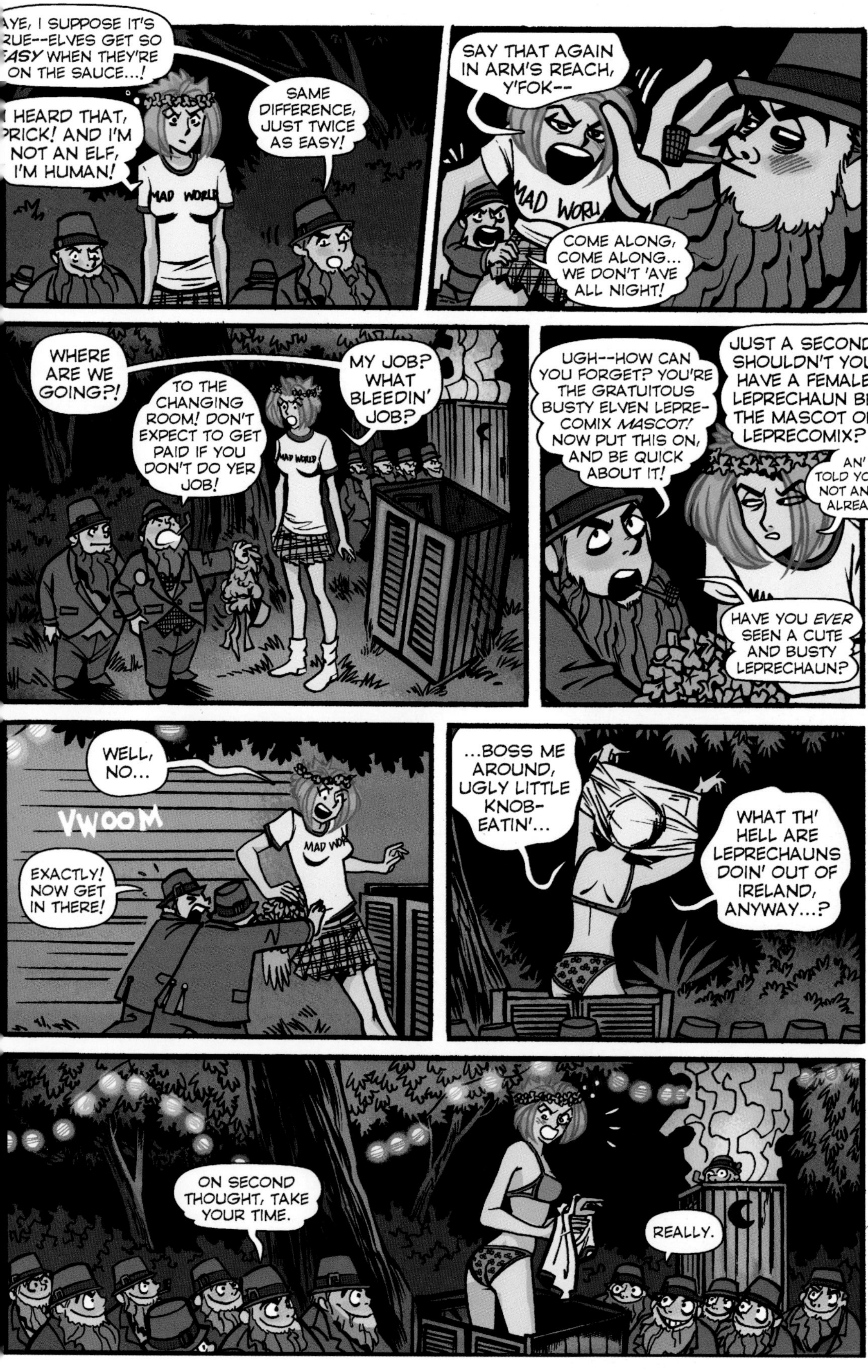
AYE, I SUPPOSE IT'S TRUE--ELVES GET SO EASY WHEN THEY'RE ON THE SAUCE...!
I HEARD THAT, PRICK! AND I'M NOT AN ELF, I'M HUMAN!
SAME DIFFERENCE, JUST TWICE AS EASY!
MAD WORLD
SAY THAT AGAIN IN ARM'S REACH, Y'FOK--
COME ALONG, COME ALONG... WE DON'T 'AVE ALL NIGHT!
WHERE ARE WE GOING?!
TO THE CHANGING ROOM! DON'T EXPECT TO GET PAID IF YOU DON'T DO YER JOB!
MY JOB? WHAT BLEEDIN' JOB?
UGH--HOW CAN YOU FORGET? YOU'RE THE GRATUITOUS BUSTY ELVEN LEPRECOMIX MASCOT! NOW PUT THIS ON, AND BE QUICK ABOUT IT!
JUST A SECOND, SHOULDN'T YOU HAVE A FEMALE LEPRECHAUN BE THE MASCOT OF LEPRECOMIX?
AN' I TOLD YOU I'M NOT AN ELF, ALREADY!
HAVE YOU EVER SEEN A CUTE AND BUSTY LEPRECHAUN?
WELL, NO...
VWOOM
EXACTLY! NOW GET IN THERE!
...BOSS ME AROUND, UGLY LITTLE KNOB-EATIN'...
WHAT TH' HELL ARE LEPRECHAUNS DOIN' OUT OF IRELAND, ANYWAY...?
ON SECOND THOUGHT, TAKE YOUR TIME.
REALLY.

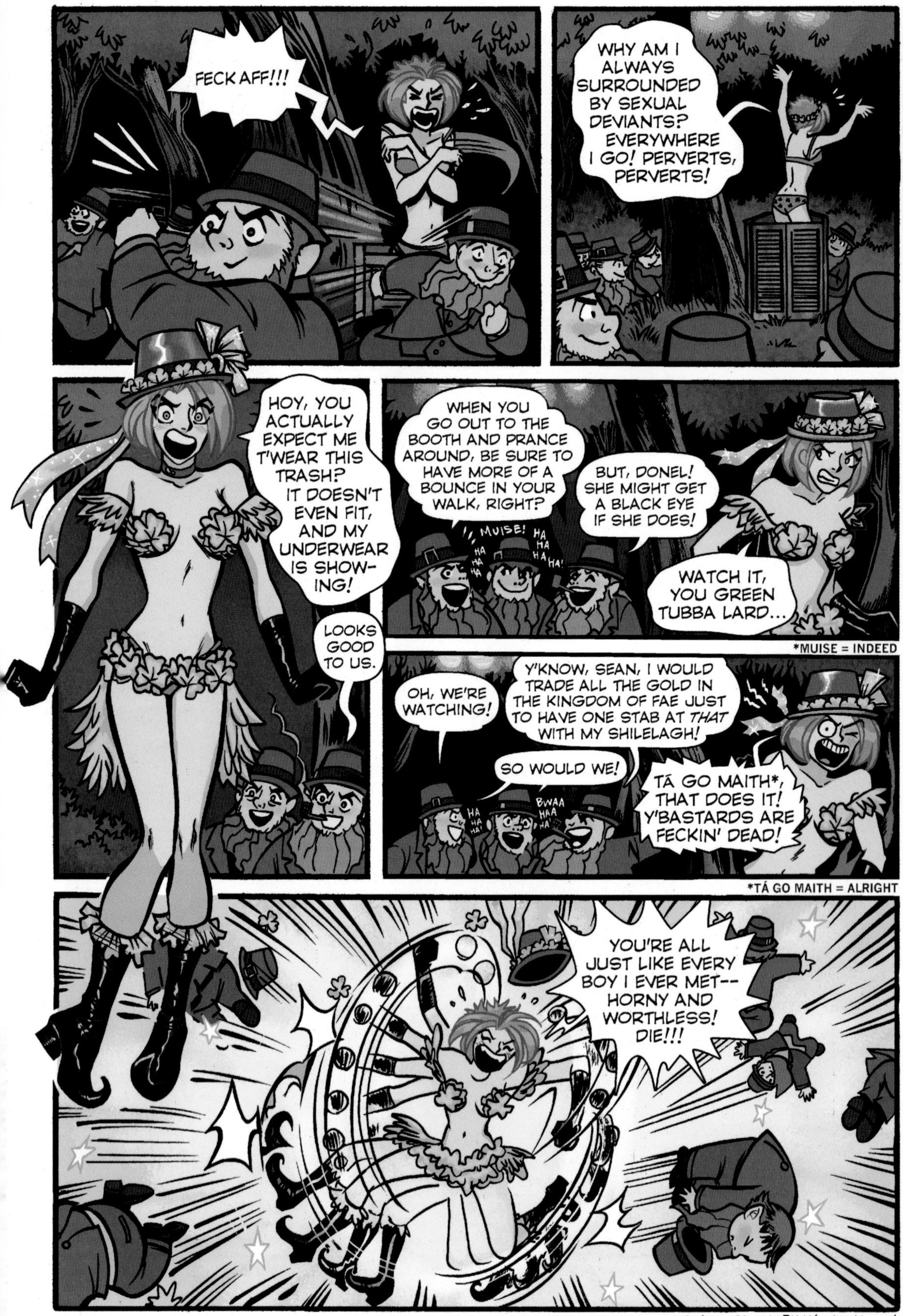
FECK AFF!!!
WHY AM I ALWAYS SURROUNDED BY SEXUAL DEVIANTS? EVERYWHERE I GO! PERVERTS, PERVERTS!
HOY, YOU ACTUALLY EXPECT ME T'WEAR THIS TRASH? IT DOESN'T EVEN FIT, AND MY UNDERWEAR IS SHOW-ING!
LOOKS GOOD TO US.
WHEN YOU GO OUT TO THE BOOTH AND PRANCE AROUND, BE SURE TO HAVE MORE OF A BOUNCE IN YOUR WALK, RIGHT?
BUT, DONEL! SHE MIGHT GET A BLACK EYE IF SHE DOES!
MUISE! HA HA HA HA!
HA HA HA
WATCH IT, YOU GREEN TUBBA LARD...
*MUISE = INDEED
OH, WE'RE WATCHING!
Y'KNOW, SEAN, I WOULD TRADE ALL THE GOLD IN THE KINGDOM OF FAE JUST TO HAVE ONE STAB AT *THAT* WITH MY SHILELAGH!
SO WOULD WE!
HA HA HA!
BWAA HAA HA!
TÁ GO MAITH*, THAT DOES IT! Y'BASTARDS ARE FECKIN' DEAD!
*TÁ GO MAITH = ALRIGHT
YOU'RE ALL JUST LIKE EVERY BOY I EVER MET-- HORNY AND WORTHLESS! DIE!!!

IT'S A PSYCHOBILLY FREAKOUT!

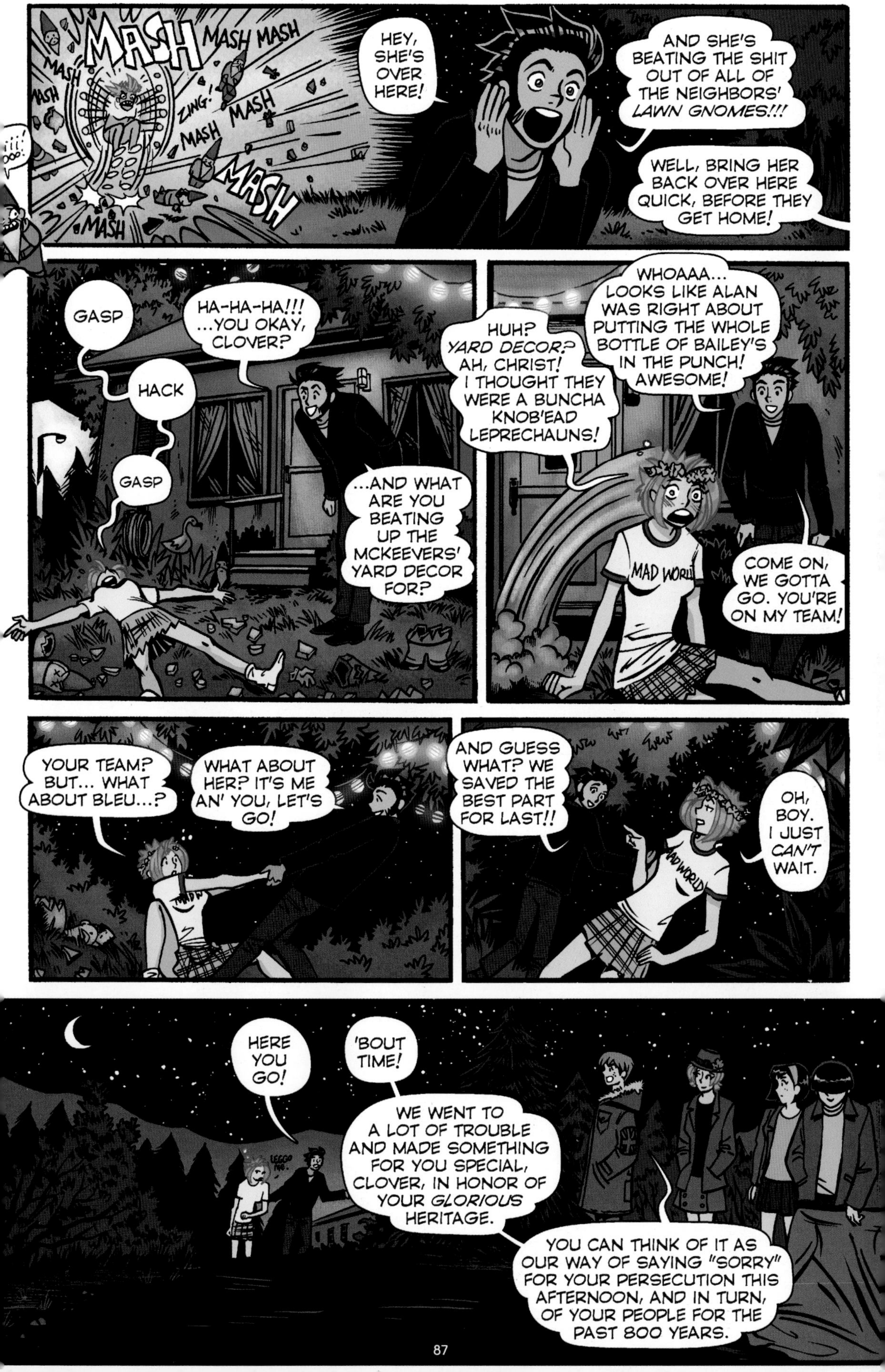
MASH MASH MASH
MASH
MASH
ZING!
MASH
MASH
MASH
MASH
HEY, SHE'S OVER HERE!
AND SHE'S BEATING THE SHIT OUT OF ALL OF THE NEIGHBORS' *LAWN GNOMES!!!*
WELL, BRING HER BACK OVER HERE QUICK, BEFORE THEY GET HOME!
GASP
HACK
GASP
HA-HA-HA!!! ...YOU OKAY, CLOVER?
...AND WHAT ARE YOU BEATING UP THE MCKEEVERS' YARD DECOR FOR?
HUH? *YARD DECOR?* AH, CHRIST! I THOUGHT THEY WERE A BUNCHA KNOB'EAD LEPRECHAUNS!
WHOAAA... LOOKS LIKE ALAN WAS RIGHT ABOUT PUTTING THE WHOLE BOTTLE OF BAILEY'S IN THE PUNCH! AWESOME!
MAD WORLD
COME ON, WE GOTTA GO. YOU'RE ON MY TEAM!
YOUR TEAM? BUT... WHAT ABOUT BLEU...?
WHAT ABOUT HER? IT'S ME AN' YOU, LET'S GO!
AND GUESS WHAT? WE SAVED THE BEST PART FOR LAST!!
OH, BOY. I JUST *CAN'T* WAIT.
HERE YOU GO!
'BOUT TIME!
LEGGO ME.
WE WENT TO A LOT OF TROUBLE AND MADE SOMETHING FOR YOU SPECIAL, CLOVER, IN HONOR OF YOUR *GLORIOUS* HERITAGE.
YOU CAN THINK OF IT AS OUR WAY OF SAYING "SORRY" FOR YOUR PERSECUTION THIS AFTERNOON, AND IN TURN, OF YOUR PEOPLE FOR THE PAST 800 YEARS.

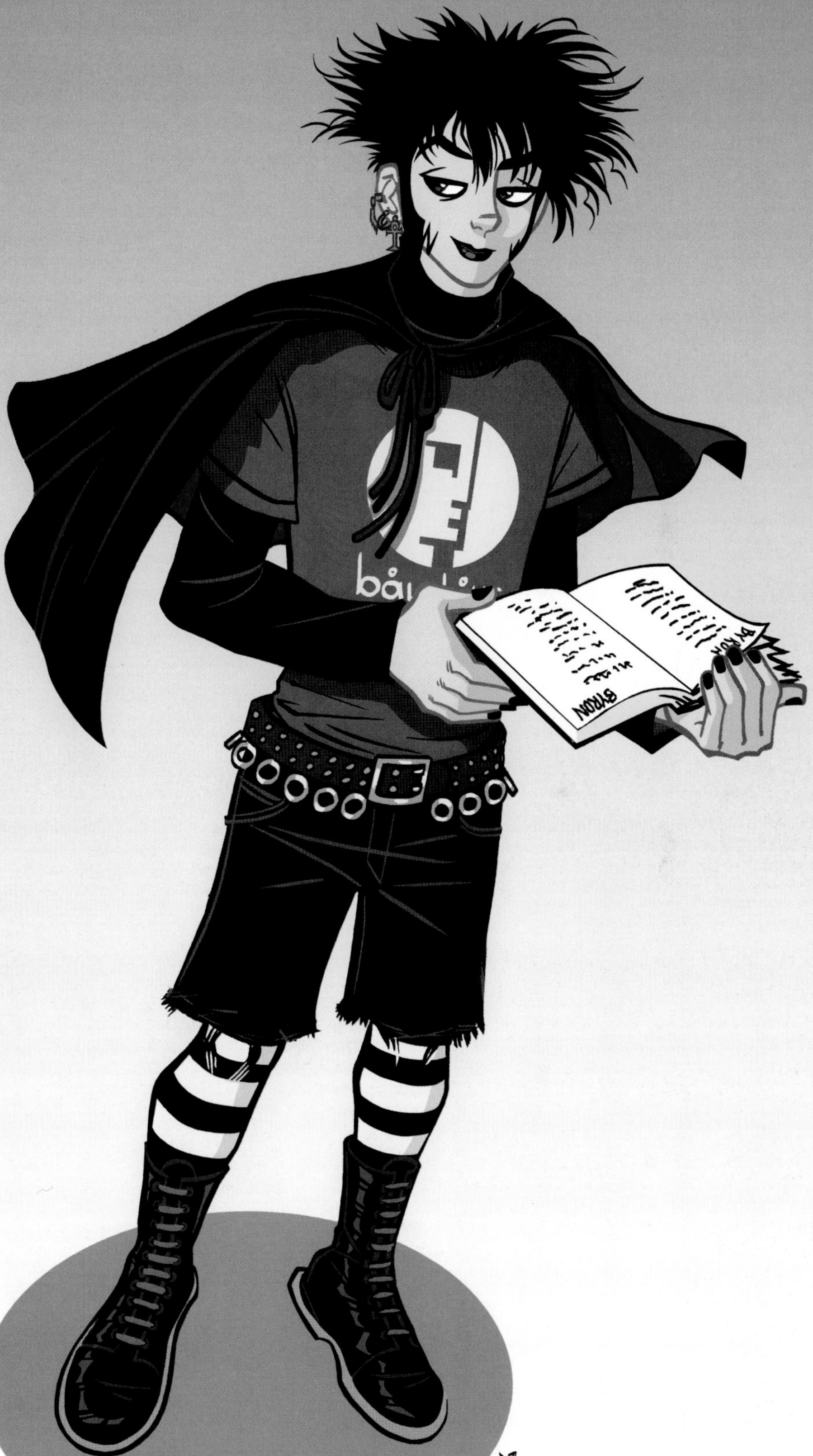

BYRON

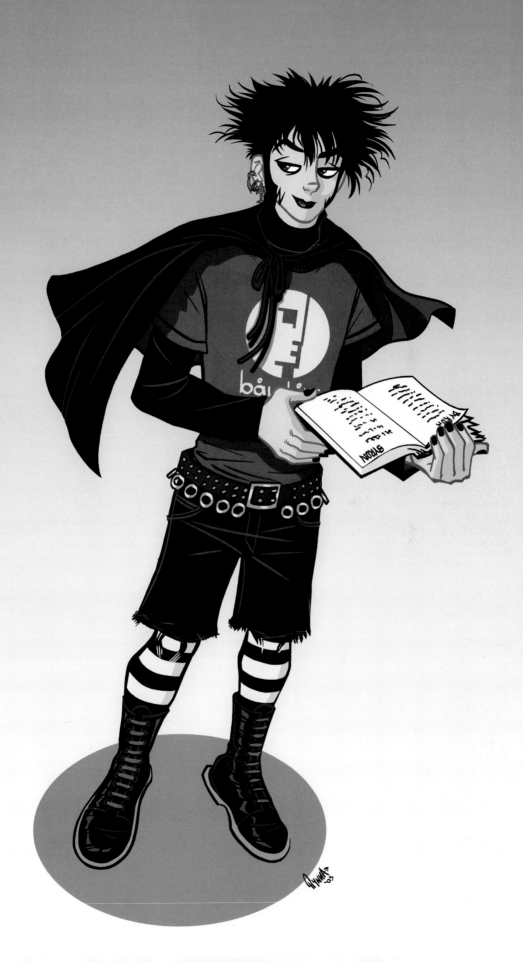

EVERY-BODY PLAYS THE FOOL

A BLUE MONDAY COMIC
BY CHYNNA CLUGSTON

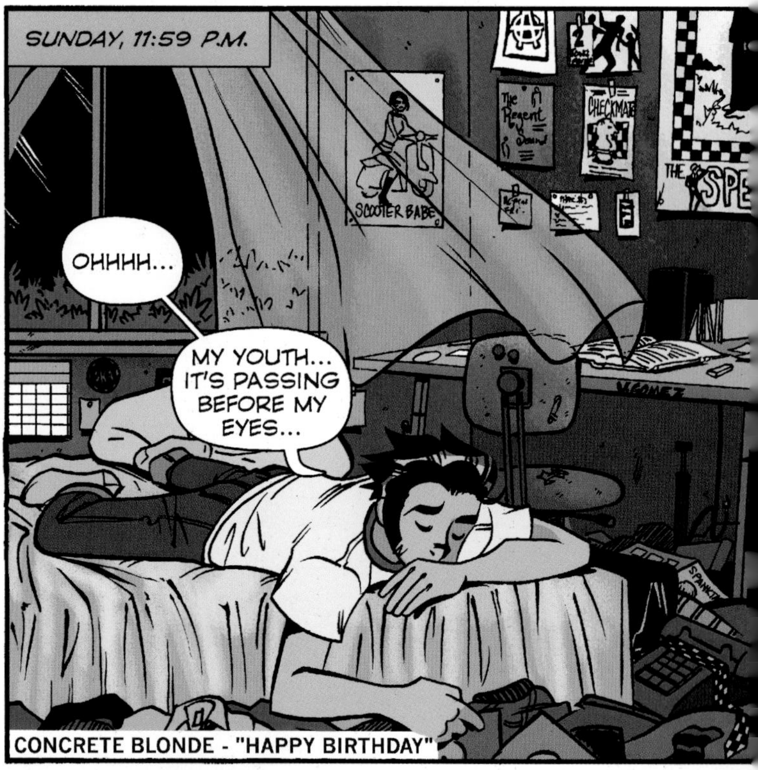
SUNDAY, 11:59 P.M.
SCOOTER BABE
CHECKMATE
OHHHH...
MY YOUTH... IT'S PASSING BEFORE MY EYES...
CONCRETE BLONDE - "HAPPY BIRTHDAY"

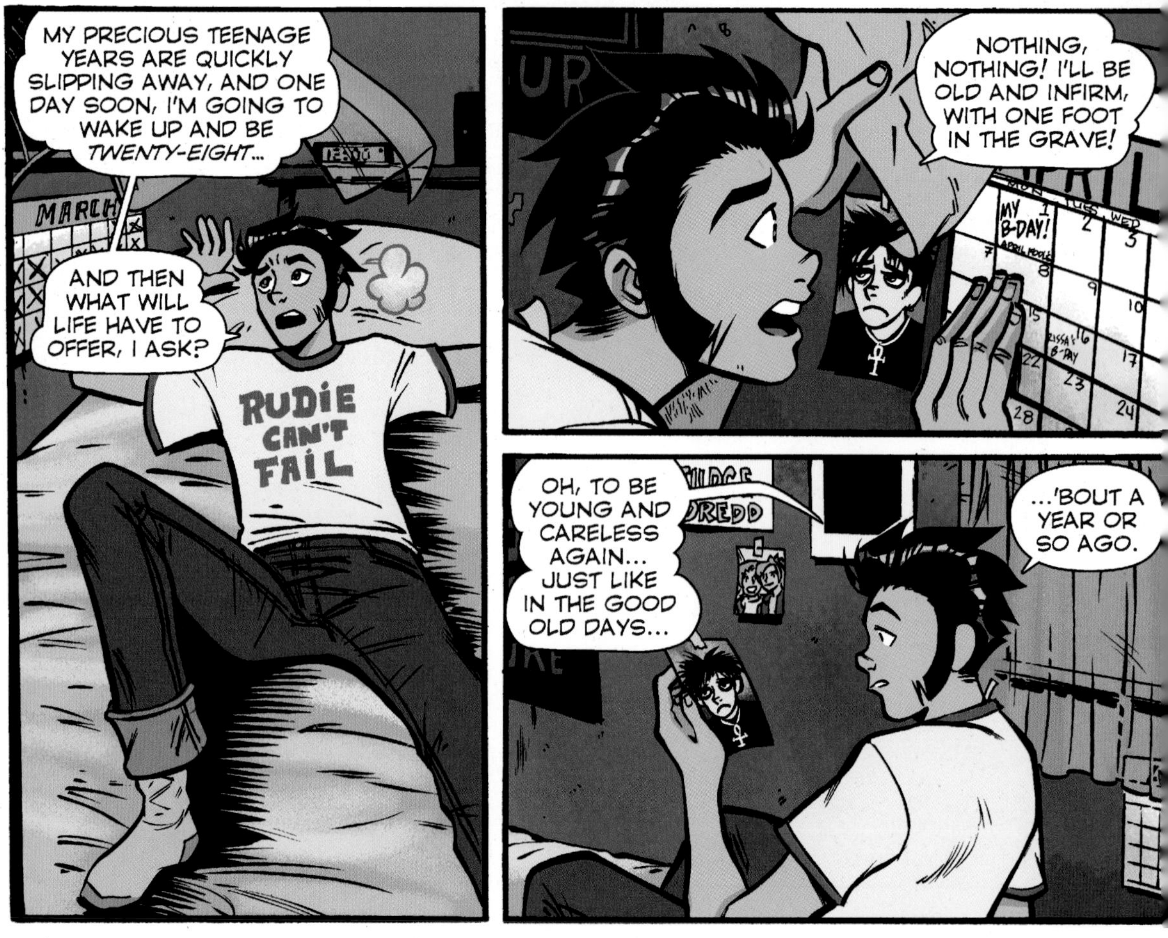
MY PRECIOUS TEENAGE YEARS ARE QUICKLY SLIPPING AWAY, AND ONE DAY SOON, I'M GOING TO WAKE UP AND BE *TWENTY-EIGHT*...
MARCH
AND THEN WHAT WILL LIFE HAVE TO OFFER, I ASK?
RUDIE CAN'T FAIL
NOTHING, NOTHING! I'LL BE OLD AND INFIRM, WITH ONE FOOT IN THE GRAVE!
MY B-DAY!
OH, TO BE YOUNG AND CARELESS AGAIN... JUST LIKE IN THE GOOD OLD DAYS...
...'BOUT A YEAR OR SO AGO.

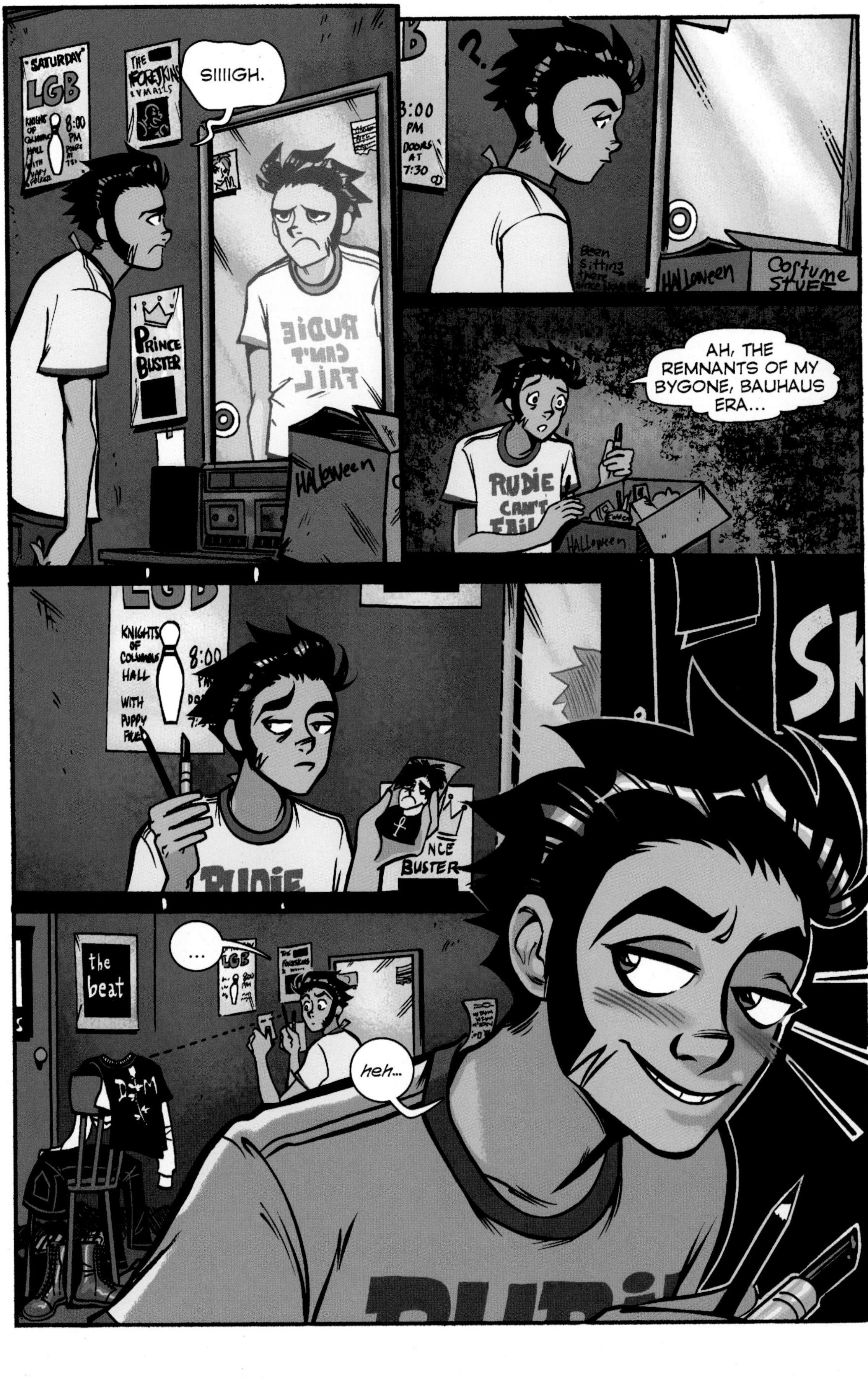
SATURDAY
LGB
KNIGHTS OF COLUMBUS HALL
8:00 PM
PRINCE BUSTER
SIIIGH.
RUDIE CAN'T FAIL
HALLOWEEN
?
Costume STUFF
AH, THE REMNANTS OF MY BYGONE, BAUHAUS ERA...
WITH PUPPY FACE
the beat
...
heh...

THE CRUXSHADOWS - "CRUELTY"

Oh, my goff.

THE CURE - "LULLABYE"

94

MORRISSEY - "THE LAST OF THE FAMOUS INTERNATIONAL PLAYBOYS"

NICE LIPSTICK, FAG!

YEAH, FAG!

I'M SO MISUNDERSTOOD! WHY...? WHYEEEE?!?

GOMEZ! SHUT UP AND BLOCK THE BALL!

GOOD ONE, DUDE.

I KNOW!

WHY-HAI-HAI-HAIIIII?!?

WHYYYYYYYYYYYYY?!

SHOOM

SLAM!

whimper

GOMEZ, ARE YOU TRYING TO INJURE YOURSELF?

PLEASURE AND PAIN GO HAND IN HAND, COACH. I LOVE SOCCER SO MUCH, IT HURTS.

BADGERS

YOU SURE HE'S NOT JOKING?

NOPE. HE'S LOST IT.

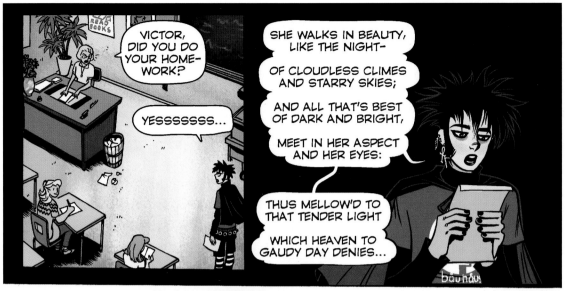

VICTOR, DID YOU DO YOUR HOME-WORK?

YESSSSSSS...

SHE WALKS IN BEAUTY, LIKE THE NIGHT—

OF CLOUDLESS CLIMES AND STARRY SKIES;

AND ALL THAT'S BEST OF DARK AND BRIGHT,

MEET IN HER ASPECT AND HER EYES:

THUS MELLOW'D TO THAT TENDER LIGHT

WHICH HEAVEN TO GAUDY DAY DENIES...

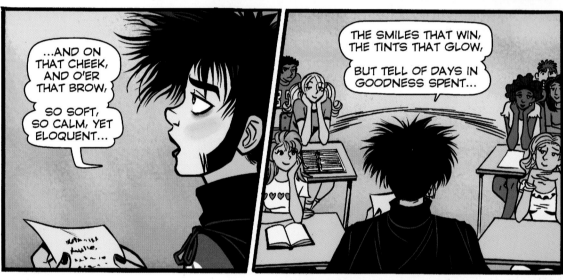

...AND ON THAT CHEEK, AND O'ER THAT BROW,

SO SOFT, SO CALM, YET ELOQUENT...

THE SMILES THAT WIN, THE TINTS THAT GLOW,

BUT TELL OF DAYS IN GOODNESS SPENT...

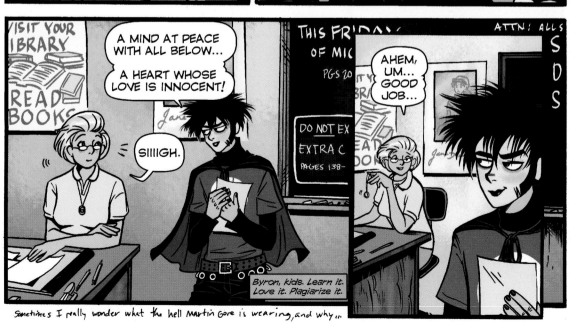

A MIND AT PEACE WITH ALL BELOW...

A HEART WHOSE LOVE IS INNOCENT!

SIIIIGH.

AHEM, UM... GOOD JOB...

Byron, kids. Learn it. Love it. Plagiarize it.

Sometimes I really wonder what the hell Martin Gore is wearing, and why...

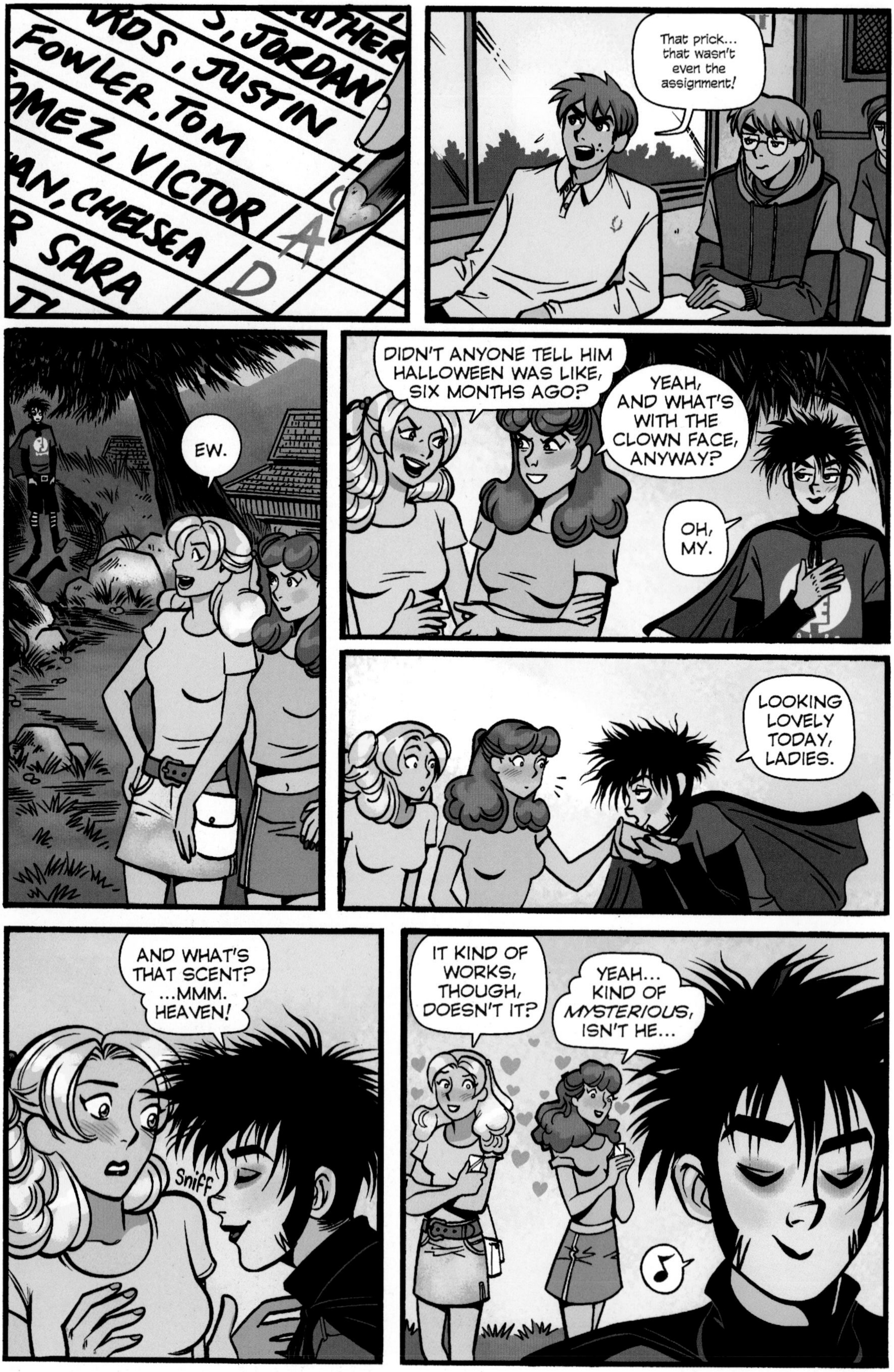

...RDS, JORDAN
FOWLER, TOM
...OMEZ, VICTOR
...AN, CHELSEA
...R SARA
...S, JORDAN
FOWLER, JUSTIN
That prick... that wasn't even the assignment!
EW.
DIDN'T ANYONE TELL HIM HALLOWEEN WAS LIKE, SIX MONTHS AGO?
YEAH, AND WHAT'S WITH THE CLOWN FACE, ANYWAY?
OH, MY.
LOOKING LOVELY TODAY, LADIES.
AND WHAT'S THAT SCENT? ...MMM. HEAVEN!
Sniff
IT KIND OF WORKS, THOUGH, DOESN'T IT?
YEAH... KIND OF *MYSTERIOUS*, ISN'T HE...
♪

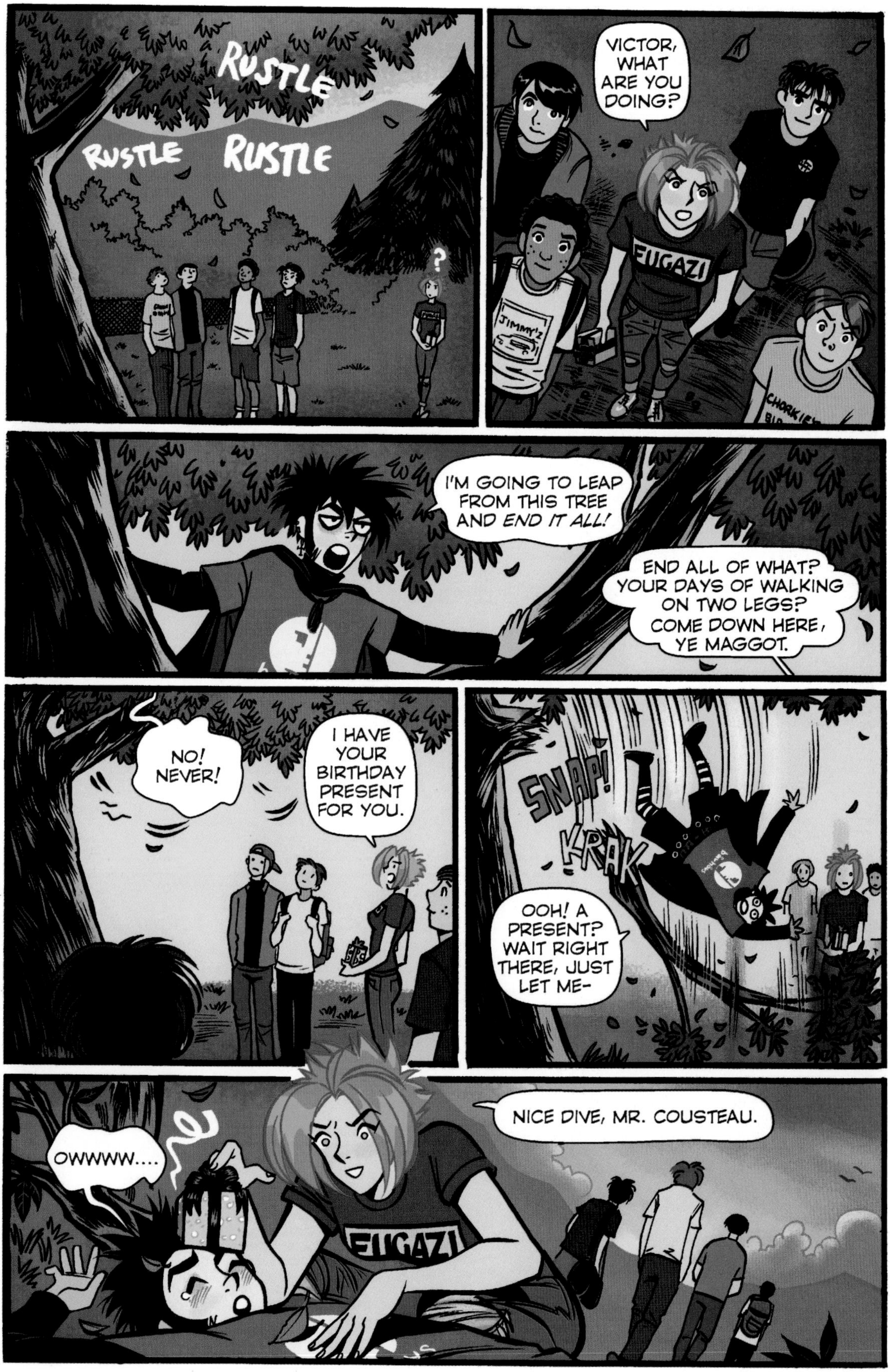
RUSTLE
RUSTLE RUSTLE
VICTOR, WHAT ARE YOU DOING?
FUGAZI
JIMMY'Z
I'M GOING TO LEAP FROM THIS TREE AND *END IT ALL!*
END ALL OF WHAT? YOUR DAYS OF WALKING ON TWO LEGS? COME DOWN HERE, YE MAGGOT.
NO! NEVER!
I HAVE YOUR BIRTHDAY PRESENT FOR YOU.
SNAP!
KRAK
OOH! A PRESENT? WAIT RIGHT THERE, JUST LET ME-
OWWWW....
NICE DIVE, MR. COUSTEAU.
FUGAZI

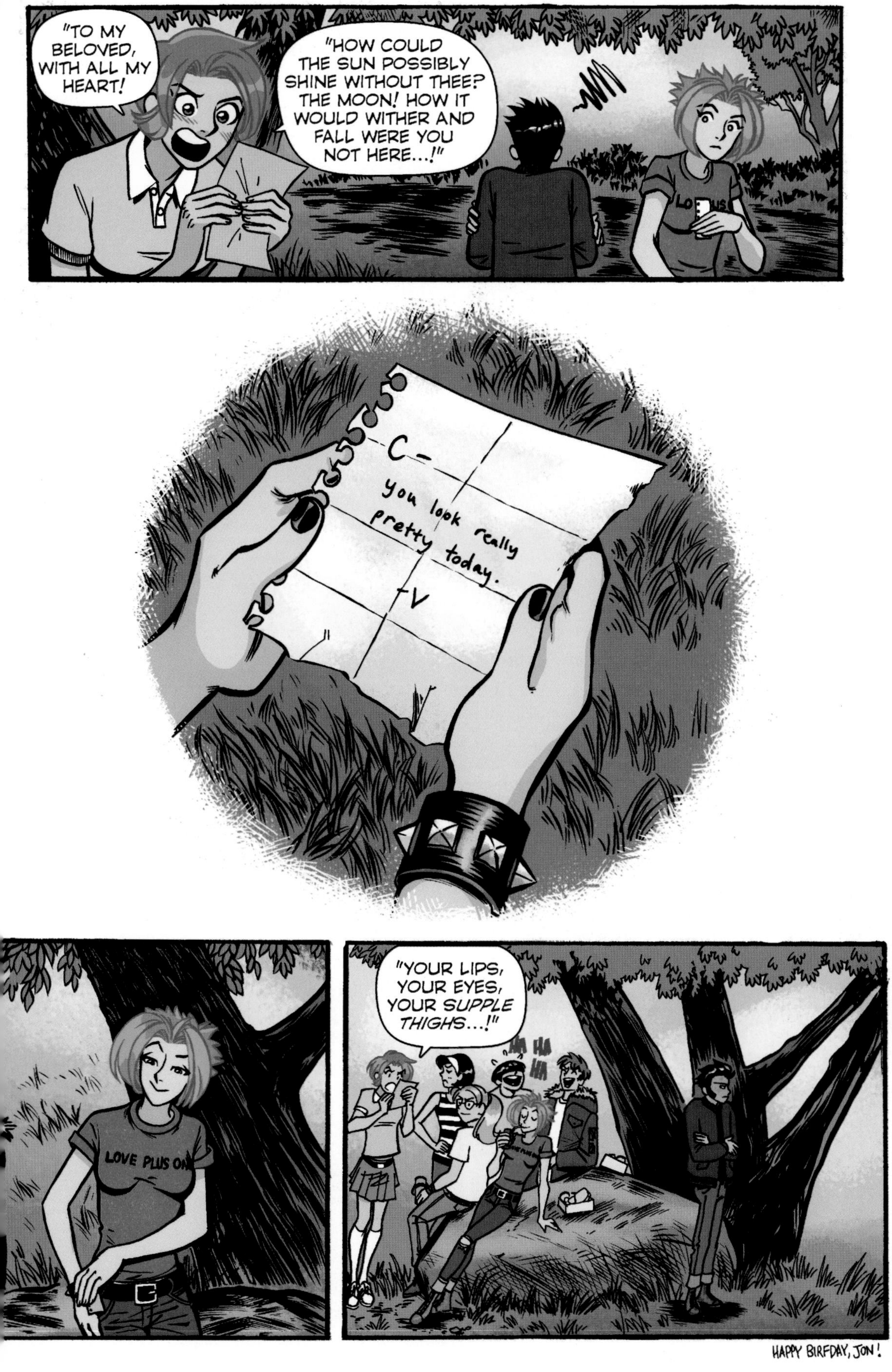
"TO MY BELOVED, WITH ALL MY HEART!
"HOW COULD THE SUN POSSIBLY SHINE WITHOUT THEE? THE MOON! HOW IT WOULD WITHER AND FALL WERE YOU NOT HERE...!"
C—
you look really pretty today.
-V
LOVE PLUS ON
"YOUR LIPS, YOUR EYES, YOUR *SUPPLE* THIGHS...!"
HA HA HA

HAPPY BIRFDAY, JON!

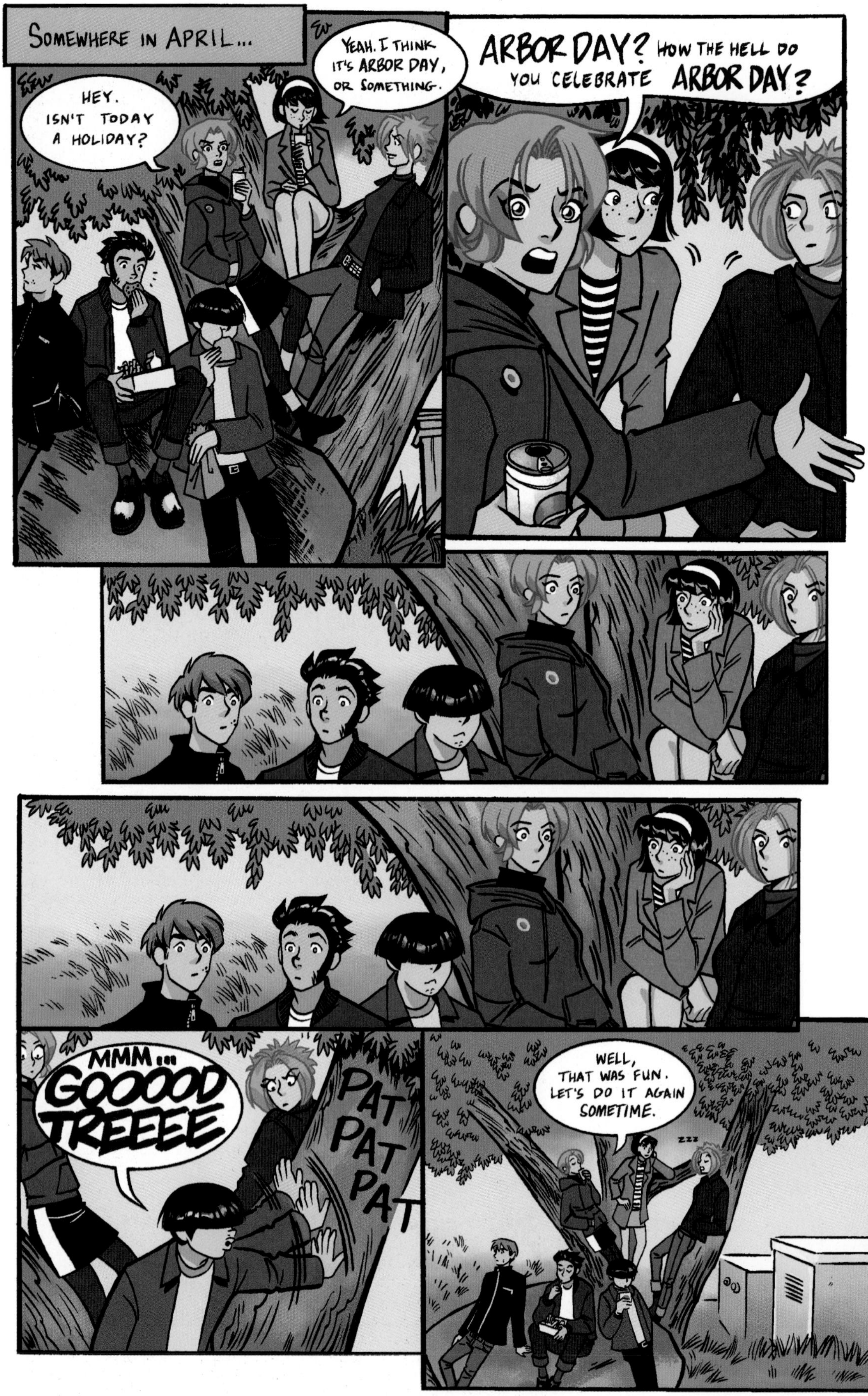
Somewhere in April...
Hey. Isn't today a holiday?
Yeah. I think it's Arbor Day, or something.
Arbor Day? How the hell do you celebrate Arbor Day?
MMM... GOOOOD TREEEE
PAT PAT PAT
Well, that was fun. Let's do it again sometime.
zzz

Bonus Material: The Lost Holiday Strips

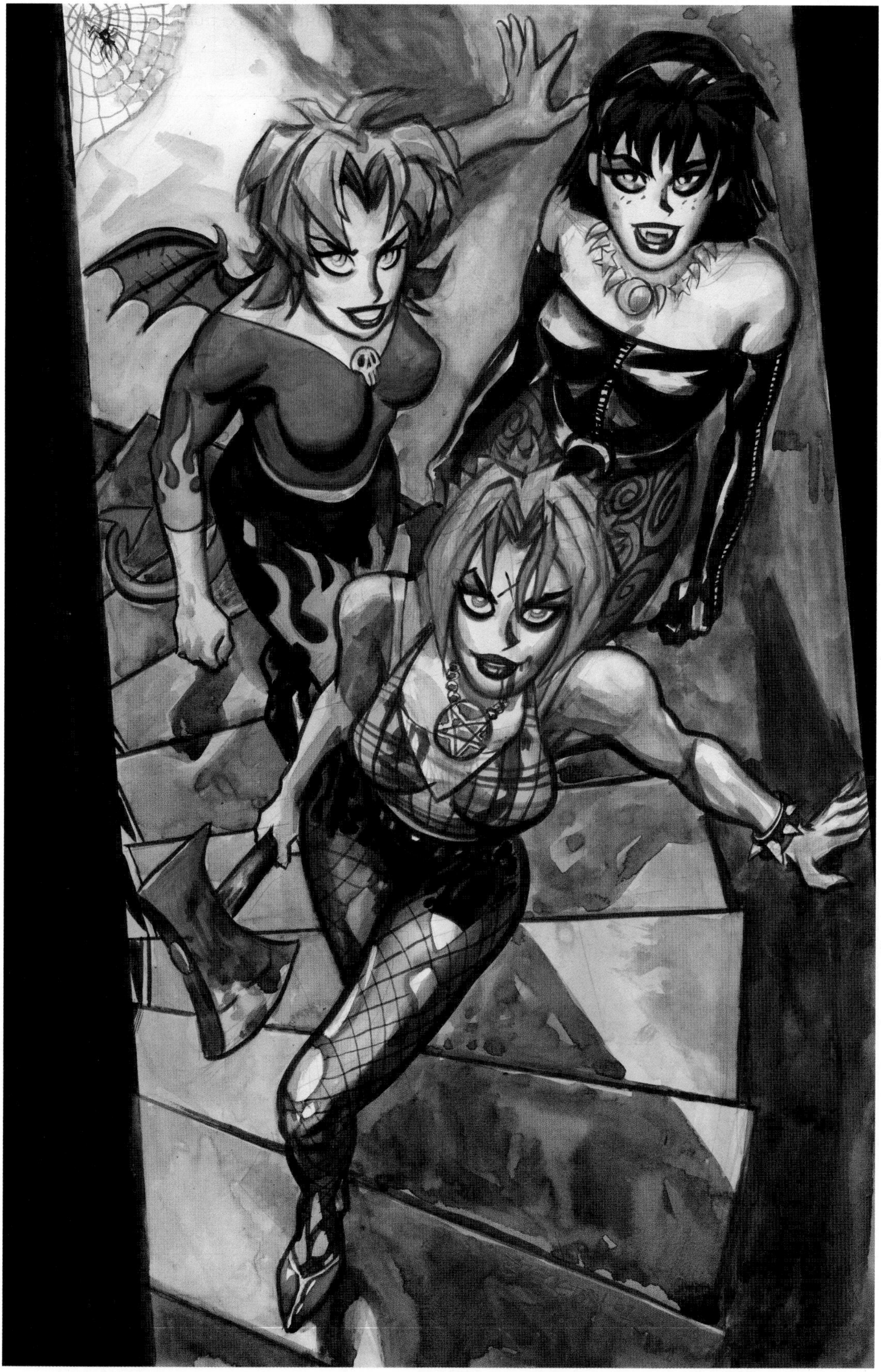

The original back cover to *Dead Man's Party*, illustration by Dan Brereton.

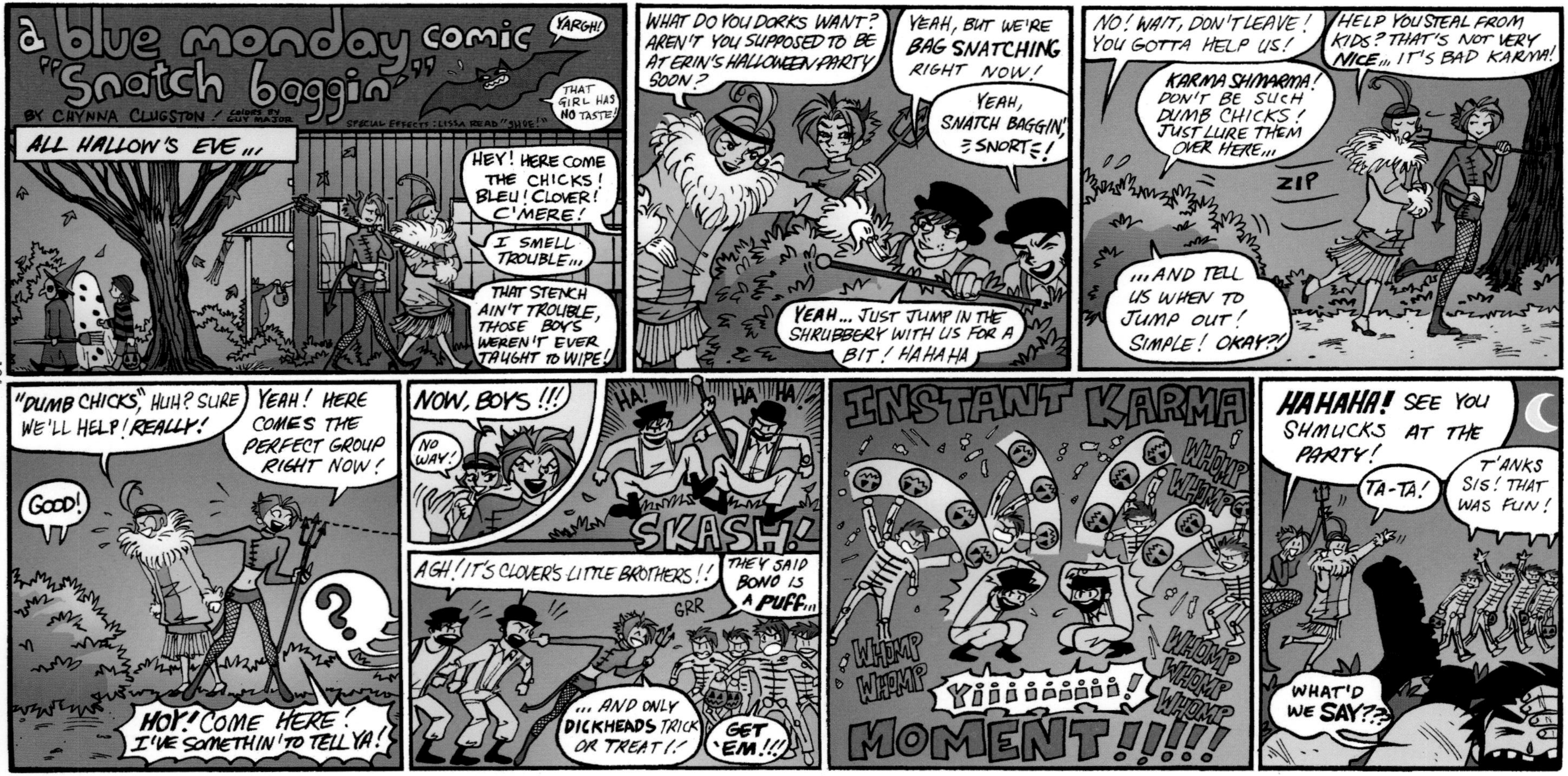
a blue monday comic
"Snatch baggin'"
BY CHYNNA CLUGSTON / COLORS BY GUY MAJOR
SPECIAL EFFECTS: LISSA READ "SHOE!"
YARGH!
THAT GIRL HAS NO TASTE!
ALL HALLOW'S EVE...
HEY! HERE COME THE CHICKS! BLEU! CLOVER! C'MERE!
I SMELL TROUBLE...
THAT STENCH AIN'T TROUBLE, THOSE BOYS WEREN'T EVER TAUGHT TO WIPE!
WHAT DO YOU DORKS WANT? AREN'T YOU SUPPOSED TO BE AT ERIN'S HALLOWEEN PARTY SOON?
YEAH, BUT WE'RE BAG SNATCHING RIGHT NOW!
YEAH, SNATCH BAGGIN', ≡SNORT≡!
YEAH... JUST JUMP IN THE SHRUBBERY WITH US FOR A BIT! HAHAHA
NO! WAIT, DON'T LEAVE! YOU GOTTA HELP US!
KARMA SHMARMA! DON'T BE SUCH DUMB CHICKS! JUST LURE THEM OVER HERE...
ZIP
...AND TELL US WHEN TO JUMP OUT! SIMPLE! OKAY?!
HELP YOU STEAL FROM KIDS? THAT'S NOT VERY NICE... IT'S BAD KARMA!
"DUMB CHICKS," HUH? SURE WE'LL HELP! REALLY!
YEAH! HERE COMES THE PERFECT GROUP RIGHT NOW!
GOOD!
?
HOY! COME HERE! I'VE SOMETHIN' TO TELL YA!
NOW, BOYS!!!
NO WAY!
HA! HA HA.
SKASH!
AGH! IT'S CLOVER'S LITTLE BROTHERS!!
THEY SAID BONO IS A PUFF...
GRR
...AND ONLY DICKHEADS TRICK OR TREAT!
GET 'EM!!!
INSTANT KARMA
WHOMP WHOMP
WHOMP WHOMP
WHOMP WHOMP WHOMP
YIIIIIIIIII!
MOMENT!!!!!
HAHAHA! SEE YOU SHMUCKS AT THE PARTY!
TA-TA!
T'ANKS SIS! THAT WAS FUN!
WHAT'D WE SAY?!?

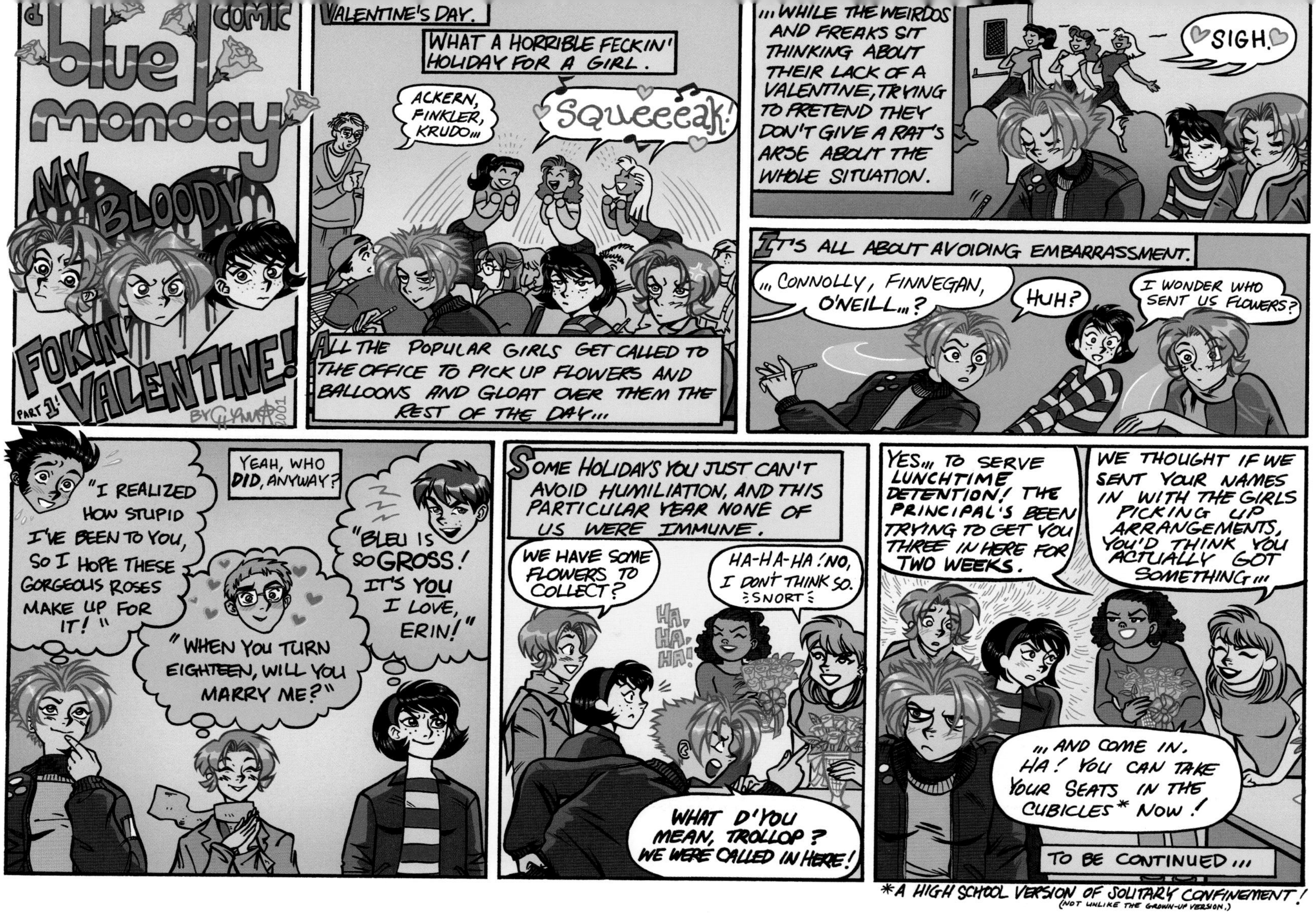
a blue monday comic
MY BLOODY FOKIN' VALENTINE! PART 1!
BY CHYNNA 2001
VALENTINE'S DAY.
WHAT A HORRIBLE FECKIN' HOLIDAY FOR A GIRL.
ACKERN, FINKLER, KRUDO...
SQUEEEAK!
ALL THE POPULAR GIRLS GET CALLED TO THE OFFICE TO PICK UP FLOWERS AND BALLOONS AND GLOAT OVER THEM THE REST OF THE DAY...
...WHILE THE WEIRDOS AND FREAKS SIT THINKING ABOUT THEIR LACK OF A VALENTINE, TRYING TO PRETEND THEY DON'T GIVE A RAT'S ARSE ABOUT THE WHOLE SITUATION.
SIGH.
IT'S ALL ABOUT AVOIDING EMBARRASSMENT.
...CONNOLLY, FINNEGAN, O'NEILL...?
HUH?
I WONDER WHO SENT US FLOWERS?
"I REALIZED HOW STUPID I'VE BEEN TO YOU, SO I HOPE THESE GORGEOUS ROSES MAKE UP FOR IT!"
YEAH, WHO DID, ANYWAY?
"WHEN YOU TURN EIGHTEEN, WILL YOU MARRY ME?"
"BLEU IS SO GROSS! IT'S YOU I LOVE, ERIN!"
SOME HOLIDAYS YOU JUST CAN'T AVOID HUMILIATION, AND THIS PARTICULAR YEAR NONE OF US WERE IMMUNE.
WE HAVE SOME FLOWERS TO COLLECT?
HA-HA-HA! NO, I DON'T THINK SO. SNORT
HA, HA, HA!
WHAT D'YOU MEAN, TROLLOP? WE WERE CALLED IN HERE!
YES... TO SERVE LUNCHTIME DETENTION! THE PRINCIPAL'S BEEN TRYING TO GET YOU THREE IN HERE FOR TWO WEEKS.
WE THOUGHT IF WE SENT YOUR NAMES IN WITH THE GIRLS PICKING UP ARRANGEMENTS, YOU'D THINK YOU ACTUALLY GOT SOMETHING...
...AND COME IN. HA! YOU CAN TAKE YOUR SEATS IN THE CUBICLES* NOW!
TO BE CONTINUED...
*A HIGH SCHOOL VERSION OF SOLITARY CONFINEMENT!
(NOT UNLIKE THE GROWN-UP VERSION.)

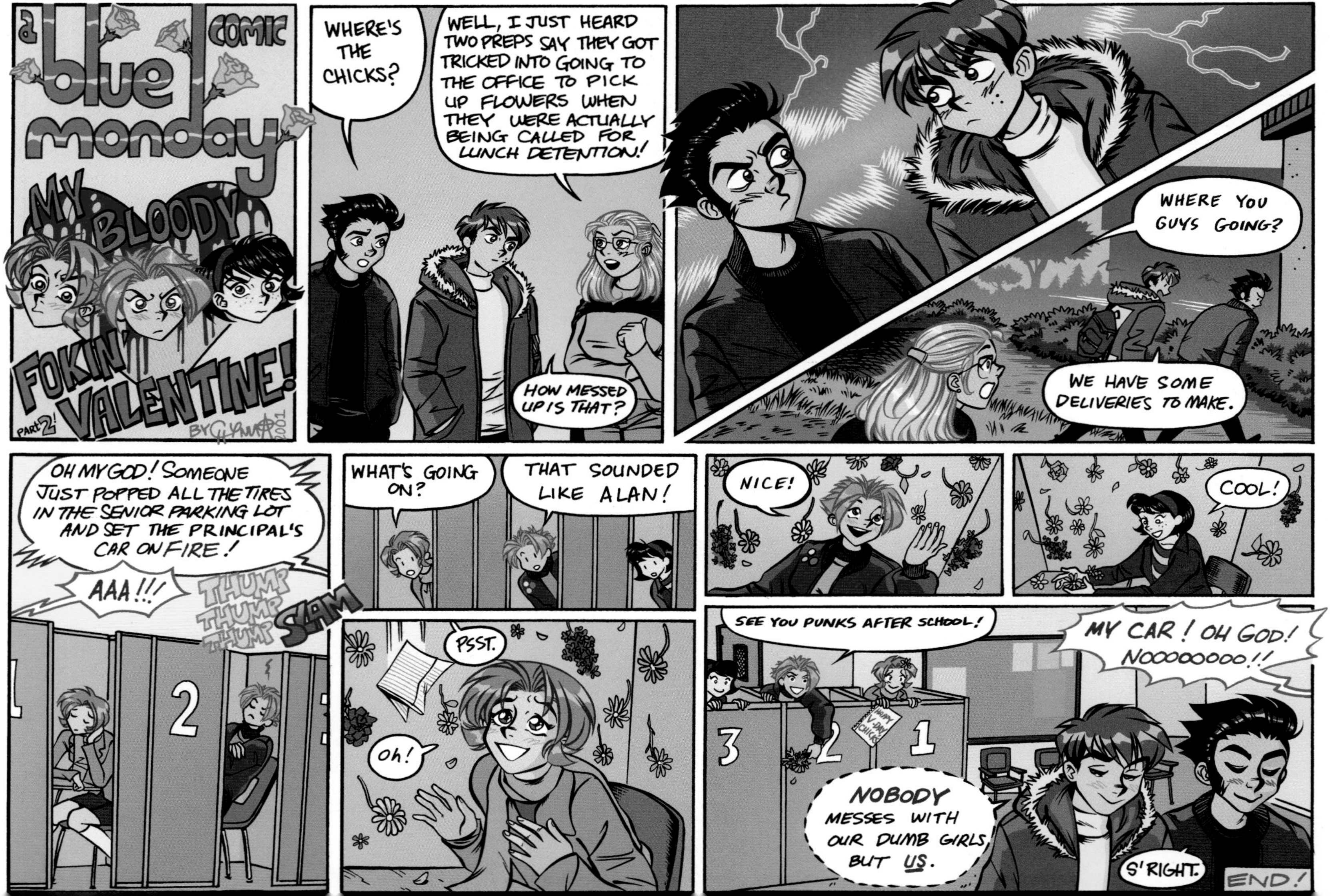
a blue monday comic
MY BLOODY FOKIN' VALENTINE!
PART 2!
BY CLYNN 2001
WHERE'S THE CHICKS?
WELL, I JUST HEARD TWO PREPS SAY THEY GOT TRICKED INTO GOING TO THE OFFICE TO PICK UP FLOWERS WHEN THEY WERE ACTUALLY BEING CALLED FOR LUNCH DETENTION!
HOW MESSED UP IS THAT?
WHERE YOU GUYS GOING?
WE HAVE SOME DELIVERIES TO MAKE.
OH MY GOD! SOMEONE JUST POPPED ALL THE TIRES IN THE SENIOR PARKING LOT AND SET THE PRINCIPAL'S CAR ON FIRE!
AAA!!!
THUMP THUMP THUMP
SLAM
WHAT'S GOING ON?
THAT SOUNDED LIKE ALAN!
PSST.
Oh!
NICE!
COOL!
SEE YOU PUNKS AFTER SCHOOL!
MY CAR! OH GOD! NOOOOOOOO!!
NOBODY MESSES WITH OUR DUMB GIRLS BUT US.
S'RIGHT.
END!

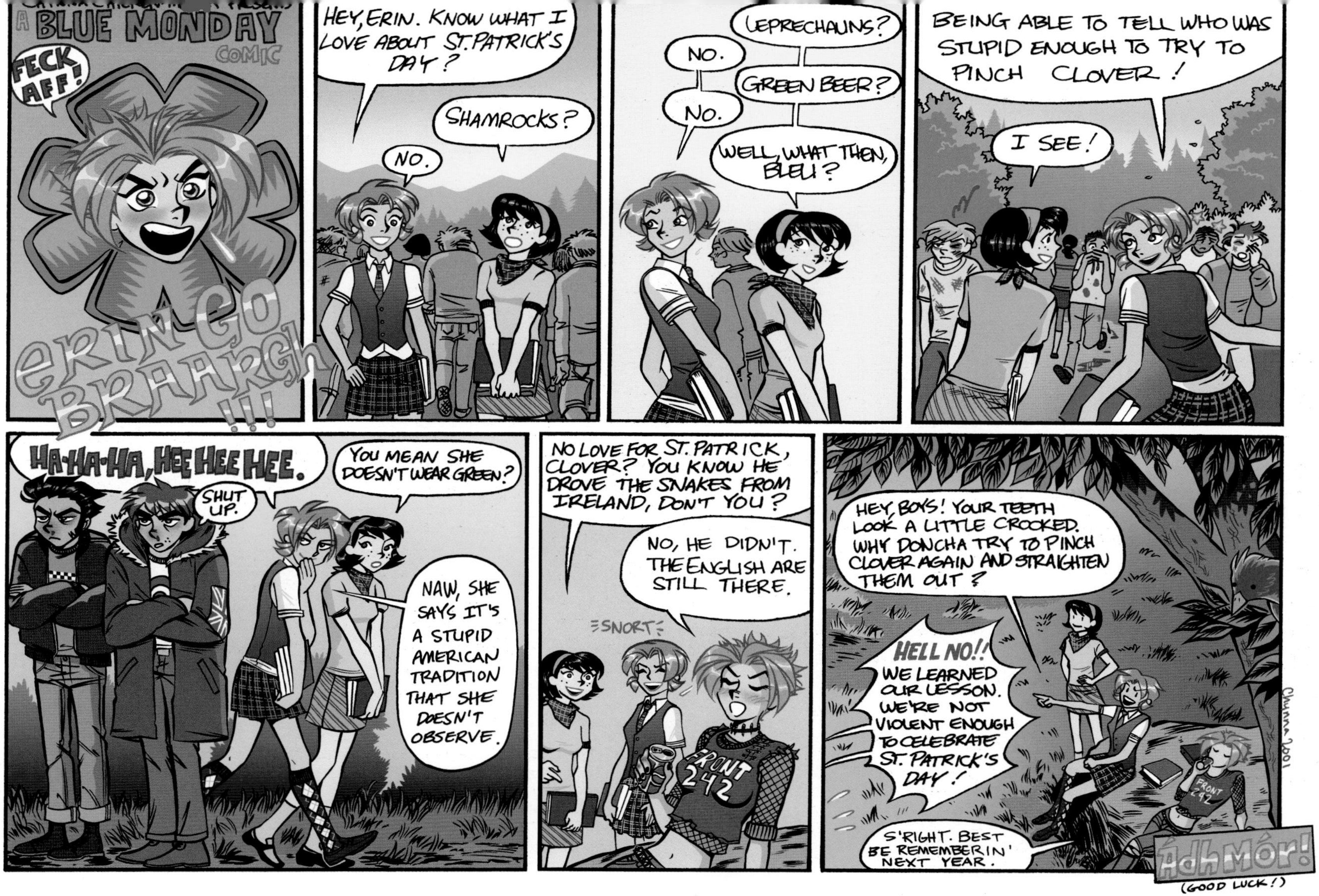
A BLUE MONDAY COMIC
FECK AFF!
ERIN GO BRAARGH!!!
HEY, ERIN. KNOW WHAT I LOVE ABOUT ST. PATRICK'S DAY?
SHAMROCKS?
NO.
LEPRECHAUNS?
NO.
GREEN BEER?
NO.
WELL, WHAT THEN, BLEU?
BEING ABLE TO TELL WHO WAS STUPID ENOUGH TO TRY TO PINCH CLOVER!
I SEE!
HA-HA-HA, HEE HEE HEE.
SHUT UP.
YOU MEAN SHE DOESN'T WEAR GREEN?
NAW, SHE SAYS IT'S A STUPID AMERICAN TRADITION THAT SHE DOESN'T OBSERVE.
NO LOVE FOR ST. PATRICK, CLOVER? YOU KNOW HE DROVE THE SNAKES FROM IRELAND, DON'T YOU?
NO, HE DIDN'T. THE ENGLISH ARE STILL THERE.
SNORT
FRONT 242
HEY, BOYS! YOUR TEETH LOOK A LITTLE CROOKED. WHY DONCHA TRY TO PINCH CLOVER AGAIN AND STRAIGHTEN THEM OUT?
HELL NO!! WE LEARNED OUR LESSON. WE'RE NOT VIOLENT ENOUGH TO CELEBRATE ST. PATRICK'S DAY!
S'RIGHT. BEST BE REMEMBERIN' NEXT YEAR.
Chynna 2001
Ádh Mór!
(GOOD LUCK!)

Extracurricular Blue Monday

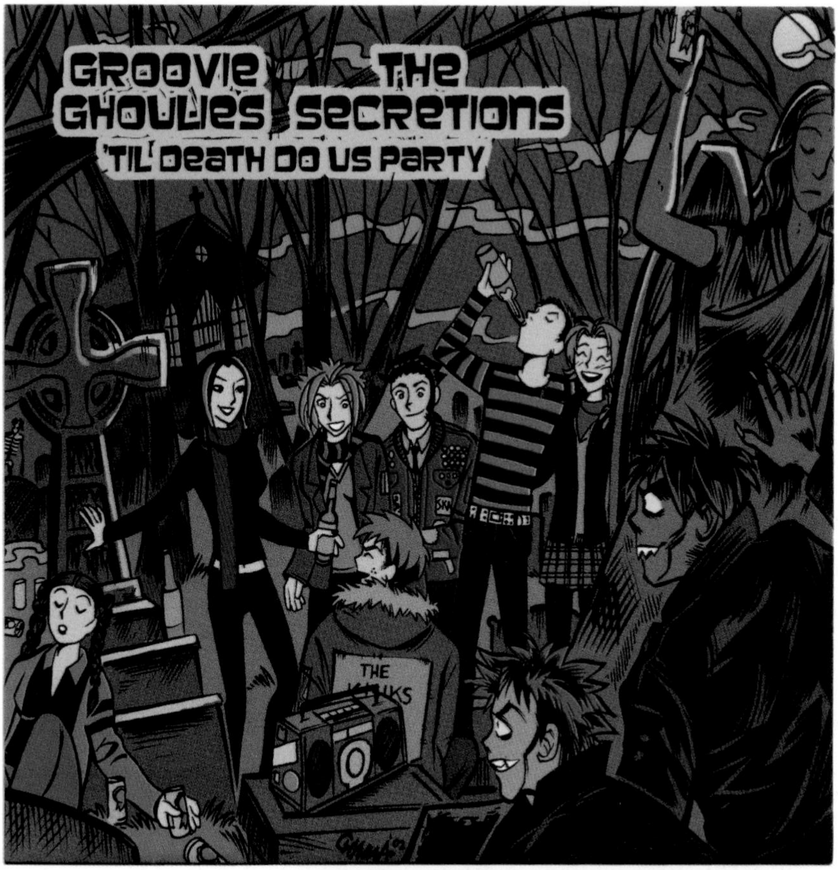
GROOVIE GHOULIES
THE SECRETIONS
'TIL DEATH DO US PARTY
THE

Cover to a split 7″ single put out by Springman Records, featuring music by the Groovie Ghoulies and The Secretions. This was a Halloween release in 2002.

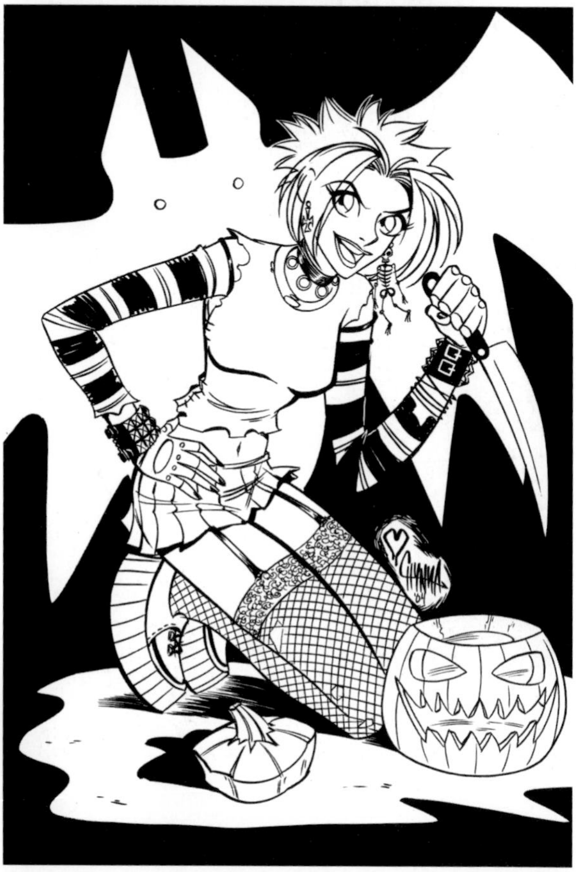

A random Halloween-themed Clover sketch from 2004, experimenting with a more exaggerated, cartoonish style.

A promotional magazine illo for a music distributor. All but two characters you will recognize, the others were made up simply for the hell of it.

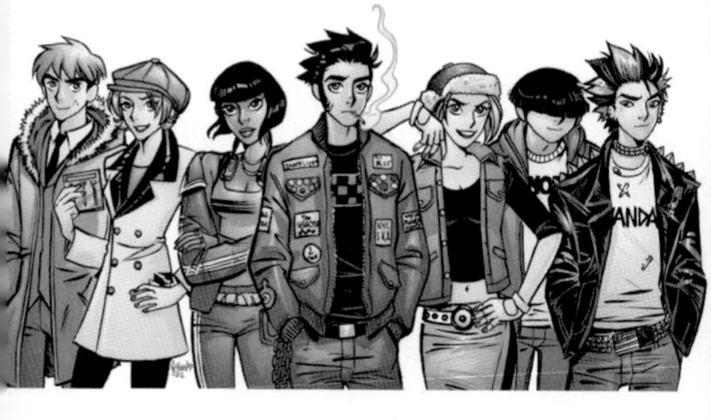

Rough initial sketches for the covers of Lovecats and the original *Inbetween Days* trade paperback collection. *The Lovecats* sketch began as a pin-up idea, but certain themes cherry-picked from it morphed into the final cover image.

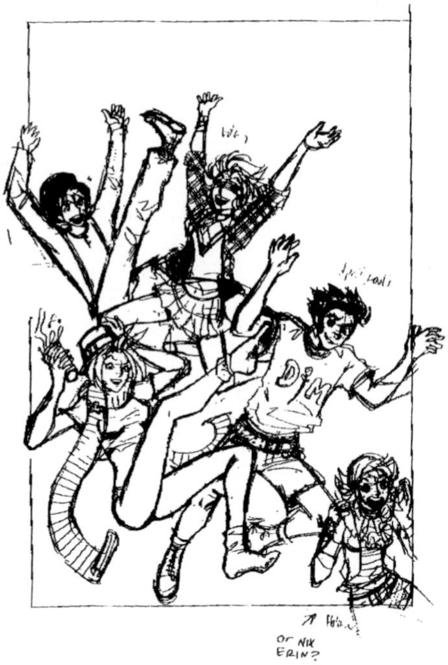

DIM
or NIK
ERIN?

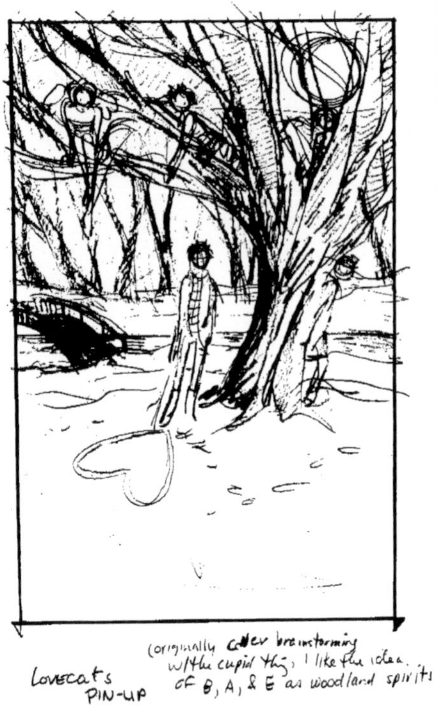

Lovecats
PIN-UP
(originally cover brainstorming
w/the cupid thing, I like the idea
of B, A, & E as woodland spirits

Cover for the December 2002 Worlds of Westfield Catalogue, also featuring characters from *Scooter Girl*.

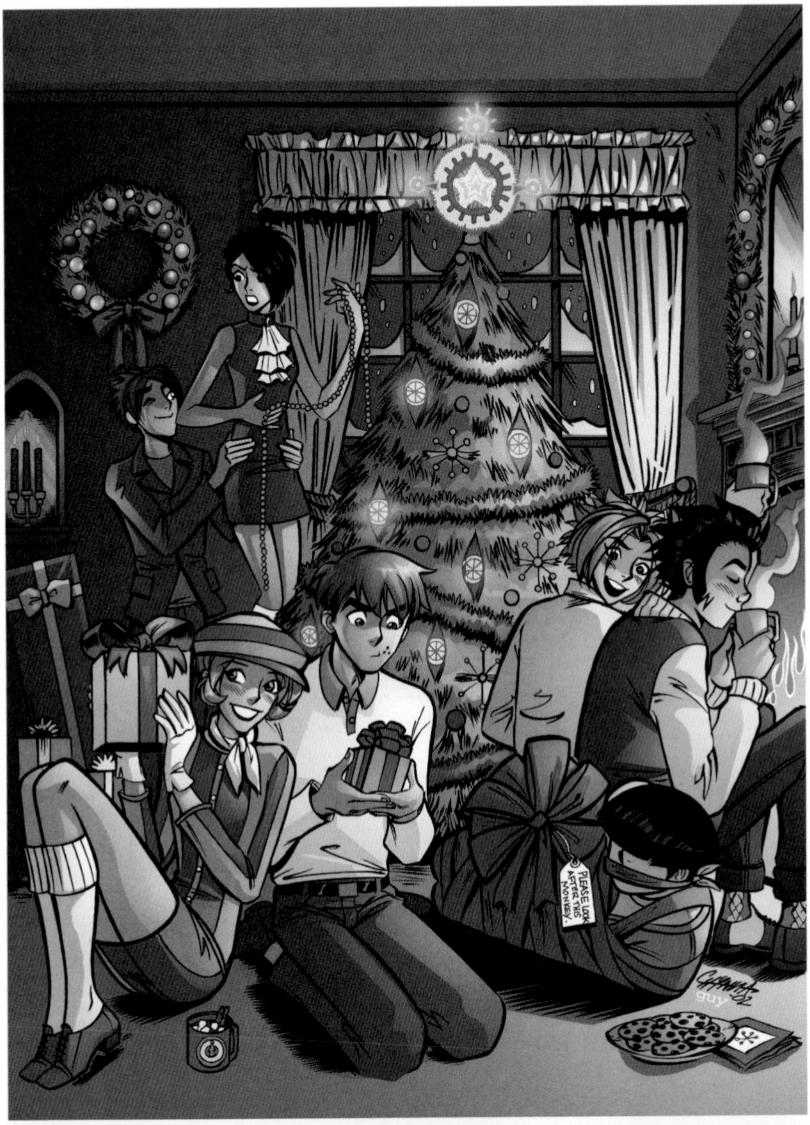

PLEASE LOOK AFTER THIS MONKEY.

Chynna Clugston Flores has been writing and drawing comics professionally since 1994. A fan of holidays in general (particularly ones involving dancing, carousing, and stuffing one's face with seasonal treats) she looks for any excuse to create stories surrounding them, especially if they involve the obnoxious gang from Jefferson High. Halloween, however, reigns supreme in the Flores household–– born with a predisposition to lurk in graveyards and toilet paper houses, there was really no way around it.

She has worked with DC, Scholastic, Lion Forge, Oni Press, BOOM!, Marvel, Dark Horse, and Slave Labor Graphics as well as working as an illustrator for books, magazines, ad companies, and as a writer, assistant editor, and colorist. Most recently she was the writer for the hit crossover *Lumberjanes/Gotham Academy*, the artist and writer on the short story *"Deadpooloween"* from Marvel, artist on bonus material for DC's *Shade the Changing Girl*, and contributed a short story on her hero, Rumiko Takahashi, to the anthology *Femme Magnifique*.

The author about age four circa 1979, already with a preference for smart-ass characters.

Chynna lives in California with her husband, Jon, and their young daughter, Luna, who even at a very young age is already plotting Halloween costumes and trick-or-treating routes months ahead of time.

Along with *Blue Monday*, Chynna's original, creator-owned series *Scooter Girl* is available through Image Comics. Follow her on Twitter @Chynnasyndrome.

Dedicated to Jon Flores, for all the Moonpies and Pennywhistles.

Special thanks to: Image Comics, Eric Stephenson, Jordie Bellaire, Ian Shaughnessy, Jamie S. Rich, Bryan Lee O'Malley, Keith Wood, Guy Major, Steven Birch, Paul Dini, Drew Gill & Jon Flores.

Jordie Bellaire is a comics creator who has worked on many titles with many publishers. Her coloring credits include *Savage Town, Injection, Batman, Deadpool, They're Not Like Us, The Vision, Pretty Deadly, The Autumnlands*, and many others. In 2016, she won her second Eisner award for Best Colorist. She makes her writing debut in August 2017 with *Redlands*, illustrated by Vanesa R. del Rey. She lives in Ireland with her famous cat, Buffy.

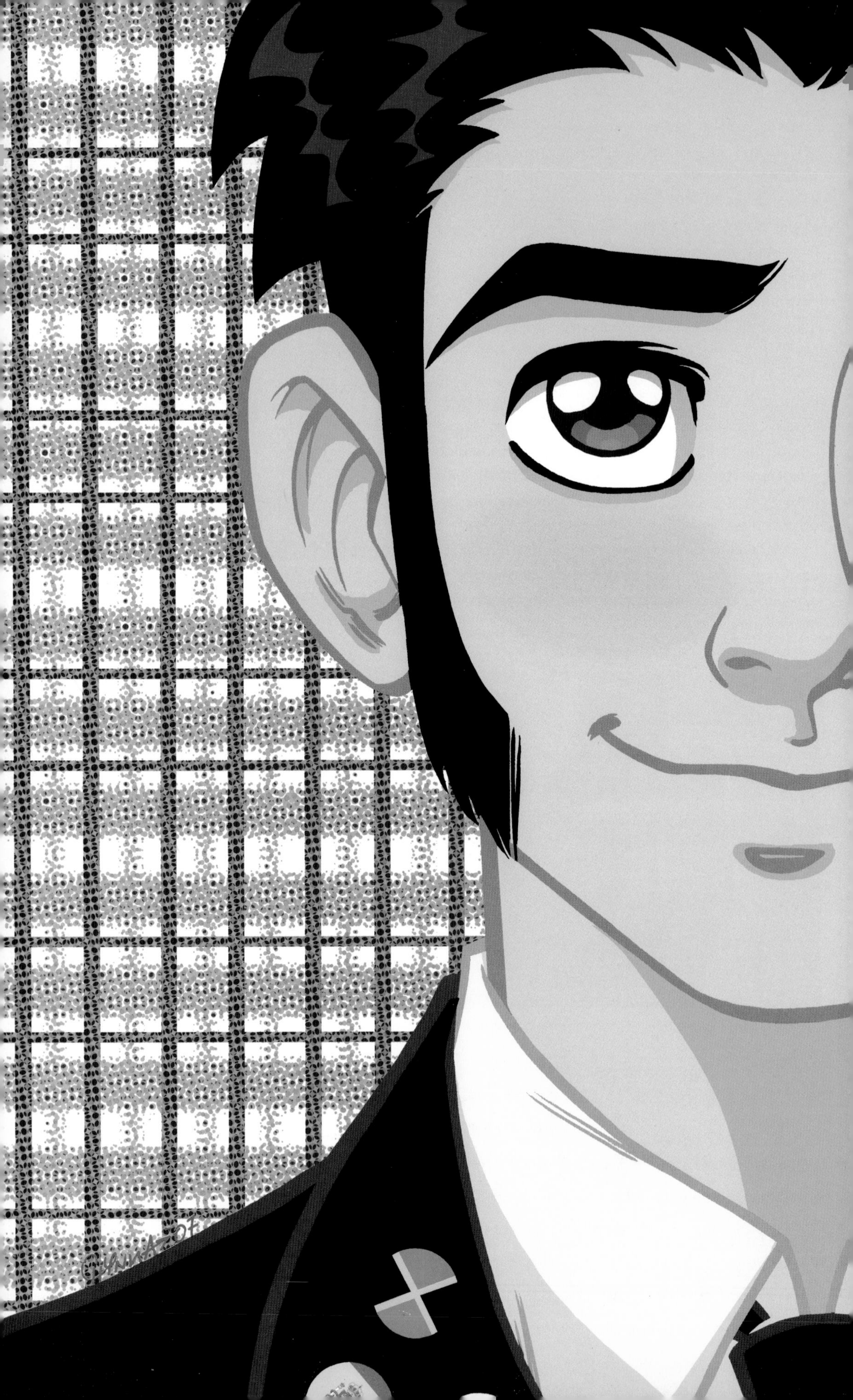